Elton John FAQ

Elton John
FAQ

All That's Left to Know About
the Rocket Man

Donald Gibson

Backbeat
Books

Guilford, Connecticut

Published by Backbeat Books

An imprint of The Rowman & Littlefield Publishing Group, Inc.

4501 Forbes Blvd., Ste. 200

Lanham, MD 20706

www.rowman.com

Distributed by NATIONAL BOOK NETWORK

The FAQ series was conceived by Robert Rodriguez and developed with Stuart Shea.

All images are from the author's collection unless otherwise noted.

Book design and composition by Snow Creative

Library of Congress Cataloging-in-Publication Data available

ISBN 978-1-61713-650-4 (paperback)

∞™ The paper used in this publication meets the minimum requirements of American National Standard for Information Sciences—Permanence of Paper for Printed Library Materials, ANSI/NISO Z39.48-1992

In memory of my grandfather, Charles Sabbides, and my uncle, Richard Sabbides.

I love and miss you both so much.

Contents

Acknowledgments

Encouragement goes a long way for a writer, especially for one who is writing his first book. Whatever self-confidence is expressed in a book's proposal disappears somewhere between the first draft and final edit. For me, every stage of bringing this book to fruition—the research, the interviews, drafts, edits—was a labor of love. On more than a few days, though, for more reasons than I care to recount, it was more labor than love. In those moments when I was overwhelmed and disillusioned, someone usually came alone to encourage me, urging me to keep my eye on the prize, so to speak, and to see this book through. To any and all of those special individuals, thank you.

Thank you as well to everyone who spoke to me on the record along the way, recalling their own shared and varied experiences over the past fifty years with Elton John. They have afforded me (and hopefully the reader) with pertinent context to many of the events that are chronicled in these pages, along with insights that enrich the impressions that are offered in critique. This book could not have been achieved without their selfless participation: Ray Williams, Caleb Quaye, Kenny Passarelli, Gary Osborne, Chris Charlesworth, and two individuals who sadly passed away before the book's publication, Romeo Williams and Russ Regan.

I would be remiss if I did not thank *Blogcritics* magazine, which gave me so many wonderful opportunities to not only write about music but to interview hundreds of musicians. My experience at *Blogcritics* shaped me into the writer I have become, and from the men and women who have run the site to the plethora of editors and writers I've encountered, and in many cases worked alongside—Eric Olsen, Lisa McKay, Connie Phillips, John Hathaway, Gordon Miller, Barbara Barnett, Jon Sobel, and Kit O'Toole—I offer my gratitude.

While writing at *Blogcritics*, my copy often found its way to Glen Boyd, who, besides being a spectacular editor with sage, practical advice— "Don't fight it! Just write it!"—also became one of my dearest pals. His

An officially sanctioned Elton John bobble-head.
Author's collection

compassion and empathy during what were some of the most difficult days of my life have never wavered in the decade I've known him, and even if I didn't acknowledge that he's a terrific writer in his own right (which, of course, I do, because, of course, he is), I definitely know he's my friend.

Through my friendship with Glen, who in 2012 wrote *Neil Young FAQ: Everything Left to Know About the Iconic and Mercurial Rocker*, I met Robert Rodriguez, who besides having created the whole FAQ series has also written a bevy a great books, including *Fab Four FAQ: Everything Left to Know About the Beatles . . . and More!* (co-written with Stuart Shea), *Fab Four FAQ 2.0: The Beatles' Solo Years, 1970–1980*, and *Revolver: How the Beatles Reimagined Rock 'N' Roll*. Without Robert, none of this would have been possible. Thank you, Robert.

In addition, I extend my thanks to Hal Leonard Publishing and Backbeat Books, and particularly to my editors, Bernadette Malavarca and Clare Cerullo. Your guidance has been essential to me along the way, and your patience has been appreciated more than I could ever hope to express. Thank you so much.

At last, thank you to my family—my mother and my father in particular—for understanding how important this opportunity was for me. I appreciate you both and I love you both dearly.

Introduction

His Gift Is His Song

The definitive book on Elton John may not be written for a long time yet to come. Within just the last few years alone, the legendary British singer/songwriter's career has continuously scaled new heights, with scarce hint of plateauing, heralded at turns by the celebrated release of his thirty-second studio LP, *Wonderful Crazy Night*, as well as two all-star tribute albums; the major-motion-picture production of John's authorized biopic, *Rocketman*; and, following the denouement of his hit Las Vegas residency, *The Million Dollar Piano*, the commencement of his *Farewell Yellow Brick Road* world tour, which is slated to be his *coup de grace* on the live stage. The man is still standing, in other words, singularly compelled to compose and entertain on top of—and arguably in spite of—all he has so far achieved.

Over the past half-century, in fact, Elton John has forged one of the most wildly successful careers in all of rock 'n' roll, selling over three hundred million albums, performing more than four thousand live concerts, and garnering countless accolades, awards, and distinctions for his music and philanthropy. Throughout each musical phase, he has cultivated a larger-than-life image that's unique in its excess and staggering flamboyance, his irreverent fashion sense having evolved from the campy, often-cartoonish stage costumes he brandished in the seventies and eighties to the comparatively conservative yet still glitzy, custom-tailored suits (designed by the likes of Gucci or Versace) he most often dons these days. However, John's artfulness has always preceded his artifice—not the other way around—and, dating back to the earliest incarnations of his career, beneath his eccentricities lays a foundation of prodigious talent and an indefatigable work ethic.

As guitarist Caleb Quaye—who first met John when they both apprenticed on England's fabled Tin Pan Alley, and who played on the latter's

Made in England

Childhood

Unlike other British rock legends of his generation whose child-hoods bore the psychic toll of World War II's still-recent aftermath, Elton John's earliest years were shaped more by conflict and anxieties in his own home. An only child fraught with insecurity and self-loathing, he struggled to cope under the strain of his parents' troubled marriage and their often-excessive expectations of propriety: "Do as you're told. Use proper utensils at the dinner table. Sit up straight. Listen to thy mother and, above all, obey thy father." Whereas, say, John Lennon and Pete Townshend harbored still-vivid memories into their adult years of breadlines and food rations (particularly on dessert items), John has often recalled how his parents forbade him from wearing Hush Puppies shoes as a child, lest they stigmatize him as a social deviant and render shame unto his family.

Growing up in such tense, restrictive conditions proved crucial in the evolution of Elton Hercules John, born Reginald Kenneth Dwight on March 25, 1947, at the government-subsidized council house he and his parents shared with his mother's sister, Win, and his maternal grandparents, Fred and Ivy Harris, at 55 Pinner Hill Road in Pinner, a suburb of northwest London, England.

Raised and Regimented

By the time of their only child's birth, Stanley and Sheila Dwight had not quite been married two years, having met three years prior at the Royal Air Force (RAF) Coastal Command complex in Northwood, Middlesex, where the latter, according to an interview her son gave to NPR's Terry Gross in 2013, had been an "Ack Ack Girl" in the war. "She was on the guns," John said to Gross. "I think life was pretty amazing. I mean, it was frightening, but it was also, you know, camaraderie at its best. So, yes, she fought, and she fired the guns."

A former milkman and trumpeter in a swing ensemble called the Millermen (named in deference to fellow band member Bob Miller, not to the world-renowned bandleader Glenn Miller), Mr. Dwight served as a flight lieutenant in the Voluntary Reserve, having ascended the ranks of the RAF during active duty (though he didn't see combat) in the waning years of the war. For the most part, during these years Mr. Dwight devoted his life to military obligations, while his wife devoted hers to the essential responsibilities of raising the couple's son.

Together, the young husband and wife shared an avid appreciation of the performing arts. Radio still reigned as the era's predominant source of home entertainment, and indeed the Dwights found much to enjoy on the dial, from BBC radio programs like *Family Favourites* and *Round the Horne* to songs by sentimental balladeers like Frank Sinatra, Rosemary Clooney, and Nat "King" Cole. Jazz pianist George Shearing's records played in frequent rotation on the family's turntable, while selections by other artists likewise enriched the musical assortment on hand. "The first records I ever heard were Kay Starr and Billy May and Tennessee Ernie Ford and Les Paul and Mary Ford and Guy Mitchell," Elton John said in 1973, to *Rolling Stone*. "I grew up in that era. I was three or four when I first started listening to records like that."

His infant ears piqued and enthralled beyond casual appreciation, Reg, as he was most commonly known throughout his early childhood and adolescence, responded to the music that filled the house by playing along to what he heard on the family's upright piano, his Auntie Win and his grandmother—Reg called her "Nan"—encouraging him along the way.

He developed a fancy for Trinidadian pianist Winifred Atwell, whose spirited boogie-woogie and ragtime-styled recordings proved a profound formative influence. "She would play some classical piece of music on a grand piano, and then she'd go over to her upright and play pub songs and ragtime," John told music journalist and filmmaker Cameron Crowe in a 2016 *Rolling Stone* interview. "She had the most infectious smile. She

Captain Fantastic lyrics with photos.   *Author's collection*

moved to Australia, and when I first went there, I managed to meet with her. It was one of the greatest moments in my life. She was one of the first people who inspired me, and I got to say thank you for it."

Indeed, family lore has it that one day his mother overheard him from another room, playing note-for-note the melody to Atwell's version of "The Skater's Waltz" (by nineteenth-century French composer Émile Waldteufel)—not exactly nursery rhyme material. Reg was just three years old.

Despite whatever childhood phases or more ordinary fancies delighted him at the time, Reg had nevertheless discovered—albeit in the most basic, intuitive sense—his life's abiding passion. In music he found refuge, a means of escape from emotions he didn't understand or know how to reconcile: grieving the death of his maternal grandfather,

Frank, as he did at age five; enduring the recurrent anxiety of his parents' increasingly fractious relationship; and bearing the brunt of his father's overbearing discipline and moral disdain.

Embroiled in a perpetual conflict of loyalties, Reg (and, in time, his mother) dreaded whenever a military leave afforded the return of his father, whose rigid disposition ratcheted up the tension that otherwise lay dormant in the house during his absence and whose reprimands sent the hypersensitive child into a nervous stupor. In a poignant and telling moment in the 1997 documentary, *Tantrums and Tiaras*, his mother concedes to her world-famous son about his father, "I don't think he liked you very much."

I Remember When Rock Was Young

Another thing his father didn't like? Rock 'n' roll. Not one bit. In fact, Stanley Dwight despised it, disparaging the music as a crude and ridiculous fad that couldn't soon enough exhaust its mass appeal, while at the same time fearing the deleterious effects it stood to wield on his suggestible young son. This was a lost cause, though, and one that Reg's mother—still quite young herself, and not as straitlaced and stern as her husband—didn't much mind her husband lose. In fact, it was Sheila Dwight who, by purchasing copies of Bill Haley and the Comets' "ABC Boogie" and Elvis Presley's "Hound Dog," most incited her son's curious enthusiasm.

"It was weird," John told the *Guardian* in 2013, "because, about ten days before, I'd had my hair cut in the local barbers, where I went as a little boy, and I'd noticed a *Life* magazine. I was reading this article on a man who looked like an alien but was so handsome. I'd never seen anything like him, and I put two and two together and said, 'That was the man I saw in the magazine!' So that was the record that really changed everything."

Reg obsessed over rock 'n' roll, its impact on his burgeoning imagination becoming all the more evident just as those closest to him recognized the promise of his musical talent. His parents signed him up for piano lessons at the age of seven, but Reg resisted the discipline such formal instruction required. All too often, when he should have been practicing his requisite Bach and Chopin exercises, young Reg instead raised an almighty ruckus on the family upright, tearing through Little Richard's "Tutti Frutti" or Jerry Lee Lewis's "Great Balls of Fire" with ecstatic abandon. To cultivate his natural gift to its fullest potential, it soon became apparent that Reg necessitated a far more structured and rigid curriculum.

In 1959, at the age of eleven, he won a scholarship to the Royal Academy of Music as a junior exhibitionist, his mandatory attendance every Saturday morning, under the tutelage of Ms. Helen Piena, obliterating the only free day of the precocious child's week (grammar school of course monopolized Monday through Friday, while Sundays were reserved for completing his homework for the week ahead). Though not a prodigy as far as musical technique was concerned—at least not as far as conventional, classically trained musical technique was concerned—Reg nonetheless possessed an uncanny ear for replicating either what he had just heard on a recording or what his instructor had first demonstrated to him on piano. In fact, because of what had heretofore been her clever student's covert skill, Piena ceased showing Reg how to play the pieces she taught, forcing him to learn to read and interpret notation on the page.

Were he to have had his way, it seems, playing the piano would have remained a casual, personal diversion—an instinctive expression, rather than one meted out by decree—and so, even at the Royal Academy, he resisted investing the necessary time and effort to bolster and refine his natural gifts. He would be grateful in the decades to come for this musical foundation, but not now. Still, he was far too timid and dutiful to mount any substantial protests. Reg knew better than to talk back, whether at school or at home.

I'd Like to Break Away from the Rut I'm In

At least within the limits of what he could get away with, Reg began to exert an identity all his own, his outward disposition reverberating rock 'n' roll. In a nod to Texan troubadour Buddy Holly, for instance, he sported black, horn-rimmed eyeglasses with clear lenses—a selective fashion statement rather than an obligatory prescription. Also, he started collecting his own records—Jackie Wilson's "Reet Petite" and Danny and the Juniors' "At the Hop" were his first 45s—which he organized with the meticulousness of a sports statistician, always taking stock of the various record companies, songwriters, and producers that appeared on the labels. He regarded each record as possessing the conscious temperament of a human being, enriched with the empathy and compassion his home life too often lacked. Whenever his parents would quarrel, Reg would retreat to the relative sanctuary of his bedroom. If he couldn't escape the chaos altogether, he could at least block it out with his favorite tunes and a pair of headphones. "I used to find solace in music when my parents used to argue," he recalled in the 2010 BBC documentary, *Madman Across the Water: The Making of Elton John*.

His parents divorced in 1962, with Stanley Dwight petitioning on the grounds of adultery, his wife having admitted to an extramarital affair with housepainter and decorator Fred Farebrother, whom she later married. While Reg welcomed the merciful end to the hostilities he'd witnessed and endured throughout his childhood, his resentment toward his father intensified as a result of the one-sided, unflattering light in which his mother was depicted in the divorce. In 1975, while at the apex of his fame as Elton John, he confided to *Playboy*, "She more or less gave up everything and had to admit to adultery, while he was doing the same thing behind her back and making her pay for it."

Stanley Dwight soon remarried, and over the next several years he fathered four additional sons, distancing himself even further from his firstborn son and solidifying a rift that would never mend. "I was afraid of my father," John told *Rolling Stone* in 2016. "I was walking on eggshells the whole time trying to get his approval. He's been dead for a long time, and I'm still trying to prove things to him. I still do things and say, 'Dad, you would've loved this.'" Stanley Dwight never attended any of his son's live performances.

If such domestic strife affected Reg in any constructive way, it did seem to instill him with the incentive, perhaps sooner than his peers, to carve out a life (if not a living) of his own. Indeed, in 1960, while still at grammar school, he formed his first band, the Corvettes, with two acquaintances, lead vocalist and guitarist Stuart Brown and bassist Geoff Dyson. The teenage trio practiced more than they performed before any live audiences, with rare gigs at local youth clubs and church halls offering little in the way of compensation beyond mere pocket change as tips. One in an interminable line of hitless sixties covers bands, the Corvettes called it quits after eighteen patchy months. Nevertheless, these three budding musicians must have recognized some sort of redemptive chemistry or potential between them, because they wound up reforming less than two years later under a new name—Bluesology—just as an emergent, charismatic quartet from Liverpool was beginning to make the idea of playing in a rock 'n' roll band seem less like an aimless juvenile distraction and more like a viable occupation.

2

It's a Long and Lonely Climb

Early Dues

In the United States, the sixties as a cultural phenomenon didn't coincide with the calendar decade. In other words, the sixties weren't "the sixties" in America until at least 1964—after the Kennedy assassination and the British Invasion, and once the Vietnam War and the Civil Rights Movement had escalated into full, violent swing. In England, though, a cultural revolution had been underway since the earliest days of the decade. In London, for instance, the nascent British blues scene drew disciples in droves to local haunts and basement dives like the Marquee, Ealing Jazz Club, and the Crawdaddy, where, into the wee small hours of the night, bands like the Rolling Stones, the Yardbirds, and Alexis Corner's Blues Incorporated (featuring one Long John Baldry, who would soon loom large in the life of Reg Dwight) held court in multiple-night engagements that inspired memories of legend.

Meanwhile, in Pinner, Reg may as well have belonged to a bygone era altogether. Like a troubadour frustratingly past his prime, every weekend inside the Northwood Hills Hotel saloon the now overweight, bespectacled teenager hunched over an out-of tune, decrepit upright piano, plucking out old cockney songs and standards (crowd-pleasers by the likes of Ray Charles, Al Jolson, and Jim Reeves), while dodging empty pint glasses thrown by the inebriated clientele. Far from resembling the sharpest hipsters and mods that marched through London's fashion district as emphatic emblems of their era, Reg's dowdy fashion sense recalled that of a humble banker or insurance salesman—occupations his estranged biological father would have preferred his son to have pursued. His pudgy physique didn't exactly turn heads, either, much less incite the sort of nubile shrieks of teenage, girlish sexuality Paul McCartney or Mick Jagger provoked from the stage. Reg was a model of mediocrity, plain and artlessly simple. Still, for a first paying job, playing in the Northwood Hills saloon served less as a deliberate first step in a conscientious career plan than as a practical means to an end—Reg needed the money he earned to purchase an electric keyboard and amplifier for his gigs with Bluesology—and the experience nevertheless provided him with an invaluable opportunity to hone his chops and ply his trade.

I Used to Be Stone Sold on Rhythm and Blues

Performing night after night as he and his mates played "the toilets," as working musicians in the know slyly referred to them—the dingy, smoky, booze-drenched joints that formed a roughshod foundation of experience on the road—instilled in Reg the resilience to overcome any adversity he would encounter in more lavish circumstances down the road. This was paying one's dues.

His band having been christened Bluesology as a riff on guitarist Django Reinhardt's 1961 LP, *Djangology*, Reg and friends reunited—along with drummer Mick Ickpen, who rounded out the lineup—with newfound commitment and, in the case of Reg in particular, single-mindedness.

On March 5, 1965, three weeks shy of his eighteenth birthday and six weeks before he was due to take his A-levels in Music and English—in other words, before he would have graduated—Reg quit Pinner County Grammar School. He couldn't foresee the auspicious fate that awaited him, of course, but he believed his talent and passion would serve him well in whatever opportunities (hopefully musical) lay ahead.

On a more practical note, thanks to a recommendation from one of his cousins on his father's side of the family, footballer Roy Dwight, Reg secured a job interview—and, in turn, a job—at West End publishing company Mills Music. Working in the trade department, his responsibilities included shuttling sheet music (and tea, among other complimentary

Elton John, *Rare Masters* cover shot.   *Author's collection*

beverages) to various publishers on England's fabled Tin Pan Alley. In so doing, Reg obtained an invaluable crash course in the music business, placing him in passing company not only of ambitious publishers but also of songwriters and artists hustling for their next hit single. Reg was also afforded unyielding and unparalleled proximity to the newest long-playing albums and singles being released by virtually every record label at the time, which soon accounted for a surge in the already growing music collection in his bedroom at home.

In July, Bluesology auditioned at the Kilburn State Cinema, before signing with the Roy Tempest Agency. No longer an amateur band on the local club scene, Bluesology was booked in venues as far off as Hamburg, Germany, to support various R&B vocalists—experienced acts like Billy Stewart ("I Do Love You"), Major Lance ("Um, Um, Um, Um, Um, Um"), the Ink Spots ("If I Didn't Care"), the Drifters ("Up on the Roof"), and Patti LaBelle and the Bluebelles ("All or Nothing")—who put the budding English musicians through their paces while at the same time invigorating their spirits.

"We couldn't believe our luck," John told *Billboard* magazine in 1997. "We were backing people whose records we used to buy . . . I mean, it couldn't get any better for me."

On the strength of two demos—"Times Getting Tougher Than Tough" and the first song Reg ever wrote, both music and lyrics, "Come Back Baby"—A&R manager Jack Baverstock signed Bluesology to Fontana Records (a subsidiary of Philips Records), the label which in the previous year had released two fleeting singles by an emerging group known at the time as the High Numbers, who would within months find a modish groove as the Who. Upon signing with Fontana, Bluesology re-recorded "Come Back Baby" for a single release in July 1965. The song garnered no chart success whatsoever. The band's follow-up single, another Reg Dwight music-and-lyrics original called "Mr. Frantic," fared only slightly better the following year.

By then, though, Bluesology had landed an audition at the Ken Colyer Jazz Club in Soho, prior to becoming the backing band for the aforementioned Long John Baldry, whom Reg met at the Cromwellian pub in September of 1966. Baldry, a British blues pioneer and mainstay of nearly a decade at this point, had just broken up with his previous rhythm-and-blues outfit, Steam Packet, which featured a rising and ever-ribald young vocalist named Rod Stewart.

After touring with Baldry—who'd scored a #1 single with a saccharine bit of pop sentimentality called "Let the Heartaches Begin" on November 22, 1967, following an appearance on *Top of the Pops*—the band transitioned from churning out purist blues and R&B to entertaining patrons at supper clubs and cabarets. This latest development frustrated Reg, who didn't appreciate performing while customers chewed their food and chatted, the clinking silverware and ceramic dishes proving a distraction he could neither ignore nor tolerate. Regardless of what the other musicians in the band decided for themselves, Reg could no longer succumb to such a dispiriting fate.

It's the Leap of Faith

Back over on Tin Pan Alley, Ray Williams was nervous. He had lied about his age to get the job, and now he was expected to actually carry it through. Only eighteen, if that, he had racked up some experience working in A&R—artist and repertoire—with artists like the Kinks and Sonny and Cher, but still he knew full well that he possessed an astute ear for recognizing talent. So he fudged his age on the application, and landed at the newly established UK subsidiary of Liberty Records as head of A&R.

"I was in a little bit of shock," Williams quips, "because I knew people like George Martin, who I considered a *proper* A&R man." Still, tasked with building Liberty's UK-based roster from scratch, Williams placed an advertisement in the *New Musical Express* (*NME*) in its issue dated June 17, 1967, seeking all manner of talent from which to build the label's roster. "I had thousands and thousands of letters and tapes, just stuff coming in," he says. "And so, being young and enthusiastic, I went through every one of those letters and tapes that were sent in."

Among those who wrote in response to the advertisement were future Electric Light Orchestra maestro Jeff Lynne, on behalf of his initial band Idle Race; songwriter and producer Mike Batt (who founded the popular children's group the Wombles and, later, discovered and produced singer/songwriter Katie Melua); and the Bonzo Dog Doo-Dah Band, whose gigantic hit "I'm the Urban Spaceman" was produced by Paul McCartney and Gus Dudgeon, the latter of whom would assume an integral role as producer of Elton John's most seminal recordings.

And then there was Reg Dwight, of whom Williams recalls:

> He said, "I'm in a band called Bluesology. Can I come in and see you?" So I said, "Sure, come on in."
>
> So, [Reg] came in and he sat down in a little chair in front of me and we just started to talk. I said that I'd seen him perform in Bluesology, and I always thought they were pretty good, but it was always Long John Baldry singing—and he wanted to sing. He said, "I just want to try and do my own thing." But, he said, "The problem is, I don't write lyrics." So, I said, "Well, look, there's

a piano there. Why don't you just go and play a few songs so I can hear you sing?"

He was a little podgy—the word I always use is *forlorn*. He was dressed in blue denim and carried stuff in a carrier bag like Tiny Tim. But he was very humble at that time. I had some sort of sympathy for him. He went along and sang some songs on the piano, and one of them was the Jim Reeves song "He'll Have to Go."

It was a peculiar choice for such a young musician—one that in retrospect seems like it was plucked from a prior, statelier generation of songs. Nevertheless, "He'll Have to Go" was, at the time, a contemporary fixture on the radio, just six years old. In fact, Jim Reeves had lost his life in a plane crash less than two years before Reg Dwight auditioned with his biggest crossover hit.

"He sang a couple of other songs," Williams continues, "and I said, 'Well, I really like your voice. Let's go and make some demos.' And that's what we did. We went down to Tin Pan Alley, which was Denmark Street in London, and we went to an old studio there where they charged about ten pounds an hour, which seemed like a fortune at the time, and we decided to make some demos."

Once the demos were complete, Williams returned to his office at Liberty, where he asked his boss, Bob Reisdorff, to listen. Reisdorff—one of the founders of Dolton Records, and a producer of such acts as the Fleetwoods ("Mr. Blue") and the Ventures ("Wipe Out")—wasn't impressed. Neither was the publisher Alan Keane, who had also listened to the demos.

"Anyway," says Williams, "I thought about it and I said to [Reg] that it didn't look like we were going to get a deal, but to leave it with me and I could introduce him to some folks that maybe ought to help him."

Meanwhile, in among the pile of responses to the Liberty Records advertisement in the *NME*, Williams had also received a letter with a postmark from Lincolnshire, sent by seventeen-year-old Bernard Taupin. "And this letter was suggesting from him that he was a poet, *potentially* a poet," Williams recalls, "but that his lyrics could be set to music."

Legend has it that Taupin's mother had fished the letter out of the trashcan and mailed it on her son's behalf. Taupin himself has disputed

eventually ascending the ranks as a virtuosic guitarist as well as a producer and engineer. "I wanted to learn every aspect about creating music," says Quaye. "We used to have a saying, 'On both sides of the glass'—the glass being in the studio. I wanted to not only be a player, performer/player, but also a writer and producer and engineer. I wanted to have an understanding about every aspect of creating music. That was my goal, so that's what I did."

Quaye may have also unwittingly saved Reg Dwight and Bernie Taupin from musical obscurity. "I got them signed to the label," he says. After the unaccounted assemblage duly exited the premises, Quaye passed the songwriting duo's demos (along with a commending endorsement) over to Dick James and his son, Stephen, who managed the day-to-day operations of the company.

Elton John and Bernie Taupin, *Rare Masters* insert photograph.   *Author's collection*

"So he heard our stuff, liked it, and signed us up," John told *Rolling Stone* in 1973. "As soon as he signed us up at ten quid a week advance royalties I left [Bluesology]. That was the best day in my life, when I quit the group."

Signed on November 17, 1967, to Dick James Music as staff songwriters, the pair was tasked with composing made-to-order songs for the reigning pop-music market. While not on a par with the classics that would evolve from their songwriting partnership, some such songs suggest the melodicism and innate soulfulness of the pair's complementing talents. For instance, "I Can't Go on Living Without You"—a cover version of which, by British songstress Lulu, finished sixth in the 1969 Eurovision Song Contest—features a freakishly cheesy, cha-cha motif, but its ascending melody and rhythm make it difficult to ignore altogether.

"Bernie and I were writing songs for two years before we even struck anything like a decent song," John recalled to British talk-show host Michael Parkinson, on his television program, *Parkinson One to One*, in 1987, "because we were told to write songs initially for people like Tom Jones and Cilla Black and Lulu. Basically, it wasn't our style . . . but then we started to write the songs that we actually liked, and things started to click."

Taupin had already moved out of his Lincolnshire family home and into the modest residence Reg now shared with his mother and step-father, Fred Farebrother—whom Reg facetiously called Derf (Fred in reverse)—in Pinner called Frome Court, the novice wordsmith taking the top bunk in Reg's bedroom while Taupin slept below. "We had so little space," John recalled to *Rolling Stone* in 2011. "We used to lie on the floor with our gatefold sleeves, listening to Leonard Cohen, Dylan, Joni Mitchell, Hendrix . . . *Electric Ladyland* blew my mind. It was an incredible time."

Taupin has reflected upon the burgeoning days of his and John's song-writing partnership with much the same sense of purpose and nostalgia. In 2013, he told the *New York Times*, "It was really, 'You and me against the world.' We were so incredibly close."

Having quit Bluesology and signed with the businessman who published the Beatles, Reg felt like a new man, and he likewise became one, if only in name rather than by formal decree—he wouldn't legally change his name via deed poll until December 8, 1972—with his first name deriving from Bluesology saxophonist Elton Dean and his surname from Long John Baldry.

From this day forward, Reg let it be known—to his friends, his fellow musicians, even his mother—that he shall be Elton John.

3

Hand in Hand Went Music and the Rhyme

Examining the Elton John–Bernie Taupin Songwriting Partnership

As a fervent student of music and an obsessive fan, John had long found fascination in an album's liner notes and the labels affixed to the vinyl, appreciating the wealth of information in their credits, whether citing producers and arrangers or stipulating those who penned the words from who composed the tune: Ira Gershwin, lyrics, George Gershwin, music; Dorothy Fields, lyrics, Irving Berlin, music; Jerry Leiber, lyrics, Mike Stoller, music. Granted, pivotal figures like Chuck Berry and Buddy Holly had emerged in the mid-fifties rock 'n' roll boom as autonomous artists who handled both tasks, but their examples loomed as singular exceptions of their era. The emergence of the "singer/songwriter," exemplified by lone-wolf talents like Joni Mitchell and James Taylor, remained, back in John's childhood, still more than a decade away.

Two songwriters forming two halves of the same whole in, as one of their songs says, "two rooms at the end of the world," together Elton John and Bernie Taupin have composed some of the most enduring and beloved pop music of the past half-century, their storied professional partnership rivaling only Lennon and McCartney's in terms of chart and critical success. Much is known about John and Taupin's propitious meeting in the Summer of Love as a result of Liberty Records head A&R man Ray Williams having placed an advertisement in the *New Musical Express* seeking talent. Much is also known, at least among fans, about the general arc of John and Taupin's songwriting arrangement—first Taupin pens the words, then John composes the melody—but less is understood about what makes their process tick.

"He has a sixth sense about what I want," John said of Taupin in 2016, to the *Telegraph*, "and I have a sixth sense about him. We're always on the same page."

By turns, John and Taupin have attributed their union to a seemingly mystic fix of destiny—or, as Bob Dylan would in his own mercurial way impart, "Blame it all on a simple twist of fate"—yet a more pragmatic analysis of their complementing qualities and contrasting distinctions reveals the features of their chemistry's success. From John's shy and still sheltered perspective in the year that saw the ascent of such landmark singles as "Respect" (Aretha Franklin), "All You Need Is Love" (the Beatles), and "Ode to Billie Joe" (Bobbie Gentry), nothing proved as pivotal—not just on a professional level but on a personal one as well—as when Bernie Taupin entered his life.

Inspiration for Navigation of Our Newfound Craft

In the rural patches of Lincolnshire, in the village of Owmby by Spital, 150 miles north and a veritable world away from suburban Pinner, seventeen-year-old Bernard Taupin's prospects looked grim. Having never ventured far from his family's residence, Flatters Farmhouse, where he was born on May 22, 1950, he has said he learned more from his mother than from the curriculum he encountered in the formal education system, having dropped out of grammar school at age fifteen. Already out of options as far as career planning was concerned, he felt dispirited by the usual opportunities that awaited most adolescents in his rural hometown community at the time—mostly agricultural and factory occupations with rigid shifts and schedules. Such discouragement was enough to make an idealistic young man reject such a society's implicit expectations outright and retreat into fictitious realms of the written word.

Thanks in large part to his maternal grandfather, who taught English literature at Cambridge University, Taupin appreciated both poetry and prose with teeming enthusiasm, and in fantastical stories like J. R. R. Tolkien's *The Lord of the Rings* he felt solace and, in a vicarious way, an innate sense of belonging. Such whimsical pastimes couldn't help but inform his writing. He found inspiration as well from such musicians as Woody Guthrie, Johnny Horton, and Leadbelly. Marty Robbins's "El Paso" was a particular favorite.

Preferring to be considered a storyteller rather than a lyricist or, least of all, a poet—"It's an insult to real poets," he said in 2012, to *Esquire* magazine—Taupin could spend weeks, even months, amassing lines. Images and allusions flowed into one another, owing no allegiance to verses or choruses. Once John would set to work on writing the melody, he would sort them out, rearranging and sometimes omitting lines altogether.

But from where does Taupin elect inspiration? "I'm pretty much drawn to the darker side of things," he said in a 1996 interview with *American Songwriter*. "I'm under the ground at times. That's where I find my ideas. To me, the dark side is much more interesting."

Titles, Taupin has said, have always held special significance to him. "I usually got the title on the top of the piece of paper," he explained to music journalist Paul Zollo, in the 2016 anthology, *More Songwriters on Songwriting*. "And I will start basically at the beginning and work my way down. Sometimes I'll just write all the verses first and then come back and write the chorus. I never usually write the chorus first. It's almost like I create a song like writing a story. The story comes alive."

I Know You and You Know Me, It's Always Half and Half

John exhibited no obvious sense of loss in abstaining from writing lyrics, just as Taupin experienced no remorse in not composing music. Each man tended to his respective specialty as a means of best serving the song he was co-writing at the moment.

"I'm just a purveyor, basically, of Bernie's feelings, Bernie's thoughts," John said in 2000, during an episode of the VH1 series *Behind the Music*. "I'm a musical mouthpiece for his lyrics, which I love."

"When we first got together, there was obviously no intention or plan for Elton to make records," Taupin says in the 2001 documentary, *Classic*

Albums: Goodbye Yellow Brick Road. "It really came about simply because we couldn't get anybody else to record our songs."

John and Taupin did not collaborate—at least not in any face-to-face manner. In fact, from the pair's earliest co-writing endeavors, each man's approach was fiercely isolationist in its distinction, most of all for Taupin. For six months following the advent of their professional union, the pair co-wrote their first songs via the postal service. Taupin would send sheaves of lyrics to his songwriting partner, from Lincolnshire to Pinner, where then John would pick out whichever words or phrases caught his roving eye and set them to music. Early songs like "Scarecrow," which was the first John–Taupin song ever recorded, and "A Dandelion Dies in the Wind," evoke some of the characteristically whimsical lyrical motifs of the late-sixties psychedelic scene.

While low-quality bootleg versions of these particular songs circulate on the Internet, none has been officially released.

They Must Have Had the Whole Thing Planned

Even in the earliest days of his professional partnership with Taupin, John acknowledged, with no sense of self-pity or sorrow, that he would never summon the lyric prowess of Bob Dylan or the lingual intimacy of Joni Mitchell, but he duly recognized his irrefutable aptitude at composing music.

Furthermore, his formative years on the road with Bluesology—reading musical charts; rehearsing and performing live with a carousel of international talent—had provided him with an invaluable crash course in composition and arrangement, for which he seemed to possess a preternatural skill.

Part impatience, part efficiency, John's process has remained much the same since he and Taupin wrote their initial songs, commencing with no deliberation beforehand, harboring no preconceived chord sequences or melodies. "I just go into the studio, look at the lyrics for the first time when I put them on the piano, and go," he told the *Telegraph* in 2013. "If I haven't got it within forty minutes, I give up. It's never changed, the thrill has never gone, because I don't know what I'm going to get next. I don't know what's going to land in front of me."

In turn, Taupin has never anticipated (successfully, at least) how the words he gives John will materialize into music.

"Sometimes," Taupin told the *New Yorker*, in its issue dated August 26, 1996, "I won't be impressed straightaway—I'll think, *You should have taken a bit more time on that, because it sounds a bit flat and repetitive.* And then I'll hear it again, and I'll pick up on all these little nuances in the songs, and, really, that's where his genius lies. He's got these hooks and turns. Instead of taking the path of least resistance—letting the melody line resolve in the obvious way—he goes against the grain."

Like a kooky superstition that evolved into a habit, the hallmark distinction of their working partnership is that the two songwriters have never composed together within the same four walls. (They have each composed within the same residence or recording studio, mind you—just not in the same exact room.) As John explained in 2002, to the *New York Times*, "I couldn't have him in the room—it would be too distracting. It's sacred to me, that selfish part of it, where, you think, 'This is my part of the baby.' Sometimes, when you've first written a song, and you've got it right, it's the best it will ever sound."

They have never discussed what the lyrics mean, either. Such an arrangement could have caused some moments of friction or resentment in the past, in Taupin's case for not having his words necessarily parlayed with what he considered the most subject-appropriate music, and in John's case for not altogether knowing what he is singing about. There could have been episodes where Taupin has submitted a song that, in his mind, should result one way, only to have John edit and rearrange his lines around or conjure a melody at odds with his original sentiment, setting the song on an otherwise ulterior course.

According to John, though, they have never argued over how any of their songs has materialized. "I'm very conscious they ultimately will be sung by him so the content cannot be overtly selfish on my part," Taupin explained in 2013, to the *New York Times*. "I'm conscious they are words that have to come out of his mouth."

Still Green and Growing

Going back to their first forays as staff songwriters in their early tenure at Dick James Music, John and Taupin were initially consigned to write songs for the prevailing mainstream marketplace of the day, not as an expression of their eccentric whims and ambitions. However, both men considered their charge a chore, their discontent manifesting in a batch of half-hearted attempts at novelty Top 40 experiments for the likes of Lulu, Tom Jones, and Engelbert Humperdinck, among others. Quite simply, they disliked their own material.

Having joined Dick James Music a year or so later than John and Taupin, Steve Brown, a promotions associate, recognized how the budding songwriters resisted the superficialities evident in their earliest tunes and in turn encouraged them to write songs that satisfied their artistic passions. Basking in the challenge (not to mention the relief), John and Taupin began writing decidedly uncommercial, non–Top 40 fare, and in so doing they inched closer and closer to distinguishing their own distinctive voice together as songwriters.

Meanwhile, John was signed to the Philips label, by way of Dick James Music, as a recording artist (in addition to his existing contract with DJM as a staff songwriter), and, on March 1, 1968, "I've Been Loving You"—which was credited to both John and Taupin, although it was written only by John—was released. It slipped promptly into oblivion.

There's a Place in the World for a Woman Like You

Fate took a turn for the better with a song recorded in December 1968 as one of the initial cuts intended for what emerged as John's debut album, *Empty Sky*, although it didn't make the cut on the original pressing. "Lady Samantha" was released as a British single on January 17, 1969.

While critics appreciated the single, the record-buying public failed to display similar enthusiasm. John performed it (and "Sails," an *Empty Sky* deep cut) live on BBC radio on July 20, 1969, the same date that Apollo 11 landed on the moon. Produced by Steve Brown (who would go on to produce *Empty Sky*), "Lady Samantha" proved if nothing else that John could compose a song appreciated by critics and disc jockeys. The public? Not yet. As a stepping-stone to more successful endeavors down the road, however, "Lady Samantha" fulfilled a crucial function, even as its dense production belied John's formidable piano playing behind grungy, hallucinogenic-sounding guitars. As a rock 'n' roll song representative of its time, though, there's nothing to suggest it would be a one-off, either. Despite its lack of sales, "Lady Samantha" nonetheless succeeded as a turntable hit—a dubious distinction where a song would benefit from multiple radio plays without its exposure translating into achievement on the charts.

A Strange New Sound You Never Heard Before

On *Empty Sky*, John was still finding his voice as an autonomous artist, barely two years after his last performances with Bluesology, where even when he sang lead he never ventured from his side-stage perch behind his keyboard. He hadn't yet learned showmanship in the manner he would come to inhabit and ultimately command.

From this vantage point, he could have reflected the embryonic stages of progressive rock as much as any characteristic singer/songwriter approach. He was still feeling out the finer translations of his talent, how they gelled with Taupin's still emerging lyrical facility. What's peculiar is that *Empty Sky* lacks any discernible nod to R&B and soul—such pivotal strains of American music that had shaped John's musical identity and appreciation since childhood.

Empty Sky was released in June 1969 in the UK, though not until 1975 in the States. For all intents and purposes, the *Elton John* album would be his official debut in America, where he would attain the most success.

Considering it marks not only the debut of Elton John in the UK and Europe as a solo artist but also the inaugural album in the John–Taupin canon, *Empty Sky* lacks the sense of significance and formality it probably should have possessed. Not that some of the individual songs pale in drastic comparison to the beloved classics that would ultimately emerge from the budding songwriters on subsequent efforts. Rather, the production by Steve Brown more often than not compromises whatever potential even the best selections may have suggested in their most elemental states. Too often submerged in ornate, staccato swaths of harpsichord rather than John's earnest piano playing, the music drifts in a post-psychedelic haze that recalls progressive bands like Procol Harum or Yes at their most sonically indulgent, rather than anything within the emergent "singer/songwriter" phenomenon (heralded by troubadours like James Taylor, Joni Mitchell, and Leonard Cohen) within which he would soon ascend. The most conspicuous instance of such musical melodrama is "Skyline Pigeon," a song that would endure as one of John and Taupin's most indelible songs in more unvarnished renditions and performances, yet here, in its original version, it is inundated with unnecessary affectations.

Elton John's debut solo LP, *Empty Sky*, was released in the UK and Europe on July 9, 1969, but not until January 13, 1975, in the US. *Author's collection*

For all the misguided production excesses, however, John's musicality—his innate gift for conceiving and shaping melodies and arrangements to even the most esoteric lyrics—resonates as almost fully formed. From the eight-minute title track (a rocker as bold and voracious as John has ever released) to such rhapsodic ballads as "It's Me That You Need," he exemplifies the sort of passion that would surface with far more frequency on far more impressive albums to come.

"To be frank," says former *Melody Maker* journalist and editor Chris Charlesworth, "*Empty Sky* was not a hit. It was the second album, the album called *Elton John*, with 'Your Song,' that introduced Britain to him, really."

Show Me Which Road I'm On

Indeed, John's self-titled sophomore album is generally the one critics and most fans start from in addressing the Elton John phenomenon, and where the nexus of his and Taupin's respective gifts as composer and lyricist merged to their first great fruition. A sense of sophistication and gravitas underscores these songs, achieved in no small part by arranger Paul Buckmaster and producer Gus Dudgeon, whose classical disposition and affinities yield heightened dimensions.

Translating influences and elements from his foundational education at the Royal Academy of Music, John infused classical distinctions within the framework of pop songs that, in their most intrinsic states, reflect a flair for the dramatic that complement such orchestral flourishes.

Recorded in London's Soho district at Trident Studios—a quantum improvement from the in-house studio welled within the Dick James Music headquarters, and where Dudgeon and Buckmaster had recently worked on David Bowie's breakout single, "Space Oddity"—the album finds John helming some of his signature tunes.

"Gus and I sat in his office and went through each song," Buckmaster recalled in a 2010 interview with the *Guardian*, "and worked out the type of orchestration which would suit each track. We effectively designed each song as an individual piece, giving it its own character."

"Border Song," with its gospel overtones (particularly in its final verse, which incidentally was written by John) that may have seemed like a fitting introduction to the American market, was released as the album's first single, though it stalled at #92 on the *Billboard* Hot 100. The song gained far more notoriety when Aretha Franklin recorded her version (which peaked at #37) and included it on her Grammy-winning 1972 LP, *Young, Gifted, and Black.*

With its unaffectedly charming lyrical illusions, not to mention its eloquent musical sophistication, it was the album's second US single, "Your Song," that most endeared John to North American listeners who were beginning to embrace the vanguard of the burgeoning singer/songwriter movement extolled by such philosophic talents as Joni Mitchell, James Taylor, and Crosby, Stills, and Nash. "Your Song" elevated Elton John well into their ranks, despite its modest origins.

Remembering when Taupin presented him with the lyrics in Frome Court, John told Cameron Crowe in 2014, for *Rolling Stone*, "'Oh, my God, this is such a great lyric, I can't fuck this one up.' It came out in about twenty minutes, and when I was done, I called him in, and we both knew."

"The great thing about that song is that the naiveté of it is truly honest," Taupin says in Paul Zollo's 2016 anthology, *More Songwriters on Songwriting.* "It's real. It's not somebody pretending to write a song that is simple and naïve. It is a simple, naïve song."

Altogether, the *Elton John* album heralded John's ascendance onto the world stage, but that was not the original intention. "It was really made as a very glamorous series of demos for other people to record his songs," Gus Dudgeon said in 2002, in an interview with *Mix Online.*

Still, as Charlesworth recalls, Elton John reflected an irrefutable charisma in his early solo performances (a trait that non-performing songwriters would not necessarily possess), like an especially thrilling one he had witnessed in the summer of 1970, at what was known as the Krumlin Festival in Halifax, England. In a rain-soaked field before two thousand undiscerning punters, John, along with drummer Nigel Olsson and bassist Dee Murray, played well enough to attract Charlesworth's attention, in print and in person.

Upon getting to know John, Charlesworth says, he recognized in him a passionate music fan, much like himself.

He'd obviously started collecting his records from a fairly early age, I would imagine, as indeed had I. He knew all about these classic recordings from the sixties. Not necessarily the obvious ones, and by that I mean the Beatles, the Rolling Stones, Bob Dylan. Everybody knows about that, but they *don't* know about Connie Francis; and they *don't* know about the Drifters; and they *don't* know about Ben E. King; and they *don't* know about the Shirelles; and they *don't* know about the one-hit wonders that were really great records from artists who never really had any more big hits. But Elton *did* know all that history of pop. He had excellent taste, of course, as a result.

Open Up Your Heart and Let Your Feelings Flow

Besides the sheer quality of its songs, one reason the *Elton John* album succeeded as it did—reaching #4 in the US on the *Billboard* Top 200 while peaking at #5 on the British album charts—is its inherent empathy. Listeners connected to songs like "Your Song" and "I Need You to Turn To" and "The Greatest Discovery" because they spoke to intimate, universal emotions, which John rendered with sophisticated musicality and vocal soulfulness. Even more lyrically abstract songs like "Take Me to the Pilot" and "Border Song" were rendered with such conviction that audiences connected with them in their own vicarious (and often improvised) ways.

"He could have easily been a one-hit wonder," says Charlesworth, noting the limited success of "Lady Samantha." "It wasn't until 'Your Song' . . . in fact, it wasn't until he established a trio with Nigel Olsson on drums and Dee Murray on bass and started performing very often—he was gigging all around the country. It wasn't until that point, which is late 1970, when he started making a name for himself. This was a year or more longer after the first album came out. It was really 'Your Song' that was the big hit when everybody started thinking, Who is this guy?"

Critics in general were similarly captivated. On the strength of the album, John was nominated as "Best New Artist" at the thirteenth Annual Grammy Awards in 1971, losing to the Carpenters, whose ubiquitous hit

Elton John, released April 10, 1970, includes John's breakout single, "Your Song" US #8 / UK #7.
Author's collection

singles the previous year, "We've Only Just Begun" and "(They Long to Be) Close to You," proved invincible. The same year, *Elton John* earned a nomination for the most coveted award of all, "Album of the Year," losing to Simon and Garfunkel's *Bridge Over Troubled Water*. Needless to say, such industry misfortunes did not hinder the popular and critical success that was to follow for John, especially in America.

4

We're Gonna Need a Helping Hand

The Musicians

Ironically, considering Elton John is among rock 'n' roll's most successful and distinctive solo artists, he has long preferred to create and play music within the group structure of a band. The endowment of ideas suggested pathways that could enrich the song that is being composed. John may have the final say—it is his name that appears on the album cover, after all—but the group dynamic is more of a democracy than it may seem, considering that he trusts the talent and instincts of those in the band—whom he chose for very specific reasons, to enhance a rhythm section or to widen out the sound with more guitars. He appreciates the camaraderie between the musicians, and the shared sense of reward upon the moment a song is fully created and produced.

In addition to John and Bernie Taupin, an insular army of musicians made everything function and thrive. John has not always been loyal to some of his most enduring bandmates—particularly in the years when his substance abuse was at its worst—but, then again, he has not played with the revolving door of lineups used by many of his contemporaries. Think of these musicians as sonic building blocks; to understand why John made the kinds of music he did at any particular time, it's wise to consider some of the defining characteristics of the musicians with whom he has worked.

Guy Babylon (Keyboards)

A Grammy Award–winning keyboardist who spent over twenty years playing live and recording with Elton John, Babylon began as a session musician in the mid-eighties. Working alongside bassist Bob Birch and guitarist Davey Johnstone, he was recruited by John in 1988 as the second keyboardist in his live band. By the time they embarked on the 1992–1993 world tour in support of *The One*, Babylon had the keys all to himself. In the studio, Babylon played on twelve of John's albums. He died of a heart attack on September 2, 2009, aged fifty-two.

"He was one of the most brilliant musicians I ever knew, a true genius, a gentle angel," John stated on his official website, "and I loved him so much."

Bob Birch (Bass)

Born and bred in Detroit, Bob Birch grew up marveling at the musicality of Motown session bassist James Jamerson, whose lugubrious grooves insulated classic sides by the likes of Marvin Gaye, the Temptations, and the Supremes. Having graduated from Wayne State University with a bachelor's degree in music education and performance—he had originally pursued a pre-med track, but changed his major—he moved to Los Angeles in 1981, playing in a small handful of fleeting bands, including an ironically named outfit called Fortune, and, presuming their modest earnings, the all-too-aptly named Pocket Change. Session work proved fleeting as well, but during the recording of Luis Cardenas's 1985 debut LP, *Animal Instinct*, Birch befriended keyboardist Guy Babylon. By 1988, both musicians were members of Ashton, but Babylon soon left that band to join Elton John's band, in time for the world tour in support of *Reg Strikes Back*. Birch soon hit the road, too, with veteran singer/songwriter José Feliciano, before joining Warpipes, which included Elton John's current keyboardist and guitarist, Guy Babylon, and Davey Johnstone, respectively, along with his former (and future) drummer, Nigel Olsson.

In 1992, John found himself in need of a bassist in a hurry, as Pino Palladino, who had played on John's most recent LP, *The One*, opted out of the massive world tour that was soon to commence in its support so that he could tend to his pregnant wife. Johnstone, impressed not only with Birch's talent but also his easygoing demeanor, recommended his Warpipes comrade for the job. Complementing a rhythm section he shared with British drummer Charlie Morgan, Birch began his tenure in the Elton John Band on May 26, 1992, in Oslo, Norway.

In the two decades during which Birch toured and recorded with John—he contributed to such albums as *Made in England*, *The Big Picture*, and *Peachtree Road*—he notched up additional opportunities on the live stage and in recording studios with artists including Tina Turner, Eric Clapton, Luciano Pavarotti, B.B. King, and Billy Joel. However, in 1995, Birch was struck by a pickup truck while walking in Montreal, suffering two broken legs and perilous damage to his spine. Though he returned to John's band after seven months of convalescence and all manner of medical treatments, he suffered from extreme back pain continually thereafter, his physical agony intensifying to the point where he needed to sit in a chair for several live performances in 2012 after suffering a fall that further exacerbated the pain he already endured. On August 15, 2012, Birch reached his breaking point, committing suicide down the block from his Los Angeles home—John's original bassist, Dee Murray, had died exactly seven months prior—his death the result of a self-inflicted gunshot wound to the head. He was fifty-six.

"I am devastated and shocked at the loss of my friend and fellow musician, Bob Birch," John wrote on his official website the following day. "To me Bob was family. He had been a member of my band for 20 years; we played over 1,400 concerts together. He was one of the greatest musicians I have ever worked with, and in all our years on the road he never played or sang a bad note. I cannot find the words to describe this tragic death, and how much I loved him."

Curt Bisquera (Drums)

Bisquera only played two full concerts with John, namely the *One Night Only* shows at Madison Square Garden on October 20–21, 2000—the drummer was also on hand when John and his band performed

"Philadelphia Freedom" with the Backstreet Boys at the 2000 Grammy Awards—but he forged an indelible impression. Recorded for a concert film and a live album produced by Phil Ramone (see chapter 6), *One Night Only* saw John and a smattering of special guests (including Billy Joel, Kiki Dee, Bryan Adams, and Mary J. Blige) gliding through expected and unexpected gems alike. All the while, Bisquera made the most of his redemptive, enduring moment in the spotlight.

Matt Bissonette (Bass)

Next to talent, versatility is probably the most valuable asset a musician can have. Consider, for example, bassist Matt Bissonette, whose credentials reflect a spectrum of projects over the past four decades, from touring with the likes of Maynard Ferguson and David Lee Roth to recording studio albums with Rick Springfield, to making live albums with Ringo Starr (along with his brother, drummer Gregg Bissonette) and Boz Scaggs, to playing on the theme song from the sitcom, *Friends*.

Bissonette relied on that same versatility when, following Bob Birch's tragic suicide on August 15, 2012, guitarist and musical director Davey Johnstone recruited him to join Elton John's band. Less than a month later, on September 11, 2012, Bissonette and his fretless bass stood onstage at the Coliseum with John and the rest of his band in Jackson, Mississippi, confronting many of the same mixed emotions that keyboardist Kim Bullard had faced when he first performed with the band after Guy Babylon's sudden death three years prior.

"You can never take a guy like Bob Birch's place in a band," Bissonette said in a statement published on John's official website. "I would love to honor Bob on this Elton tour and while playing all these great songs remember how great he was, as a bass player and all-round musician."

Paul Buckmaster (Arrangements, Strings)

Paul Buckmaster's talents transcended his inveterate arrangements. After working with David Bowie on his breakthrough single, "Space Oddity," in

1969, he was recruited to arrange John's eponymous sophomore album, released the following year. On songs like "Sixty Years On," "The Greatest Discovery," and especially "Your Song," Buckmaster complemented John's earnest piano and vocal with discreet, delicate instrumentation—decisions that enriched rather than overwhelmed their musical essence.

"Adding orchestral passages and textures should give added depth and dimensionality, physically, psychologically and aurally speaking," Buckmaster explained in 2010, in an interview with the *Guardian*. "I feel I've succeeded when the goose-bump thrill factor kicks in."

Opportunities begat subsequent opportunities for Buckmaster, who went on to work with such artists as Miles Davis, Carly Simon, Harry Nilsson, Leonard Cohen, Guns N' Roses, and Stevie Nicks. Buckmaster died of undisclosed causes on November 7, 2017, aged seventy-one.

"He helped make me the artist I am," Elton John said in a statement on his social media channels. "A revolutionary arranger who . . . took my songs and made them soar."

Kim Bullard (Keyboards)

Following the sudden death in 2009 of keyboardist Guy Babylon from a heart attack, Kim Bullard was chosen for the delicate yet necessary task of replacing him. At first, Bullard humbly followed as best he could in the creative footsteps of his predecessor, but after just a few performances, John encouraged him to embrace his own artistic muse—to contribute his own ideas and instill his own style within the existing framework of the music he was tasked with performing each night onstage.

After eight years of playing with the band on countless stages around the world, Bullard entered Village studio in Los Angeles in 2016 along with John, producer T Bone Burnett, and the rest of John's touring band to record *Wonderful Crazy Night*, the first Elton John studio album to feature his contributions.

Ray Cooper (Percussion)

The members of Blue Mink were no slouches on the British music scene. The five-piece band boasted a string of hit singles in the late sixties and early seventies, some which featured Reg Dwight on piano. By the time he first laid his madcap percussion on 1971's *Madman Across the Water*, Ray Cooper was already his own singular tour de force, a gesticulating percussionist with a homicidal stage presence galvanized by an indefatigable fire. Over the past four decades, Cooper's on-again/off-again presence in the band has only continued to amplify John's music with the same requisite heat.

James Newton Howard (Keyboards, Orchestral Arrangements)

Music obsessive that he is, John already knew about James Newton Howard when the keyboardist was summoned to join the band in 1974. Having recorded and toured with the likes of Melissa Manchester and Ringo Starr, Howard had recorded a solo album in 1974, which John had sitting on his table when he and Howard first met. John played Howard the entirety of *Captain Fantastic and the Brown Dirt Cowboy*, which had not been released to that point, then offered the young musician a spot in the band. Howard's first gig? A sold-out Wembley Stadium, headlining a bill that also included Joe Walsh, the Eagles, and the Beach Boys, among others.

In the ensuing years, Howard proved a crucial accompanist and arranger, especially considering his contributions to John's 1976 double album, *Blue Moves* (on such songs as "Sorry Seems to Be the Hardest Word" and "Tonight"). In 1986, Howard assumed the mantle of conducting the Melbourne Symphony Orchestra during John's historic Tour de Force in Australia, culminating with the tour's final night being recorded for the 1987 LP, *Live in Australia with the Melbourne Symphony Orchestra*. In July 2004, he reprised his role as maestro, conducting a ninety-nine-piece orchestra and choir culled from students at New York's Juilliard School and London's Royal Academy of Music for four performances John staged at Radio City Music Hall—John's first-ever shows in the US with a full symphony orchestra.

Davey Johnstone (Guitar)

Though he was content with his Scottish-folk band, Magna Carta, at the time—Gus Dudgeon had produced the band's LP, *Songs from Wasties Orchard*—Davey Johnstone accepted Dudgeon's invitation to play on a session for the title track of *Madman Across the Water*, adding mandolin, sitar, and banjo to "Holiday Inn." The next day, he was officially invited to join the band. In later years, as his stature in the band grew, he became the band's musical director.

John Jorgenson (Guitar/Various Instruments)

Classically trained, Jorgenson has nurtured his virtuosity since early childhood, and his skills have yielded a smorgasbord of opportunities to record and tour with a range of musicians, including Bob Dylan, John Prine, Barbra Streisand, and Willie Nelson. Joining Elton John's band in 1994 for what amounted to a six-year stint, Jorgenson not only complemented a plethora of live performances, such as the one heard on *One Night Only*, but also select session work, including that which manifested on *The Big Picture*.

Jody Linscott (Percussion)

Percussionist Jody Linscott's credentials are packed with a slew of superstars, including live performances (Paul McCartney, the Who, and Bob Dylan) and studio credits (Pete Townshend's *All the Best Cowboys Have Chinese Eyes*, Kirsty MacColl's *Electric Landlady*) galore. After contributing percussion to John's 1986 LP, *Leather Jackets*, Linscott was enlisted to perform on his world tour in support of the album, culminating in John's Australian tour with the Melbourne Symphony Orchestra.

John Mahon (Percussion, Backing Vocals)

If the talent is a given, connections are important things to have in the music business, too. One opportunity leads to another, and after playing with the likes of jazz great Peter White and vocalist Rita Coolidge, Mahon earned gigs like producing Ray Charles in a television commercial—which quite a lot of people noticed at the time. He debuted with Elton John in 1997, playing just percussion at first, as expected, but soon enough his vocal talents set him up for prime slots singing backup with John and the other musicians, including Davey Johnstone and Nigel Olsson.

Jonathan "Sugarfoot" Moffett (Drums)

A longtime drummer for Michael Jackson (and, before M. J.'s solo career, the Jacksons), Moffett also recorded and performed with such superstars as Madonna and George Michael before Elton John recruited him for his *Reg Strikes Back* world tour. He remained in the band for the recording sessions in Switzerland and subsequent world tour in support of *Sleeping with the Past*. Attacking the groove with pathological funk—think of the insistent beat that drives "Billie Jean," for instance—Moffett got all up in the groove at hand.

Charlie Morgan (Drums)

Though he'd recorded with Elton John in the studio by this point, drummer Charlie Morgan faced what a select few other band members had also endured: their first live gig was in front of an enormous audience. In Morgan's case, it was 1985's Live Aid at Wembley Stadium—not exactly a small club within which to hone one's chops. In fact, before what was a thirteen-year tenure with John, Morgan had run in many of the same circles as John since the seventies, having played with the likes of bassist David Paton, John Jorgenson, and Kiki Dee, along with former Rocket Records artist Judy Tzuke.

In the studio, Morgan played on albums including *Ice on Fire*, *Leather Jackets*—his arm, in a Warholian illustration, graces that album's cover—as well as *Live in Australia with the Melbourne Symphony Orchestra*.

Dee Murray (Bass)

Born in Kent, Dee Murray played in a band in the sixties called the Mirage, before joining the last iteration of the Spencer Davis Group—long after the group's founding member, Steve Winwood, had graduated to Traffic. In 1967, Murray recruited drummer Nigel Olsson to join the band on a US tour—the Summer of Love in America, not a bad gig.

With Olsson, Murray appeared on John's earliest and most classic albums, and was a founding member of the Elton John Band until John fired his band prior to his historic double-header at Dodger Stadium in 1975. Murray was recruited once again in the eighties, performing at the Central Park concert as well as on the albums *Too Low for Zero* and *Breaking Hearts*, before being dismissed again. His final appearance on an Elton John album came with 1988's *Reg Strikes Back*, on which he sang backing vocals. After battling skin cancer, Murray died of a stroke on January 15, 1992, in his adopted hometown, Nashville, Tennessee. He was forty-five.

Nigel Olsson (Drums)

The singer in a group called Sunderland before discovering his love for drumming in another group called Plastic Penny—a sixties group signed to Dick James Music the same time John and Taupin were staff songwriters—Nigel Olsson gave his first live performance with John on April 21, 1970, at the Roundhouse in London, supporting the Who. Olsson played Keith Moon's drum kit, which would by show's end lay scattered and destroyed on the stage; during the Who's set, guitarist and principal songwriter Pete Townshend dedicated what would be his band's last performance of the rock opera *Tommy* to John.

In an association that has lasted off and on for half a century—Olsson's debut on an Elton John recording was on the *Empty Sky* song "Lady What's Tomorrow"—the drummer has contributed with not only his drumming but his backing vocals (the latter often alongside Dee Murray and Davey Johnstone) to John's signature sound, forging a place in John's band that has proven integral, though not always indispensable.

Depending on whose version of history is to be believed, he was notably replaced (or fired) in 1975, upon the release of *Captain Fantastic and the Brown Dirt Cowboy*, just prior to the Mid-Summer Music Festival at Wembley Stadium, as well as, a decade later, just prior to the *Ice on Fire* sessions and John's performance at Live Aid, once again at Wembley Stadium.

After singing backing vocals on John's *The Road to El Dorado* soundtrack, Olsson was officially reinstated to the band for the *One Night Only* concerts in 2000 at Madison Square Garden, and has remained in the lineup ever since. Having idolized Ringo Starr's discreet style of playing, Olsson adapted a similarly discreet style of his own, reveling in performing ballads in particular, and in not playing loud in general. Aside from his predilections behind the kit, Olsson also forged a reputation for wearing workman's uniforms (like those of a gas station attendant or an automobile mechanic), replete with golfer's gloves.

Kenny Passarelli (Bass)

No sooner had bassist Kenny Passarelli joined the band than he was playing his first gig—at a sold-out Wembley Stadium. Recommended to Elton John by Joe Walsh, with whom he had previously performed as a co-founding member of Colorado-based trio Barnstorm and co-written such classics as "Rocky Mountain Way," Passarelli stepped into a situation unlike the comparatively laid-back one he had enjoyed back in his native state. (Barnstorm was the first band to record at the then-new Caribou Ranch recording studio, where John would make a handful of albums in the mid-seventies, including *Captain Fantastic and the Brown Dirt Cowboy* and *Rock of the Westies*.)

John had just fired his band, and the new bassist (and other band members) had to learn an album they hadn't played on, *Captain Fantastic and the Brown Dirt Cowboy*, before performing it in full at Wembley Stadium before an unsuspecting, sold-out audience. The band soon found its groove, however, and went on to play the historic two-night stand at Dodger Stadium and record *Rock of the Westies* and *Blue Moves* before John disbanded this group of musicians, out of the blue, as well.

On August 13, 2017, Passarelli was inducted—as a member of Barnstorm, along with guitarist Joe Walsh and drummer Joe Vitale—to the Colorado Music Hall of Fame.

David Paton (Bass)

Best known as the lead vocalist for British pop group Pilot, whose hit single "Magic" (which was produced by Alan Parsons) remains a staple of oldies pop-and-rock radio, Paton has played with a variety of artists, including Paul McCartney, the Pretenders, and Kate Bush. Responsible for the bass part on "Nikita," among other Elton John songs, Paton's association in the band included the historic 1986 tour of Australia with the Melbourne Symphony Orchestra.

Roger Pope (Drums)

Hailing from Whitstable, Kent, Pope supplied the drumming on several of Elton John's earliest, most template-setting works; he then contributed to John's mid-seventies albums *Rock of the Westies* and *Blue Moves*. Known as "Popey" to friends, he played in the Countdowns before joining the Soul Agents, which featured an up-and-coming vocalist named Rod Stewart, who then renamed the group Rod Stewart and the Soul Agents. Then came Loot, which morphed into Hookfoot (along with bassist David Glover, guitarist Caleb Quaye, and harmonica player Ian Duck); and then Pope's affiliation with Dick James Music and, ultimately, Elton John.

After John "retired" from performing in 1976, Pope went on to play in Davey Johnstone's short-lived group China, before reuniting once again with Quaye in Hall and Oates's touring band. Pope died of cancer on September 17, 2013, aged sixty-six.

Caleb Quaye (Guitar)

While John has played with other band members for longer, more consistent periods, no musician shares as much history or as many references with him as guitarist Caleb Quaye. From his days working for Dick James Music on Tin Pan Alley to touring in the later iteration of Bluesology to the heights of John's superstardom, Wembley Stadium, Dodger Stadium, and several indispensable albums, Quaye could be described as the unsung catalyst of his career.

Ken Stacey (Guitars, Backing Vocals)

While his talents on the acoustic guitar have come in handy when certain songs call for an influx of strings, Stacey's ticket to ride has correlated to his abilities as a vocalist, particularly as a harmonist. His other credits range from appearing on two seasons of *American Idol* as a voice coach to landing a coveted spot as a backup singer on Michael Jackson's ill-fated *This Is It* residency (which was canceled in the wake of the King of Pop's 2009 death) at the O2 Arena in London—the rehearsals for which were captured for posterity on what has now become the most successful concert film of all time.

Romeo Williams (Bass)

Following the throat surgery he received in Australia in early 1987 and the subsequent recording of his 1988 LP, *Reg Strikes Back* (which saw original bassist Dee Murray return to the fold as a backing vocalist), John sought a band that could toughen up his songs for his return to the concert stage. "I think he was just looking for a different sound," bassist Romeo Williams, who replaced David Paton, told me in 2016. "Maybe a little bit more soulful sound." New songs like "I Don't Want to Go on with You Like That" and "A Word in Spanish" certainly merited the added punch, and the rhythm section of Williams and newly acquired drummer John Moffett had the chops to deliver. "[Elton] had a lot more movement than usual onstage because his other bands pretty much kind of stayed still," Williams continued. "And we were more with the girl background singers dancing back there, me jumping around like a madman."

That relative looseness onstage gave John the confidence to take his new lineup into the studio after the tour, recording 1989's *Sleeping with the Past* over a six-month stretch at Puk Recording Studios in Denmark. The camaraderie and chemistry the band had enjoyed on the road (during the world tour in support of *Reg Strikes Back*) now extended to the sessions. "It was fantastic," Williams recalled. "The vibe, the style, the method of recording was very relaxed. Most sessions are more intense. His were very relaxed."

Such stress-free conditions resulted in one of John's strongest albums in years, yielding an instant classic in "Sacrifice" and producing additional hit singles like "Club at the End of the Street" and "Healing Hands." Brief as it was, Williams looked back on his experience alongside John with nothing but fondness. "I love him to death—love him to death," he said of John. "It wasn't my choice I got out of the band, that's for sure, because I enjoyed working with him." Williams died on May 8, 2017.

Richie Zito (Guitars)

Zito had just turned twenty-eight when he stepped onto the makeshift stage at Central Park before an estimated audience of over four hundred thousand frenzied fans. As the guitarist for Elton John, Zito may have considered that performance as the peak of his career, but he was only just beginning, his credits as a guitarist and producer (or co-producer) appearing on albums by the likes of Joe Cocker, Heart, and Glenn Frey.

5

Well, I Looked for Support from the Rest of My Friends

Special Guests

Some artists consider it professional courtesy, but one of the major perks of achieving a certain level of stardom in the music business is having the opportunity to collaborate with an array of other artists. As one's stature increases, so too, generally, does the quality of artists at one's disposal. The caliber of musicians and vocalists who have in various ways contributed to Elton John's studio albums over the past half-century speaks not only to the integrity of his talent but also to the respect he inspires among his peers. In this chapter, we will survey the special guests—artists who were not credited as session musicians or as members of John's band—who have appeared on his official studio albums.

Rick Astley

In the late eighties, few artists were played as often on mainstream pop radio as Rick Astley, whose ubiquitous 1987 hit single, "Never Gonna Give You Up," topped the charts in twenty-five countries, including the US and his native UK. Granted, at the height of his fame, he scored other hits as well (three from his debut album, no less, including "Together Forever" and "It Would Take a Strong, Strong Man"), but "Never Gonna Give You Up" proved to be an albatross that Astley (or his audience) couldn't shake, inciting both ecstatic reverence and fierce ridicule. In fact, thirty years after "Never Gonna Give You Up" exited the charts, the song spawned one the Internet's most popular (and, depending on one's perspective, exasperating) memes—"Rickrolling," an online prank that duped the unsuspected into watching the song's official music video, further illustrating Astley's unique power to unite and divide music lovers.

Whether or not Astley's distinctive brand of soul-inspired pop music is everyone's cup of tea, his robust singing style remains difficult to dismiss altogether. In fact, his backing vocals on "Can You Feel the Love Tonight," from the 1994 soundtrack to *The Lion King*, immersed though they are in the final mix, suitably resound like a mighty roar.

The Backstreet Boys

By the late nineties, mainstream pop had evolved into a conglomerate of prefabricated mass productions, glossy hit singles cobbled together by small armies of songwriters for up-and-coming singers ranging from former Disney starlets like Britney Spears and Christina Aguilera to burgeoning boy bands like NSYNC and the Backstreet Boys.

At the peak of their popularity, the Backstreet Boys were savoring the gargantuan success of their most recent album, *Millennium*, which had entered the *Billboard* 200 chart at #1 (a feat achieved for the first time ever by Elton John with 1975's *Captain Fantastic and the Brown Dirt Cowboy*) and sold over a million copies in its first week of release, when they appeared with John on the 2000 soundtrack to *The Road to El Dorado*, singing backup on "Friends Never Say Goodbye."

Gary Barlow

At the height of his success with British boy band Take That, whose album, *Everything Changes*, had recently topped the UK album charts, lead vocalist Gary Barlow added his backing vocals to "Can You Feel the Love Tonight" on the 1994 soundtrack to *The Lion King*. By 2001, as a bona-fide solo superstar in his own right, he contributed backing vocals to "This Train Don't Stop There Anymore," the closing track on John's twenty-sixth studio LP, *Songs from the West Coast*.

Curt Boettcher

Having produced acts like the Association and Tommy Roe in the late sixties, Curt Boettcher attained a cultish success as a singer/songwriter. In the seventies and early eighties, he also sang backup for a host of artists, including John, contributing to his 1976 duet with Kiki Dee, "Don't Go Breaking My Heart," along with two songs his double album of the same year, *Blue Moves* ("Chameleon" and "Someone's Final Song"), and his 1980 LP, *21 at 33*. Boettcher died in 1987 of a lung infection, aged forty-three.

The Brecker Brothers

Throughout the seventies, the Brecker Brothers—Randy on trumpet, Michael on tenor sax—simmered in clubs and on albums by the best of the best, including the original lineup of Blood, Sweat, and Tears. Their appearance on *Blue Moves* in 1976 preceded their iconic performance on the title track of Paul Simon's *Still Crazy After All These Years* by more than a year. For the siblings, who played on "Boogie Pilgrim," "Shoulder Holster," and "Idol," an extensive career awaited. On January 13, 2007, Michael Brecker died of leukemia, age fifty-seven.

Paul Carrack

For more than four decades, Paul Carrack has cultivated one of the most eclectic careers in popular music. Known initially as the lead vocalist of the British band Ace, whose 1974 single "How Long" (#3 US, #20 UK) has become a staple of adult contemporary radio ever since, he is perhaps best known for his soulful lead vocals on the 1981 Squeeze single "Tempted" (#49 US, #41 UK) and the 1988 Mike and the Mechanics single "The Living Years" (#1 US, #2 UK), not to mention a commendable solo run of his own, including the 1987 hit "Don't Shed a Tear" (#9 US). Through session work and a steady stream of live itineraries, Carrack has continued to expand his oeuvre, working with the likes of Joe Cocker, Ringo Starr, Eric Clapton, Roger Waters, and Roxy Music.

In 1995, he played the Hammond organ on "Man," which features on John's twenty-fourth studio album, *Made in England*. Two years later, he reprised his post behind the Hammond once again, summoning a gospel punch on "Something About the Way You Look Tonight," which, when released as a double A-side with "Candle in the Wind 1997" following the tragic death of Princess Diana, became the second-biggest-selling single of all time, with over thirty-three million copies sold.

Bill Champlin

The veteran singer/songwriter and longtime member of Chicago provided backing vocals for two songs ("Little Jeannie" and "Give Me Love") on 1980's *21 at 33*, and three more on the following year's *The Fox* ("Breaking Down Barriers," "Chloe," and "Heels of the Wind," the latter two of which he also played tambourine on).

Robert Englund

The most peculiar and conspicuous name to appear on the credits to an Elton John album, the man otherwise known the world over as iconic horror-film villain Freddy Krueger from the *Nightmare on Elm Street* film franchise sang backup on, of all songs, "Can You Feel the Love Tonight," from the 1994 soundtrack to *The Lion King*.

Eric Clapton

A mutual respect between "Slowhand" and the Rocket Man has existed since 1970, when John, on his maiden American tour (following his triumphant residency at the Troubadour in Hollywood), opened for Derek and the Dominos. In 1991, for the album and documentary, *Two Rooms: Celebrating the Songs of Elton John and Bernie Taupin*, Clapton complimented John (while voicing his utter confusion at John and Taupin's songwriting process) and recorded a bluesy version of "Border Song," which stands among the tribute LP's finest performances. The following year, the pair converged to record *The One* scorcher "Runaway Train," as blistering a song as John had released since the edgiest material on *Rock of the Westies*, more than a quarter-century before.

Reverend James Cleveland

A legend in gospel circles, particularly in his association with Aretha Franklin's seminal 1972 live album, *Amazing Grace*, Reverend Cleveland conducted the Cornerstone Institutional Baptist and the Southern California choirs on a trio of *Blue Moves* songs in 1976—"Boogie Pilgrim," "Where's the Shoorah?," and "Bite Your Lip (Get Up and Dance!)"—as well as, in 1981, providing a spoken part and directing the Cornerstone Baptist Church Choir on *The Fox* song "Fascist Faces." Cleveland, a four-time Grammy Award winner, died of congestive heart failure on February 9, 1991, aged fifty-nine.

B. J. Cole

The veteran pedal-steel guitarist, whose diverse credentials include recordings with the likes of T. Rex, Katie Melua, and Robert Plant, played on "Tiny Dancer" on 1971's *Madman Across the Water*, as well as on "Georgia" from 1978's *A Single Man*.

David Crosby and Graham Nash

These frequent collaborators paired up in 1976 on the *Blue Moves* tracks "Shoulder Holster" (which was the B-side to "Sorry Seems to Be the Hardest Word"), "The Wide Eyed and Laughing," and the Édith Piaf elegy "Cage the Songbird."

Andraé Crouch

The gospel singer and songwriter directed his own choir on "The Power," John's potent duet with his childhood hero, Little Richard, on 1993's *Duets*. Crouch also worked with John the next year on *The Lion King* soundtrack. Crouch died on January 8, 2015, after suffering a heart attack at the age of seventy-two.

John Deacon and Roger Taylor (Queen)

Queen's indomitable rhythm section, Deacon (bass) and Taylor (drums) brought a bit of cheek to "Too Young," from John's 1985's LP, *Ice on Fire*, as well as to "Angeline," from his critically maligned 1986 LP, *Leather Jackets*.

Kiki Dee

While best known for her duets with John on "Don't Go Breaking My Heart" in 1976 and "True Love" in 1993—not to mention seventies solo hits "Amoureuse" and "I've Got the Music in Me"—Dee has sung backup for a plethora of artists, including Dusty Springfield, Tom Jones, and Alice Cooper, among others. She even composed the sumptuous ballad "Sugar on the Floor," which John played on and produced alongside Clive Franks for her 1973 album, *Loving and Free*, before releasing his own version as the B-Side to "Island Girl" two years later.

On John's albums, Dee sang backup on *Goodbye Yellow Brick Road* ("All the Girls Love Alice"), most of the tracks on *Rock of the Westies*, *Too Low for Zero* ("Cold as Christmas (In the Middle of the Year)"), most of *Ice on Fire*, *Leather Jackets* ("Slow Rivers"), *The One* ("When a Woman Doesn't Want You," "On Dark Street," "Understanding Women"), and the soundtrack to the Disney motion picture *The Lion King* ("Can You Feel the Love Tonight").

Lesley Duncan

Best known for writing "Love Song," one of the earliest cover songs on an Elton John album (1970's *Tumbleweed Connection*), Duncan was among the UK's first wave of late-sixties singer/songwriters—and certainly one of its first female singer/songwriters. In the early seventies, she sang backup on a number of milestone albums—including the soundtrack to *Jesus Christ Superstar* and Pink Floyd's *Dark Side of the Moon*—but she was most closely associated with John, singing on several of his albums, including *Elton John* ("Take Me to the Pilot," "Border Song," and "The Cage"), *Tumbleweed Connection* ("Ballad of a Well-Known Gun," "Son of Your Father," "My Father's Gun," and "Love Song," on which she also played acoustic guitar), *Madman Across the Water* ("Tiny Dancer," "Levon," "Holiday Inn," and "Rotten Peaches"), and the soundtrack to the motion picture *Friends* ("Honey Roll," "Can I Put You On," "Friends," and "Michelle's Song").

Following a modest career as a solo recording artist in her own right, Duncan stepped away from making music after the release of her fourth album, *Maybe It's Lost*, in 1977. Having devoted herself in the intervening decades to her family and to various charitable (often ecological) causes, Duncan died on March 12, 2010, from cerebro-vascular disease, at the age of sixty-six.

Glenn Frey, Don Henley, Timothy B. Schmit (Eagles)

In 1980, this Eagles threesome provided backing vocals to "White Lady White Powder" on *21 at 33*. Henley and Schmit also harmonized on "Without Question," from the 2000 soundtrack to *The Road to El Dorado*. Frey died January 18, 2016, of pneumonia, aged sixty-seven.

David Gilmour

The Pink Floyd guitarist played on one of the lesser-known tracks from John's first album after rehab, 1992's *The One*, "Understanding Women."

Jim Horn

The L.A.-based saxophonist, whose eclectic and extensive credentials include some of the most inimitable saxophone solos in popular music, is known for his session work for Phil Spector, performing at the Concert for Bangladesh, and recording sides by the likes of Aretha Franklin, Steely Dan, Boz Scaggs, U2, and Tom Petty, among countless others.

In 1980, on *21 at 33*, Horn played tenor saxophone on "Two Rooms at the End of the World," and, most notably, alto saxophone on "Little Jeannie." The following year, he played alto on "Just Like Belgium," from *The Fox*.

Freddie Hubbard

Hubbard handled the flugelhorn and trumpet solo on "Mona Lisas and Mad Hatters Part II," from 1988's *Reg Strikes Back*.

Bruce Johnston (the Beach Boys)

Unlike his typically breakneck efficiency in composing melodies to Bernie Taupin's lyrics, John labored on composing "Chameleon" for six solid months in the hope that the Beach Boys, whom he had always revered, would record it. Much to John's disappointment, the group passed on recording the song, but John was nonetheless able to land one of the Beach Boys' vocals on his own version of the song, which appears on 1976's *Blue Moves*.

Booker T. Jones

As Bluesology's gawky teenage keyboard player, Reginald Dwight's inherent predisposition to rhythm and blues no doubt indoctrinated him early on into the thick-as-molasses soul classics Stax Records was producing in Memphis, particularly the viscous Hammond organ grooves wrought by Booker T. Jones. The future Elton John must have dug the unctuous rhythms chugging through Booker T. and the MG's sides like "Green Onions" and "Hip Hug-Her," not to mention the indispensable classics from Otis Redding, the Staple Singers, and Albert King on which Jones sprinkled his superlative touch.

The mutual renown both John and Leon Russell had long since encouraged among their contemporaries and protégées culminated during the 2010 sessions for *The Union* in a full-circle experience of sorts for John, as Jones laid down his B-3 musicianship on four songs: "If It Wasn't for Bad," "The Best Part of the Day," "Hearts Have Turned to Stone," and "I Should've Sent the Roses."

Nik Kershaw

Having crossed paths while both were signed to MCA Records in the eighties, during which time both played sets at Live Aid, Kershaw and John joined together on the latter's 1985 LP, *Ice on Fire*, with the former playing guitar on three tracks: "Act of War," John's collaboration with R&B firebrand Millie Jackson; "Satellite"; and "Nikita," on which Kershaw also sang backup. On John's 1993 LP, *Duets*, the pair sang the appropriately titled "Old Friend" together.

LaBelle

The R&B supergroup—Nona Hendryx, Sarah Dash, and Patti LaBelle, who in their late-sixties incarnation as Patti LaBelle and the Bluebelles had employed Bluesology as their backing band during assorted UK gigs—supplied their mighty soulful pipes to the medley of "Yell Help / Wednesday Night / Ugly" that sets off 1975's *Rock of the Westies*.

John Lennon

During his ironically productive "Lost Weekend"—a nearly two-year period of separation from Yoko Ono, during which, among some comparatively illicit dalliances and chemical misadventures, Lennon wrote and recorded with the likes of David Bowie ("Fame"), Harry Nilsson, and Ringo Starr, while also making his own *Rock 'n' Roll* and *Walls and Bridges* LPs—the ex-Beatle recruited John to play and sing on "Whatever Gets You Thru the Night" and "Surprise, Surprise (Sweet Bird of Paradox)." The following year, Lennon, credited as "Dr. Winston O'Boogie," played rhythm guitar on John's cover of "Lucy in the Sky with Diamonds," while John added harmonies to the B-side of Lennon's *Mind Games* solo track "One Day at a Time." Lennon also played tambourine on "The Bitch Is Back" (under the same alias). Lennon was murdered on December 8, 1980, aged forty.

Publicity photographs of John Lennon dated 1988.   *Author's collection*

Michael McDonald

Still with the Doobie Brothers at the time, McDonald was no stranger to singing backup on albums by other artists, including LPs by Steely Dan, Kenny Loggins, and Carly Simon. On the title track to John's misguided 1979 release, *Victim of Love*, McDonald sang backing vocals with fellow Doobie Brother Patrick Simmons.

George Michael

Elton John had warmed to Wham! from the get-go—actually, it was when he first heard "Wake Me Up Before You Go-Go," the monster hit from George Michael and Andrew Ridgeley's blockbuster 1984 LP, *Make It Big*, because it reminded him of the many classics of Motown. For the British duo's follow-up, 1986's *Music from the Edge of Heaven*, John played piano on "Edge of Heaven," which topped the British singles chart and reached #10 in the US. Showcasing his continued support for Michael, John invited him onstage during his prime-time set at Live Aid, on July 13, 1985, at London's Wembley Stadium, during which Michael assumed lead vocals (and Ridgeley handled indiscriminant backing vocals like a champ) on "Don't Let the Sun Go Down on Me," while John, grinning ear to ear, played piano.

By this time, Michael had already made his debut appearance on an Elton John album (no small feat, considering he had idolized John when he was a teenager buying copies of *Rock of the Westies* and *Blue Moves*), singing on two tracks from the 1985 LP, *Ice on Fire*: "Nikita," on which he sang backup, and "Wrap Her Up," a campy duet between the two of them. Five years after Wham! disbanded, and while Michael was enjoying a stratospherically successful solo career, he reprised (and reversed) John's gesture at Live Aid, now inviting John onto his stage at Wembley Arena in March 1991 for a duet version of "Don't Let the Sun Go Down on Me." Released as a single in November of the same year, the song shot to #1 in both the US (for one week) and the UK (for two weeks). While their friendship endured some on-again, off-again moments that fueled much tabloid fodder, John and Michael had reconciled by the winter of 2016, not long before Michael died of what authorities described as natural causes on Christmas Day, aged fifty-three.

Randy Newman

In a performance that was either ironic or all too appropriate, depending on one's sense of humor, Newman dispensed his driest wit on "It's Tough to Be a God," his duet with John for the 2000 soundtrack to *The Road to El Dorado*.

Peter Noone

The Herman's Hermit's front man sang backing vocals on two songs on John's 1980 LP, *21 at 33*, "Sartorial Eloquence" and "Dear God."

Jean-Luc Ponty

The renowned French violinist added electric violin to the *Honky Château* ballads "Amy" and "Mellow." Having within the previous three years experimented with the language and possibilities of rock with Frank Zappa, among others, Ponty had by 1972 established a familiarity and vocabulary for communicating within the pop-rock idioms that John explored on *Honky Château*, the first Elton John album to reach #1 in the US, beginning a streak of seven consecutive chart-topping albums in America.

Billy Preston

One of the few musicians who could have made an effective case for being considered the "fifth Beatle" for his Hammond organ grooves on the "Get Back" sessions, which evolved (or devolved, depending on one's perspective) into the 1970 LP, *Let It Be*, Billy Preston played with the best of the

Randy Newman, performing on November 19, 2017, at the Capitol Theatre in Clearwater, Florida. Newman appears on the soundtrack to the 2000 film *The Road to El Dorado*, duetting with John on "It's Tough to Be a God." *Photo by Donald Gibson / Author's collection*

best. From learning at the foot of mentor Ray Charles as a youngster to playing alongside the likes of George Harrison, Eric Clapton, and the Rolling Stones, he debuted on an Elton John album by playing Hammond B-3 on the 1993 *Duets* version of "I'm Your Puppet," John's collaboration with fellow British vocalist Paul Young. (Technically, Preston had played on an Elton John song far earlier—specifically, Aretha Franklin's 1972 cover of "Border Song.") On 2001's *Songs from the West Coast*, he brought his infectious electric-organ magic to "I Want Love," while adding his B-3 artistry to two other album highlights, "Love Her Like Me" and "Wasteland."

After an especially fertile and busy period, during which he recorded with various artists (including his mentor, Ray Charles) and toured once more with Clapton, Preston succumbed to the kidney-related health troubles that had plagued him for years. He died on June 6, 2006, aged fifty-nine.

Robert Randolph

The pedal-steel prodigy, who has earned rave endorsements from the likes of Eric Clapton (with whom he has toured), among others, laid down some licks on *The Union*'s "There's No Tomorrow" and "Monkey Suit."

Mickey Raphael

A staple on seventies albums by the likes of Emmylou Harris, Guy Clark, and Willie Nelson, harmonicist Mickey Raphael played on the title track to John's 1981 LP, *The Fox*. In the nearly four decades since, he has only added to his résumé, appearing on albums by such artists as Vince Gill, Norah Jones, and Johnny Cash.

Cliff Richard

One of Britain's preeminent pop-music pioneers, dating back to the fifties phenomenon of Cliff and the Shadows, Richard teamed with John on "Slow Rivers"—the only track from 1986's *Leather Jackets* to make it into the set list of the latter's historic Australian tour the same year with the Melbourne Symphony Orchestra.

Mick Ronson

Still flinging off the glitter from his tenure in David Bowie's Spiders from Mars, the diminutive, blond-locked guitarist soared in similar orbits to John in the early seventies, when both Bowie and John recorded at Trident Studios. He played on what ended up as an alternate version of

"Madman Across the Water" that wasn't officially released until 2008, as part of the deluxe, two-disc edition of *Tumbleweed Connection*.

Not long after John, Bowie, and a legion of other legends assembled at Wembley Stadium for the Freddie Mercury Tribute Concert (who had died of AIDS-related pneumonia), Ronson died of liver cancer on April 29, 1993, aged forty-six.

David Sanborn

As one of the most in-demand session saxophonists around, David Sanborn had already played on a multitude of albums—including sets by Stevie Wonder (*Talking Book*), Todd Rundgren (*A Wizard, a True Star*), David Bowie (*Young Americans*), Paul Simon (*Still Crazy After All These Years*), and Bruce Springsteen (*Born to Run*)—when he contributed his versatile talents to John's 1976 double LP, *Blue Moves*. Sanborn played on three tracks: "Boogie Pilgrim," "Shoulder Holster," and "Idol."

Patrick Simmons

The voice behind such instantly identifiable Doobie Brothers staples as "Black Water" and "Listen to the Music," Simmons in all likelihood wishes his backing vocals (with then-fellow Doobie Brother Michael McDonald) on the title track to John's insufferable 1979 LP, *Victim of Love*, weren't so, uh, identifiable.

Sister Sledge

The familial disco act behind "We Are Family," penned by Nile Rodgers of Chic, Sister Sledge provided backing vocals to "This Town" on 1985's *Ice on Fire*.

The Spinners

One would think that such a vehement soul-music fan as Elton John would have leaped at the opportunity to have the Spinners—the smooth Detroit crooners behind such classic staples as "I'll Be Around," "One of a Kind Love Affair," and "Could It Be I'm Falling in Love"—sing backup on some of his songs. Indeed, he probably did grin from ear to ear upon listening to "Mama Can't Buy You Love," which became a #9 hit single in the US in 1979 (and a #1 hit on the Adult Contemporary chart), but John wasn't thrilled with the production that Philly soul architect Thom Bell had applied to other tracks from the same sessions. He called one such song, "Are You Ready for Love," saccharine, alleging that the Spinners' vocals were mixed louder than his own. John and Bell never worked together again, and, as the Spinners themselves would attest, it's a shame.

Dusty Springfield

One of John's undisputed idols, the enigmatic chanteuse (and unspoken gay icon) behind such seminal pop recordings as "I Only Want to Be with You," "The Look of Love," and "Son of a Preacher Man" provided some of her quintessentially opaque, breathy vocals to two tracks on 1971's *Tumbleweed Connection*, "Ballad of a Well-Known Gun" and "My Father's Gun," credited, as she was on a variety of records of the day to which she wasn't contractually obliged to contribute, as Gladys Thong. In 1974, under the same pseudonym, she provided vocals to "The Bitch Is Back" and an unreleased version of "Don't Let the Sun Go Down on Me," both recorded at Caribou Ranch Studios.

On the night of her death from breast cancer, on March 2, 1999, at age fifty-nine, John paid tribute to Springfield during a solo concert in Peoria, Illinois, performing her first big hit, "I Only Want to Be with You."

"Dusty, wherever you are, this one's for you, my love," he said, before playing the classic tune "with all my love." The following week, John inducted Springfield into the Rock and Roll Hall of Fame.

Toni Tennille

Guitarist Davey Johnstone didn't know who the Captain and Tennille were when he was first introduced to the couple in the mid-seventies, at Caribou Ranch. The long-haired rock 'n' roll guitarist didn't exactly swim in the same sentimental circles as the matrimonial duo ultimately responsible for "Love Will Keep Us Together" and "Do That to Me One More Time." In addition to singing on "Don't Let the Sun Go Down on Me" from John's 1974 LP, *Caribou*, and a batch of songs from 1976's *Blue Moves* ("Crazy Water," "Chameleon," "Someone's Final Song"), Tennille also sang along with an all-star batch of California stars (including Glenn Frey and Don Henley of the Eagles) on "Sartorial Eloquence," from John's 1980 LP, *21 at 33*.

Chris Thompson

Thompson's earliest bouts of fame included singing lead for the multi-generational British band Manfred Mann in its seventies lineup (most notably on the band's #1 hit cover of Bruce Springsteen's verbose epic "Blinded by the Light"), and he sang backup for John during his 1977 benefit gig at Wembley Arena, which featured a surprise appearance from Stevie Wonder. Thompson also sang backup on "I Don't Care" and "Part-Time Love" from John's 1979 LP, *A Single Man*.

Tower of Power Horns

In 1974, the T.O.P. horns were recruited to play on *Caribou* tracks "The Bitch Is Back," "Don't Let the Sun Go Down on Me," "You're So Static," and "Stinker."

Pete Townshend

The Who's rhythm guitarist, principal songwriter, and guiding visionary played jangling acoustic guitar on "Ball and Chain" (featuring Gary

Pete Townshend, performing with the Who on March 25, 2007, at the Ford Amphitheater in Tampa, Florida. Townshend plays acoustic guitar on both "Ball and Chain" from John's 1982 LP *Jump Up!* and "Town of Plenty" from his 1989 LP *Reg Strikes Back*.

Photo by Donald Gibson, Author's collection

Osborne's lyrics), from 1982's *Jump Up!*, and took another acoustic swing on "Town of Plenty" (featuring Bernie Taupin's lyrics), from 1989's *Reg Strikes Back*. "I was using a little cocaine and drinking Rémy," Townshend writes of the "Ball and Chain" session in his 2012 autobiography, *Who I Am*, "and after a few takes I started to feel in the presence of God." His playing on the song doesn't sound quite so awe-inspired (and neither does the song overall), but Townshend on his worst day is far better than most other guitarists on their best.

Granted, the eighties were a period when Townshend concentrated more on pop-oriented solo works than his band's edgier rock efforts, but considering his brilliance on an electric guitar, it would nevertheless have been far more thrilling to hear him inject a shot of circuited rage through one of John's songs.

Rufus Wainwright

With his often-whimsical yet fiercely sentimental 1998 debut album, *April Fools*, Canadian singer/songwriter Rufus Wainwright attracted an empathetic and loyal fan base, including Elton John, who began singing his praises almost immediately. During the sessions for his 2001 LP, *Songs from the West Coast*, while recording the song "American Triangle," which describes in gruesome detail the kidnapping and murder of gay college student Matthew Shepard, John asked Wainwright, who is gay as well, to add harmonies to the track. The symbolism of John and Wainwright, two openly gay men, paying musical tribute to a young man who was killed for simply being who he was, spoke volumes.

Rick Wakeman

As keyboardist for Yes in the early seventies, Wakeman was a busy man. Yet much of his hectic schedule, particularly at Trident Studios in London's Soho district, had nothing to do with his recording with Yes. Before capping off 1971 by laying down his seminal piano part on David Bowie's "Life on Mars" in August, Wakeman also worked on a few Elton John sessions, recording organ parts for "Razor Face," "Rotten Peaches," and the title track to 1971's *Madman Across the Water*.

Brian Wilson

God only knows the sheer poignancy of Brian Wilson's peerless appearance on backing vocals on "When Love Is Dying," from John and Leon

Russell's 2010 collaborative LP, *The Union*, leaves a lump in the throat of anyone who listens to the song. Check out the Cameron Crowe documentary on the making of the album, though, to witness how the Beach Boys genius elicited tears from the eyes of all who beheld his touching performance.

Carl Wilson (the Beach Boys)

The Beach Boys vocalist on "God Only Knows" and "Darlin'," among other hits, provided backup vocals on "Don't Let the Sun Go Down on Me" during sessions for the 1974 LP, *Caribou*. Fourteen years later, Wilson and Bruce Johnston reprised their signature harmonies on "Since God Invented Girls," from 1988's *Reg Strikes Back*. Wilson died on February 6, 1998, of lung cancer, aged fifty-one.

Stevie Wonder

In the mid-to-late seventies, thanks to a dizzying run of prodigious albums like *Innervisions*, *Fulfillingness' First Finale*, and *Songs in the Key of Life*, Stevie Wonder had transcended his original image as Motown's child superstar, emerging as a musical genius with the stature of a beloved icon.

When, during Elton John's 1977 benefit concert at Wembley Arena, John escorted Wonder from the wings to the ecstatic surprise of everyone, the joint went bonkers. Sitting alongside John at the piano, Wonder clapped along and played harmonica during an interminable yet otherwise exuberant version of the concert closer, "Bite Your Lip (Get Up and Dance!)." Five years later, on John's 1982 return to form, *Too Low for Zero*, Wonder provided harmonica on "I Guess That's Why They Call It the Blues." Wonder reprised his harp once more, along with a clavinet, on "Dark Diamond," from 2001's *Songs from the West Coast*.

Neil Young, performing on September 22, 2010, at Ruth Eckerd Hall in Clearwater, Florida. Young sings backup on "Gone to Shiloh," from Elton John and Leon Russell's 2010 LP *The Union*.   *Photo by Donald Gibson, Author's collection*

Neil Young

Intensely beholden to no one and nothing but his own muse, Neil Young has for more than fifty years represented a sense of integrity most artists would like to believe they too possess, but, when push comes to shove, are reticent to express. (Just ask David Geffen, who tried to force Young to conform to his preconceived notion of what "Neil Young" should have sounded like during his bitter and tumultuous tenure on Geffen Record in the eighties. Like most battles he has fought, Young won.)

Having attended John's historic appearance at the Troubadour in August of 1970, Young recognized a similar distinctiveness in England's newest hit-maker. "I thought it was great," Young recalled of John's performance, in the 1990 documentary, *Two Rooms: Celebrating the Songs of Elton John and Bernie Taupin*. "It wasn't like rock 'n' roll, but it wasn't like pure pop either. I didn't know what it was."

Young sang backup on "Gone to Shiloh," from John's 2010 album with Leon Russell, *The Union*.

6

From the Day That I Was Born I Waved the Flag

Made in America

F rom sea to shining sea, the United States of America is the promised land for immigrants seeking a better way of life. Yet as with any industry, much less the music business, success on its shores has never been a sure thing for even the most prodigious artists. When, in 1947, French chanteuse Édith Piaf made her US debut at the Playhouse Theater in New York City, for instance, audiences were slow to appreciate her extraordinary gifts, despite her already proven appeal back in her native country, and indeed throughout Europe.

Elton John had cherished American music all his young-adult life, his enthusiasm emboldened by his mother having introduced him as a young child to the reverbed, sexually suggestive revolution personified by Elvis Presley. Throughout his adolescence and now into his twenties, having added to the ever-flourishing record collection that congested his modest bedroom at Frome Court, he further absorbed America's most venerable and extraordinary, though all-too-often overlooked, music: the resilient blues mythologies that had migrated with ancestors of slaves from the cotton fields to the Crossroads; the uplifting rhythms from Motown to Muscle Shoals; the shimmering pop symphonies of John's most beloved American group, the Beach Boys, whose songs, like "Don't Worry, Baby" and "Wouldn't It Be Nice," spoke to an inner maturity at play in the culture of the American youth.

As enamored as he was of the possibility of carving out his own stake of the American dream, however, he had experienced enough hard knocks of the music business by this point to recognize that such ambitions wouldn't pan out on the merits of talent and passion alone. For all the support he had received (both financial and moral) from Dick James Music, he also needed to sign with a record label based in the States that could help build his profile there as well.

As events transpired, however, beginning with a six-night run of trailblazing performances at Doug Weston's fabled Troubadour nightclub on Santa Monica Boulevard in West Hollywood, Elton John introduced himself as America's latest overnight sensation, heralding the irreverent and seemingly instantaneous arrival of the decade's most successful solo artist. Still, his Wild West redemption almost didn't happen at all.

This chapter chronicles the risks and enduring rewards of John's American introduction, and how the music he was making at the time reflected aspects of the nation's "land of the free" culture.

For Things Are Getting Desperate

"Well, here's an interesting thing, which I don't think a lot of people realize," says guitarist and producer Caleb Quaye.

> When [Elton] was sent to America on that first tour, that was a last-ditch attempt. For some reason, we'd put some records out, some recordings out in England, but he'd never taken off. It never quite caught hold in England. And of course we always loved American music, so the idea was, "Let's get him to America and see if something will click in America."
>
> So, Dick James had spent, I forget what it was, a certain amount of money on the first album—or what was considered the first album, the *Elton John* album, with "Your Song" and everything. The single was released over there, started to pick up airplay. "Okay, let's send him over." The thinking from Dick James was, *Well, we'll do this, and if this don't work out, forget it. It's over.* The pressure was on, big time. It was either sink or swim.

One factor in John's favor was that the "singer/songwriter" movement was concentrated in and around the Troubadour at the time. On any given night, innumerable artists who penned intensely personal songs based upon their own innermost thoughts and experiences—as-yet-unaffected, self-reliant artists like James Taylor, Joni Mitchell, Neil Young, Laura Nyro, and Jackson Browne—converged inside the venue, some of them carousing by the bar, others eying the action onstage, everyone eager to discover the new kid in town.

Elton John was a virtual unknown entity in such a tight-knit scene, yet with a buzz-worthy new album boasting the sort of esoteric songs that such a scene should embrace, he stood a fighting chance of being welcomed in its ranks.

Lennie Hodes, the New York representative of Dick James Music, had hand-delivered a copy of John's 1969 debut LP, *Empty Sky*, to Russ Regan, president of the MCA Records subsidiary Uni Records in Los Angeles, but Regan wasn't impressed. Upon hearing John's new, self-titled album, however, he changed his tune. In 2016, Regan recalled:

> When I heard the second album, which was the *Elton John* album, I literally at the end of it looked up to the sky and said, "Thank you, God." I thought this was the most incredible piece of music I'd ever heard. It was incredible. I shut down the company—there were about thirty people working for us at Uni Records at the time—[and] I had everybody come in my office and sit on the floor and all that kind of stuff and listen to it. After it was over everybody just went crazy, so I knew I had something special. And so basically when I heard it, I said, "I'm the luckiest man in the record business."

The next logical step was to deliver John to the States, to show off this prodigious British export to the movers and shakers of the L.A. music scene. This boy wonder could create a mighty buzz indeed.

Ray Williams, John's manager at the time, remembers:

> I got this offer for fifty bucks to appear in New York from Howard Rose, who was working for Chartwell Artists in New York. I said, "You've got to be joking." I said, "That's just enough for me, not enough for Elton." So that didn't fly. Then I get another call from the same agency from a guy called Jerry Heller, and [he] tells us that we can get a gig at the Troubadour in L.A. for about a

hundred-and-twenty-five bucks. I said, "Jerry, that's a hell of a long way to go for a hundred-and-twenty-five bucks."

Long story short, we ended up getting two-hundred-and-fifty or two-hundred-and-seventy bucks, I can't remember, with a replay clause, and we had to play at the Troubadour in San Francisco, which was nothing like the Troubadour in L.A.—and that was it. The whole thing was set.

Still, Regan's over-the-moon enthusiasm hadn't convinced John that the time was right. "The *Elton John* album had come out, and I'd been on the road [in Europe] with Nigel Olsson and Dee Murray, and we'd been getting a good reputation playing festivals and getting good reviews," he recalls in the 2001 documentary, *Classic Albums: Goodbye Yellow Brick Road*. "The buzz was happening in England, and I thought it was the wrong time to go to America. And the record company in America said, 'No, no, we want to bring you over.' So, I thought, *Well, if I go over, at least I can go to a record shop and buy a few records.*"

And I Can't Forget That Trip to the West

Having grown up fascinated by westerns and the iconography of the American outback—not to mention having invested his passion into his songs, most recently in John's finished yet unreleased LP, *Tumbleweed Connection*—Taupin reacted a bit different to California than his song-writing partner. "When I got here," he said in 2013, to the *Telegraph*, "it really was a case of thinking, *I've come home.*"

"I'd been to L.A. a few times before that," Ray Williams recalls.

I said, "I've got some friends out here. Why don't we go relax and do something?" Everybody said, "Let's go. Let's go to Palm Springs." So we invited these two ladies that I knew, friends, they joined us. We had a brilliant time, but Elton didn't want to go. So he stayed at the hotel. We had a great time, and we came back, everybody was up. And then, the following morning at breakfast, Elton came down and said, "I'm not doing this gig at the Troubadour. I'm just not doing it."

He threw a big wobbly. You've got to understand that we were basically chums—friends who found ourselves in this situation. And, suddenly, there was a lot going on because there was a bit of a vibe out there, with Russ Regan and Norman Winter, the PR guy. What they did in retrospect was an amazing job. At the time Elton wouldn't have understood what they were doing. So we had this argument.

Cooler heads prevailed, fortunately, and Elton John stepped into destiny.

Tumbleweed Connection, released on October 30, 1970, reached #5 on the *Billboard* 200 and #2 on the UK Albums chart, but yielded no singles.   *Author's collection*

Burn It Down

Russ Regan met Elton John for the first time prior to John's debut Troubadour performance. "A very nice young man," said Regan, remembering his initial impression of the young artist. "He was terribly passionate about his music and the music business."

As a full-court press heralded his auspicious arrival in the States, John stepped into the epicenter of the singer/songwriter culture with a six-night residency at Doug Weston's Troubadour, commencing on August 25, 1970. "The Troubadour, there was something magical about that place," said Regan. "Neil Diamond had played there, and he did very well, created a lot of sizzle out of there. So, anyway, I said, 'The only way to do this is to bring him to America and present him at the Troubadour and ask Neil Diamond to introduce him,' which he did."

A melee of music-business bigwigs—from Quincy Jones to Gordon Lightfoot to Danny Hutton of Three Dog Night, who had covered the John–Taupin songs "Lady Samantha" and "Your Song," much to both composers' delight—crowded inside the three-hundred-seat club to witness this unfamiliar artist become an overnight sensation. Opening the show was singer/songwriter David Ackles, whose placement on the bill baffled the modest headliner to no end (John and Bernie Taupin were such ardent fans of Ackles that John dedicated his forthcoming album, *Tumbleweed Connection*, to him).

While John's American dream lay on the line, so too did Russ Regan's professional reputation. Having signed John to Uni Records, sight unseen, on the quality of the *Elton John* album, the music executive had never seen him play live. "I had one concern," Regan said, "because the album is so beautifully orchestrated by Paul Buckmaster that I said, 'Can three people produce the sounds in a small venue like that?'"

"It was very hot and smoky and a great vibe," John told *Mojo* in 2006. "We came on—I was in flying boots and hot pants—and did 'Sixty Years On' and they weren't expecting it. They thought that it was going to be a really low-key David Ackles type thing because the music on the *Elton John* album was very orchestral. But with a three-piece band, we went out and did the songs completely differently and just blew everyone away."

Regan knew his initial anxiety was unfounded even sooner than that. "Nigel Olsson and Dee Murray and Elton John, the three of them together were like a symphony orchestra," he recalled. "They were just incredibly loud and they played flamboyantly—all of them—and so it was just all good. Everything was positive."

On the second night, while barnstorming through "Burn Down the Mission" to close the set, John noticed one of his biggest idols, Leon Russell, watching intently, his demonic-looking eyes shielded behind his signature mirrored shades. "I was onstage and I could see him in the audience—you can't miss that hair and those glasses—and it was pure fright," John told the *Telegraph* in 2010. The same year, in the Cameron Crowe documentary on the making of John and Russell's album, *The Union*, the grizzled "Master of Space and Time" conceded, much to John's surprise, that he'd attended that Troubadour performance not just to check out this buzz-worthy new artist but to attempt to sign him to Shelter Records, the label he ran with Denny Cordell (the British impresario and producer of such artists as the Moody Blues, Procol Harum, and J. J. Cale, among others).

The audience, which either had no idea what to expect or (for the few who had already listened to John's eponymous album, which had only been released in the States a few weeks prior) perhaps anticipated the brooding, solemn figure suggested by the album's obscured cover, the burgeoning young artist was an exhilarating revelation.

Among the club regulars and luminaries on hand sat Robert Hilburn, who, as the chief pop music critic at the *Los Angeles Times*, was accustomed to seeing artists not live up to their hype. In his 2009 memoir, *Cornflakes with John Lennon and Other Tales from a Rock 'n' Roll Life*, he confides that John didn't set the house on fire at first. Recollecting how, at the outset, John seemed "extremely shy and nervous," Hilburn writes, "He kept his eyes on the piano and the microphone in front of him. Someone next to me whispered that Elton had better be a good songwriter, because he certainly wasn't a very compelling performer."

With his chops and innate charisma on his side, though, John gained composure, confidence, and, with each song he performed, momentum. By the time he'd reached "Burned Down the Mission," Hilburn recalls,

"Suddenly, the Troubadour audience was on its feet. The guy next to me wasn't whispering any longer. He joined in the thunderous applause."

Lord Have Mercy, You Can't Sit Still

"Rejoice!" Hilburn raved the next day in the *Los Angeles Times*. "Rock music, which has been going through a rather uneventful period lately, has a new star. He's Elton John, a twenty-three-year-old Englishman whose United States debut Tuesday night at the Troubadour was, in almost every way, magnificent."

Word spread far, wide, and fast.

"The review from Robert Hilburn at *The Los Angeles Times* really did make us a star in the main cities in America before we played there," John says in the 1992 documentary, *Two Rooms: Celebrating the Songs of Elton John and Bernie Taupin*. "Word of mouth spread very, very quickly: 'This is the new person. This is it. This is the new big thing.'"

John soon found himself on the road and in demand, opening for the likes of Leon Russell and Derek and the Dominos in such major markets as San Francisco, Philadelphia, and New York City; making his US television debut with a performance of "Your Song" on *The Andy Williams Show* (which aired January 16, 1971, on NBC); and recording the *11–17–70* live album in New York City at A&R Studios.

"I wasn't surprised," says former *Melody Maker* journalist and editor Chris Charlesworth, recalling the splash John had made in America in such a short span of time. "I could tell that he had boundless enthusiasm. He had a lot of ambition, as well."

John's talent and ambition soon put him in the rarified company of his heroes—musicians whose albums he owned and played back home. "I met Bob Dylan, I met George Harrison," John said in a 2010 interview with *ShortList*, reflecting on his rapid rise to fame in America following his Troubadour residency. "Neil Young came and sang the whole of *After the Gold Rush* at my flat in Edgware Road [in London]. I enjoyed the success because it brought me into contact with people who I really admired and they validated what I was doing."

The patience and energy—and, of course, money—that Dick James Music in London and Uni Records in Los Angeles had invested in this fledgling yet nevertheless promising artist paid off like gangbusters. In fact, the buzz emanating from the States about this new artist named Elton John had the ironic effect of making him seem like an American artist to many people back in Great Britain. Reminiscent of America's belated recognition of its blues pioneers, John's own country didn't quite appreciate what it had in this emergent artist until another country acknowledged and appreciated him first. "He became a big star in America much, much quicker than he became a star in England," said Regan. "Why, I don't know."

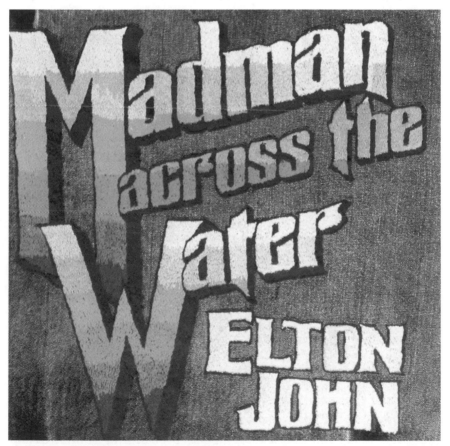

Madman Across the Water, released on November 5, 1971, reached #8 in North America while peaking only at #41 in the UK. Two of its songs, "Tiny Dancer" and "Levon," have since become staples of John's legendary live performances.   *Author's collection*

When the Bells of Freedom Ring

For anyone paying attention to the lyrics that accompanied the music on John's albums in 1971, American imagery and ideas abounded. Stagecoaches, log cabins, and shotguns litter the sepia-toned scenes of *Tumbleweed Connection*, John's third album (and his second to be recorded at Trident Studios), on which he and Taupin pay lyrical homage to America's provincial past. A concept album more in cumulative themes rather than narrative storytelling, it found Taupin emblazoning rustic nineteenth-century American iconography throughout epic, cinematic sagas, it was not unlike when Robbie Robertson wrote "The Night They Drove Old Dixie Down" for the Band's 1969 self-titled second album. The only difference is that Robertson had traveled to America—once—prior to composing "Dixie," whereas Taupin had yet to set foot anywhere near an American McDonald's, let alone a mythologized Southern battlefield. Plus, Robertson's band boasted an actual American southerner, drummer and vocalist Levon Helm, to give the songs credence and heart.

"Gospel and soul and country," John says in the 2010 BBC documentary, *Madman Across the Water: The Making of Elton John*, "basically that's my favorite kind of music, American music that embraces all those three, like Elvis Presley did, in a way. He came from R&B, gospel, and country. You fuse those together and you've got a pretty soulful combination."

For an artist aiming to make a name for himself in a new country, that *Tumbleweed Connection* yielded no singles whatsoever seems, from a marketing perspective, unorthodox to say the least. "It seemed like he was everywhere," says Chris Charlesworth. "He was almost over-productive because a lot of albums came out very quickly."

The *Elton John* album made a splash, Charlesworth recalls. "Then there was *Tumbleweed Connection*, then there was the [*Friends*] film soundtrack, then there was a live album, which was recorded in America. All these albums seemed to come out within the space of a year. Most acts put out an album one a year, basically, and here he was putting out four albums."

Besides its obvious American allusions to Los Angeles street life and Jesus freaks and the *New York Times* proclaiming "God is dead," on *Madman Across the Water*, the last album recorded in full at Trident Studios, John and Taupin synthesized their American dreams with the orchestral embellishments that Paul Buckmaster and Gus Dudgeon had been perfecting since the *Elton John* album. "The challenge we made for ourselves," said Dudgeon, in a 2002 interview with *Mix Online*, "was to try and marry a big orchestra with a rock 'n' roll section and make it work, and not have one of them lose out to another."

The first phase of his recording career complete, a new direction beckoned for Elton John—not so much geographically but sonically and, as his solicitor advised him, economically. He needed a new place to write and record, which prompted a hunt for a new studio—possibly one where the band could hang out and kick back as well.

7

The Change Is Gonna Do Me Good

The Honky Château

lton John had established a signature sound and style with his previous three studio albums (four, if you count the soundtrack to the 1971 motion picture *Friends*), based on dense yet enthralling orchestration, taut string arrangements, and the occasional ornamental flourishes of progressive rock. Such complicated sonic territory, under the mutual tutelage of producer Gus Dudgeon and arranger Paul Buckmaster, had certainly yielded no dearth of indelible songs, but now both John and Bernie Taupin sought to make a change.

At the time, John had acknowledged new, looser music like Leon Russell's eponymous album (featuring classics like "Delta Lady" and the immortal "Song for You") and the Allman Brothers' *Eat a Peach*. Music in the early seventies was getting funkier, for sure, ingrained with influences culled from gospel and soul—the kinds of music John had loved the most since Little Richard first blew his timid English mind as a child growing up in the conservative fifties in the equally conservative suburban Pinner, England.

While his three previous studio albums—*Elton John*, *Tumbleweed Connection*, and *Madman Across the Water*—showcased his and Taupin's emergent sophistication as songwriters, as well as the superb production and arrangements of the Gus Dudgeon and Paul Buckmaster studio alliance, they tended to reflect comparable sonic, orchestra-accentuated terrain that in some rather fanciful moments flirted with the dense, kaleidoscopic textures of progressive rock. (In fact, John had auditioned for progressive-rock bands King Crimson and Gentle Giant back in 1969.)

Itching to reveal new dimensions of John's talent and musicality, he and Taupin now pursued a more elemental and eclectic approach—one that incorporated their inherent appreciation for American gospel, soul, country, and pop.

Having prospered in finding their own unique (and, early on, eccentric) voice as songwriters—and having found success with what they wrote—John and Taupin now stood at a creative precipice. They recognized the breadth of their abilities now more than ever, especially in John's case, and could expand beyond the musical template they had established on their previous albums. With experience comes knowledge, and, indeed, self-awareness.

Beginning with his next album, John would dispense with utilizing session musicians, as he had done previously, in favor of working with his touring band, bassist Dee Murray and drummer Nigel Olsson. He also sought a guitarist to flesh out the sound, to give the music more of a pop distinction. Caleb Quaye had appeared prominently on John's studio albums up to that point (and would do so again within a few short years), but he was committed at the time to his own band, Hookfoot, which featured drummer Roger Pope, who had also played on prior Elton John albums, and would resume doing so in the not-so-distant future.

Guitarist Davey Johnstone had played on the session for the song "Madman Across the Water," but the long-haired Scottish folk musician didn't seem like the best fit to join the band—at least not at first. However, with his group Magna Carta, which Gus Dudgeon had produced, he demonstrated a remarkable versatility with a range of stringed instruments—a talent that no doubt impressed the man at the piano. With that, the musician who would become the most consistent presence in Elton John's career joined the band.

Better Get Back to the Woods

A change of scene was in order as well, as British tax laws were causing plenty of headaches for some of the most affluent artists of the era, whose ranks John was now ascending. The Rolling Stones, most notably, had relocated from their native English residences to the South of France to

Honky Château, released on May 19, 1972, was John's first US #1 album.   *Author's collection*

work on what emerged as the double LP, *Exile on Main Street*. John resisted having to agree to such provisions, but with his solicitor at the time urging him to record outside of his home country, he conceded.

In a June 2002 interview with the Elton John fanzine *Hercules*, conducted shortly before his tragic death in an automobile accident, Dudgeon explained, "The plan was, he would arrive in France and write the songs when he got there, and then send his mum a letter about the songs he'd just written, which would give him the proof if he ever had to go into court to defend it, that he wrote them in France." In other words, the postmarks on the sealed envelopes, along with the specific information contained within, would verify that he'd written certain songs abroad.

"I said I'd go only if we could find someplace peaceful without any interruptions," John told *Rolling Stone* in 1973. "We started getting a dossier on all European studios and this Chateau leaflet came through."

In 1972, Château d'Hérouville was not exactly France's answer to Abbey Road. However, like other makeshift recording studios—be it the erstwhile movie theater that housed Stax's recording studios in downtown Memphis, or the actual house that housed Motown's recording studios in suburban Detroit—it boasted its own unique ambience and history. Constructed in the seventeenth century, Château d'Hérouville—christened by John, upon his arrival, the Honky Château—was once a romantic refuge in the nineteenth century for Polish composer Frédéric Chopin and his mistress, novelist George Sand, and allegedly housed Chopin's ghost.

For John and his band and crew, though, the bohemian, thirty-bedroom compound (complete with tennis courts, Ping-Pong tables, swimming pools, and enough distance from urban civilization to seem utterly isolated from the distractions of the then-modern world) offered just the right kind of comfort and self-contained accommodations. "It wasn't technically the greatest studio in the world," John says of the French villa in the 2001 documentary, *Classic Albums: Goodbye Yellow Brick Road*, "but it was a great environment."

A plethora of other pop artists followed John's lead to compose at Château d'Hérouville, including David Bowie, who recorded 1973's *Pin-Ups* there, as well as portions of 1976's *Low*; the Bee Gees, who wrote and recorded some of the songs that comprised their blockbuster 1977 soundtrack to *Saturday Night Fever* on site; and Fleetwood Mac, who used it for their 1982 LP, *Mirage* (featuring hit singles "Gypsy" and "Hold Me"). For the better part of two years, the Château served as home base for Elton John and his musical entourage, accommodating their insular creativity during the making of three classic albums.

"While recording at the Château, we lived there for a month," drummer Nigel Olsson told *Modern Drummer* magazine in 2007. "Elton would get the lyrics from Bernie, sit down and write the melody, and we'd be right there in the studio. So we were with those songs from their conception, which was the beauty of all of it."

Whether by concerted design or from the organic chemistry that evolved among the musicians in the band, the albums that marked this new phase of John's still burgeoning career were distinguished by their eclecticism as much as their mainstream musical accessibility.

Released in 1972, *Honky Château* signified Elton John's transition from an underrated singer/songwriter with an almost cultish appeal into a mainstream pop sensation. Without sacrificing the sonic integrity of his three prior studio albums, the production was now distilled to predominant piano and vocal. The songs hung together with the ease of a well-oiled live band, a veritable gumbo of styles and influences, blending moments of raw-and-aching soulfulness ("Mellow") complemented by Cajun-flavored, carnival-esque mirth ("Honky Cat," "I Think I'm Going to Kill Myself"), gospel and boogie-woogie influences ("Salvation"), and countrified Americana (à la the Band) like "Amy," heralding the shift from using session players in favor of the musicians who comprised John's touring band.

"Rocket Man" ascended to the top of the US singles chart—the first such feat for John. "Actually," Taupin said in a 2016 video about the song, "the interesting thing about 'Rocket Man' is that people identify it, unfortunately, with David Bowie's 'Space Oddity.' It actually wasn't inspired by that at all; it was actually inspired by a story by Ray Bradbury, from his book of science-fiction short stories called *The Illustrated Man*. In that book there was a story called 'The Rocket Man,' which was about how astronauts in the future would become sort of an everyday job. So I kind of took that idea and ran with it."

Musically, however, the song owes much to Bowie's 1969 hit, as when John heard the song he specifically requested to work with its producer, Gus Dudgeon; arranger Paul Buckmaster was added to the Elton John team shortly afterward as well.

The album reached #1 on the *Billboard* chart (where it remained for a total of five weeks), wresting the Rolling Stones' *Exile on Main Street* from the coveted top spot. It also initiated a run of seven consecutive #1 albums over the next four years.

They'll Never Kill the Thrills We've Got

On John's next album, *Don't Shoot Me I'm Only the Piano Player*, "Daniel" and "Crocodile Rock" further distinguished him as a pop star with mass appeal, but the album cuts are what made this album so enduring. With songs like the achingly innocent "Blues for Baby and Me" and "Have Mercy on the Criminal"—the latter one of Paul Buckmaster's most riveting arrangements—John was cultivating one of the most serious—and seriously great—catalogues in all of pop music. As for "Crocodile Rock,"

Don't Shoot Me I'm Only the Piano Player, released on January 26, 1973, was John's second straight US #1 album, and features "Crocodile Rock," his first US #1 single. *Author's collection*

it was John's first million-selling single, and a familiar one at that, its melody lifted from the 1962 Pat Boone hit "Speedy Gonzalez."

"Daniel" in particular inspired myriad interpretations, thanks to John cropping out the last verse because, he said, it made the song too long. It also explained the song, but the enigma its omission generated has only enhanced the song's enduring appeal. "Daniel" could have been about one's brother heading to Spain after going to Vietnam, but its sense of loss could spark any number of more immediate and personal interpretations for listeners. There is no literal "correct" way to perceive the storyline. What's personal and compelling for one listener may not be the same for someone else.

Incidentally, the album's title stems from an off-the-cuff comment John made to Groucho Marx at a party, when the iconic comedian ribbed him about how his name should be "John Elton" instead of Elton John. "Don't shoot me," John replied, quipping to one of the sharpest comedic tacks of all time, "I'm only the piano player." Marx is subtly credited on the album cover, a mock setup of a movie theater marquee, which includes a poster for the 1940 Marx Brothers film *Go West*.

John and Taupin and company would soon take another tip from the Rolling Stones (having already traveled to France to mediate John's tax situation) by flying everyone to Jamaica, where the Stones had just finished recording *Goats' Head Soup*, to lay down tracks for John's next album. A bit of misadventure and danger loomed over the trip, however, and, soon enough, everyone had returned to the their familiar stomping grounds at Château d'Hérouville. The songs that emerged, which in short order comprised John's first double album, *Goodbye Yellow Brick Road*, reflect the sense of ecstatic distraction that had sent their whole crew to the Caribbean in the first place—and what in turn compelled them to get back to where they once belonged.

8

Solid Walls of Sound

The Producers

Perhaps there's a tendency to lump all the music he's made together as "Elton John music," but truth be told there have been several distinct periods, underscored by who was producing his records at the time. Giving anyone the reins to shape and create the sonic landscape of his musical compositions requires much trust from any artist, but for Elton John—an artist whose talent is so single-minded and ingrained—the level of trust has been nothing less than extraordinary.

Any artist with the career longevity of Elton John will pass through certain periods and phases, but for such an insular songwriter and composer as John, the changes have tended not to be in reaction to the times or even the various musicians who've played on his albums. Rather, such changes have for the most part occurred because of who was producing the albums. "Look at some of the other groups turning out album after self-same album," John explained to *People* in 1975. "A good producer will keep you from such self-indulgence."

In the 2016 PBS documentary, *Soundbreaking*, John says, "That's the whole point of having someone like that, who can sit in the booth, hearing something that you might play that you would just discard, and he'll say, 'Hang on a minute, that was really good. Go back to that.'"

In renowned producer Phil Ramone's picaresque 2007 memoir, *Making Music—The Scenes Behind the Music*, John is quoted as saying, "A producer knows when a song should be changed or a vocal isn't good, because he isn't as close to it as the artist is. The knowledge and experience that a producer brings to the control room when a musician is playing and singing on the other side of the glass is very reassuring."

In this chapter, we will survey the producers who have helped to shape the way the songs John has recorded and released have sounded throughout his career.

Steve Brown

A good producer does more than supervise recording sessions. Instead, the role involves guiding the musicians to play at their fullest potential, while at the same time distinguishing which elements—a bad take, a bum note, a missed opportunity—necessitate a change. A good producer also recognizes what specific set of skills is best suited to embracing the task at hand. Such was the determination made by Steve Brown, who, after familiarizing himself with the material slated for John's eponymous second album, bowed out of producing it altogether. The songs John and Taupin had written (including austere moments like "Your Song" and "I Need You to Turn To," but also more emphatic ones like "The King Must Die" and "Take Me to the Pilot"), bolstered by Paul Buckmaster's intricate arrangements, called for a distinctive ingenuity at the helm that, in Brown's estimation, eclipsed his abilities. (That's not to say he lacked talent altogether, however, as he proved his worth the previous year in producing John's idiosyncratic debut, *Empty Sky*.)

In the decades that followed his close, early association with Elton John, Brown went on to produce such acts as Wham!, Alison Moyet, and Freddie Mercury. He died on December 24, 2017, aged seventy-two.

Albums produced

- *Empty Sky*

Gus Dudgeon

The songs Elton John and Bernie Taupin wrote for what became the *Elton John* album differed from the ones that preceded them on *Empty Sky*. They were more mature, both musically and thematically. "The songs were very classically orientated," John said, reflecting for the audience at the Wiltern Theatre in Los Angeles on January 13, 2016. "I didn't know who I wanted to use. Then I heard a record which blew me away. It's called 'Space Oddity.'" As John discovered, David Bowie's debut hit had been produced by a then-relatively unknown Gus Dudgeon.

No one is more responsible for distinguishing the way Elton John has sounded throughout his most quintessential recordings than Dudgeon—the man most responsible for transforming John's stark, stripped demos into pristine, indelible performances on par with the greatest productions of their time, and indeed of all time.

Faced with the caliber of compositions that John and Taupin had composed for their sophomore album, Steve Brown, who had been one of John and Taupin's earliest champions—both songwriters have credited Brown with encouraging them to write the sorts of songs they preferred to compose, rather than the disposable pop tunes they were churning out beforehand for a coterie of British vocalists—acknowledged that the material deserved the best possible producer. In 1970, mere months after the critically hailed release of *Abbey Road*, the best possible producer was George Martin, who expressed interest in taking on the project—the whole project, as it turned out. He not only wished to produce but also to handle all the arrangements, which Paul Buckmaster was already involved in composing. Thus, Dick James Music declined Martin's services. "Of course, Paul was very touched that they would stick with him," Dudgeon told *Mix Online* in 2002, "because he was relatively untried as an arranger."

When Dudgeon listened to twelve demos intended for the forthcoming album, he embraced the opportunity to produce what would emerge as *Elton John*. Still, in listening to the demo for "Your Song," in particular, he voiced apprehensions about the intenerate song's prospects in the comparatively provocative pop-music climate of the moment—doubts that would ultimately disappear when the song catapulted John to stardom.

Dudgeon enjoyed untold amounts of freedom to sculpt and shape each song the way he saw fit. In an interview published in the 2000 anthology *Behind the Glass: Top Record Producers Tell How They Craft the Hits, Volume 2*, he explained:

If I said to him, "This song would be great with an orchestra," he'd just go, "Fine." The most amazing thing about Elton was that, as soon as he'd finish doing what he had to do, he was off. He was either going to go and listen to some records or watch a football game or play some tennis or something. He never hung around for any overdubs, be they strings, backing vocals, whatever.

It wasn't that he wasn't interested—don't get the wrong impression. It was just that, for some reason, he trusted us, right from the word go.

Dudgeon's results were irrefutable. "He was *brilliant* in the studio," Taupin said in 2014, in a video commentary celebrating the fortieth anniversary of *Goodbye Yellow Brick Road*. "He was absolutely extraordinary. You just have to listen to those records. Sonically, there's nothing to touch them."

Having produced what are generally considered John's classic albums, beginning with 1970's *Elton John* and culminating with 1976's *Blue Moves*, Dudgeon parted ways with John's organization (Rocket Records) in a dispute over potential future earnings. He wouldn't return to the fray for nearly a decade, when he produced a pair of studio albums, 1985's *Ice on Fire* and 1986's *Leather Jackets*—neither of which rivaled John's strongest works of the seventies—and 1987's *Live in Australia with the Melbourne Symphony Orchestra*. Disgruntled by the poor sonic fidelity of John's "classic" albums on previously existing compact discs, in 1995 Dudgeon oversaw the digital remastering of that most venerated era comprising John's vast catalogue.

On July 21, 2002, in Berkshire, England, Dudgeon was driving his Jaguar, with his wife, Sheila, by his side, when he nodded off, according to an inquest held on November 7, 2002. As the car accelerated at a speed upward of one hundred miles per hour, it veered off the M4 motorway before crashing upside down in a storm drain. Both died at the scene. Gus Dudgeon was fifty-nine. As the inquest further revealed, he had been driving while more than one and a half times above the legal limit, his intoxication most likely a contributing factor in him having fallen asleep at the wheel.

"I am devastated by the tragic news about Gus Dudgeon," John said in a statement released to the press shortly after news broke of Dudgeon's death. "He was an incredibly talented producer and a very dear friend for many years. I will miss him terribly."

As the fortieth anniversary of John's most popular (and perhaps Gus Dudgeon's most innovatively produced) studio album, *Goodbye Yellow Brick Road*, approached, John expounded on Dudgeon's ingeniousness while at the same time underscoring the late producer's invaluable relevance to his legendary career. "The actual sound and the quality of the recording is extraordinary," he says in a 2014 video commentary, "and that was down to him. He was our fifth member. Like, the Beatles had George Martin. We had Gus."

Albums produced

- *Elton John* (1970)
- *Tumbleweed Connection* (1970)
- *Friends* (1971, original soundtrack)
- *Madman Across the Water* (1971)
- *Honky Château* (1972)
- *Don't Shoot Me I'm Only the Piano Player* (1973)
- *Goodbye Yellow Brick Road* (1973)
- *Caribou* (1974)
- *Captain Fantastic and the Brown Dirt Cowboy* (1975)
- *Rock of the Westies* (1975)
- *Blue Moves* (1976)
- *Ice on Fire* (1985)
- *Leather Jackets* (1986)
- *Live in Australia with the Melbourne Symphony Orchestra* (1987)

Chris Thomas

Some producers invoke a hallmark sonic distinction all of their own, from Phil Spector's bombastic Wall of Sound to Gamble and Huff's svelte

Philly soul orchestrations. However, British producer Chris Thomas hasn't impressed such a unifying characteristic, instead yielding to the service of whichever artist he's working with at the time. A former student himself at the Royal Academy of Music, Thomas has produced more albums by Elton John than by any other artist, but the list of other artists he's produced is colossal. He's said in the very few interviews he's granted that he prefers working with songwriters, and his credentials corroborate as much.

His career began, auspiciously enough, with the Beatles, who were at the time recording their 1968 eponymous double album (otherwise known as *The White Album*). Despite a plethora of high-profile assignments thereafter, whether working within the realm of progressive rock (Pink Floyd, Procol Harum), punk (the Sex Pistols), new wave (the Pretenders), or mainstream pop (Paul McCartney, INXS), Thomas has maintained a low profile.

"Chris Thomas and I have known each other thirty-two years," John said in 1991, in the liner notes to the *To Be Continued . . .* boxed set. "He was at the Royal Academy of Music with me, and Paul Buckmaster was there too. Chris only hears out of one ear, and I've never really worked out how he produces records. The thing I love about Chris . . . and Gus also . . . is that they were very good at structuring songs."

Albums produced

- *The Fox* (1981, co-produced with Clive Franks and Elton John)
- *Jump Up!* (1982)
- *Too Low for Zero* (1983)
- *Breaking Hearts* (1984)
- *Reg Strikes Back* (1988)
- *Sleeping with the Past* (1989)
- *The One* (1992)
- *The Lion King* (1994, original soundtrack, co-produced with Hans Zimmer)
- *The Big Picture* (1997)

Clive Franks

One of the prevailing figures in Elton John's career, Clive Franks has for decades mostly occupied the position of sound engineer, including at John's live concerts.

Albums produced

- *21 at 33* (1980, co-produced with Elton John)
- *The Fox* (1981, co-produced with Chris Thomas and Elton John)

Greg Penny

Greg Penny grew up with two musical idols: George Martin and Elton John. After working with such artists as Rickie Lee Jones and Canadian songstress k.d. lang, he was invited to produce a duet between lang and Elton John, "Teardrops," on the latter's aptly titled 1993 LP, *Duets*. The opportunity led to him co-producing (with John) 1995's *Made in England*. Recorded at George Martin's AIR Studios in Hampstead, North London, from February to April 1994, *Made in England* pays both obvious and subtle nods to Martin's production work with the Beatles. Martin himself arranged the string and French horn charts for one of the album tracks, "Latitude."

Penny has since remastered John's classic catalogue in 5.1 surround-sound audio.

Albums produced

- *Made in England* (1995, co-produced with Elton John)

Pat Leonard

To produce two albums by an artist boasting over thirty studio albums could seem like a footnote. But considering that one of them is *Songs from the West Coast*, Pat Leonard (whose production credits include albums by the likes of Madonna, Leonard Cohen, and Boz Scaggs, among others) succeeded in making one of the most compelling albums of John's latter-day career. Beginning with its lead single, "I Want Love," with its Lennon-esque chord progression and unaffected, bone-dry vocal summoning the sort of earnest inflections inspired by John's earliest classics, the album veers through moments of melancholic nostalgia ("This Train Don't Stop There Anymore") and carnal mischief ("Love Her Like Me") like the best of John's past classics. In the album's liner notes, John thanks Leonard, "who delivered exactly what I wanted."

Albums produced

- *The Road to El Dorado* (2000, original soundtrack, co-produced with Gavin Greenaway and Hans Zimmer)
- *Songs from the West Coast* (2001)

Phil Ramone

One of the most versatile and revered music producers of the past half-century, the late Phil Ramone is perhaps best remembered in rock and pop circles for his work on seminal albums by the likes of Billy Joel (*The Stranger*, *The Nylon Curtain*) and Paul Simon (*There Goes Rhymin' Simon*, *Still Crazy After All These Years*), but his résumé reflects everyone from Barbra Streisand to Tony Bennett to Frank Sinatra to Quincy Jones, among others.

His experience with Elton John dates back—literally—to 11–17–70, John's first official live album (see chapter 28), which he engineered and produced. Originally broadcast live on New York's WABC-FM radio, the performance, staged at A&R Studios in Manhattan, quickly surfaced on the burgeoning bootleg market, before John's record label released it officially. Showcasing John in the first blush of recognition in America, coming less than three months after his triumphant sets at the Troubadour in Los Angeles, the release soon earned a place among the all-time great live albums, and, thanks to Ramone's productions, has remained a visceral, vital remnant of an artist on the threshold of his own glory days.

In 1999, Ramone produced John's all-star soundtrack to *Aida*, which saw John collaborating with lyricist Tim Rice (with whom he had co-written "Legal Boys" from 1982's *Jump Up!*) and also with such artists as Tina Turner, Shania Twain, James Taylor, Janet Jackson, and Lenny Kravitz, to name but a few.

Considering he was a producer whose primary work environment was the recording studio, it's perhaps curious that Ramone's professional relationship with John occurred mostly in the realm of live albums and performances. Even so, his most fundamental responsibilities—meticulously preparing for and documenting a performance, albeit one in front of an audience of thousands—remained much the same. But there are more opportunities for mistakes when producing a concert, which is what happened with the making of the 2000's album, *One Night Only* (see chapter 28). Recorded at New York City's Madison Square Garden over two nights (and edited, delivered to the label, and released in stores within a week), the greatest-hits performance featured John along with select special guests like Mary J. Blige and Anastasia, but Ramone remembered the events in his memoir more for many an unfortunate technical malfunction and John's mood swings on the stage in response.

The mishaps occurred during what was considered to be the live album's dress rehearsal, on the first of two nights—the mixing board's computer, connected by cables snaked from inside the arena to a recording console built inside a truck parked outside, froze—which compelled the irritated artist to announce his immediate retirement. Thankfully, John returned for the second scheduled performance—"I'm full of shit," he quipped, of the haste with which he expressed his frustration the previous night—and such technical difficulties were mercifully avoided.

There was even less room for error when Ramone produced four of the most audacious gigs of Elton John's career to date, in July 2004, at Radio City Music Hall. Backed not only by his band but by a full symphony orchestra and choir, John was delivering the kind of shows he helmed in Australia in 1986 for the first time on American soil. While not released as a live album (as of yet, anyway), one of the performances was later broadcast on cable television's Bravo Network.

A Radio City Music Hall marquee advertising Elton John's July 2004 performances with band and full symphony orchestra with choir.   *Photo by Donald Gibson, Author's collection*

While Ramone for the most part was accustomed to negotiating his craft against the often-temperamental whims of technology, in his final experience of producing John he had to contend with the fragility of life itself. The session was for the 2004 Ray Charles album, *Genius Loves Company*, on which the soul music legend duetted with such artists as B.B. King, Norah Jones, and Willie Nelson, among others. Charles was near death at the time, suffering from liver cancer, and his performance with John on the latter's "Sorry Seems to Be the Hardest Word" ended up being the last recording of his life. For Ramone, having the artists rehearse and run through multiple takes (as is common practice) in the hope of landing on a technically or otherwise precise one was out of the question. He had to capture the ailing icon summoning his soul in real, precious time. Even on his best days, though, Charles could be persnickety and even indignant in the studio. Ramone had already learned that much first hand, having produced him singing "Baby Grand" with Billy Joel on the Piano Man's 1986 LP, *The Bridge*. This time, two takes, which were ultimately edited together to create the recording that's on the album, were all Ramone could get. "By the end of the second take, all of us were in tears," Ramone recalls in his memoir, *Making Music—The Scenes Behind the Music*, "but we wouldn't let Ray catch us crying."

Albums produced

- *Elton John and Tim Rice's Aida* (1999)
- *Elton John One Night Only—The Greatest Hits* (2000)

Matt Still

While *The Captain and the Kid* boasts his only (co-)production credit on an Elton John album, Matt Still has worked with John in various other capacities, including engineering and backing vocals, dating back to 1993's *Duets*, as well as *The Road to El Dorado* and *Peachtree Road*.

Albums produced

The Captain and the Kid (2004, co-produced with Elton John)

T Bone Burnett

T Bone Burnett witnessed Elton John's US debut firsthand at the Troubadour in August 1970, and he has known throughout the five decades since what potential still lay untapped in John's talent. Having been a vocal fan of Burnett at least since his stellar production of Elvis Costello's 1986 LP, *King of America*, John sought out the enigmatic record-maker after hearing his work on the Grammy-winning Robert Plant–Alison Krauss album, *Raising Sand* to produce his and Leon Russell's 2010 LP, *The Union*.

Known for utilizing an insular crop of top-flight session musicians, Burnett (who has amassed thirteen Grammy Awards to date) afforded John the best-case scenario of what he had sought in working with other producers—especially Thom Bell and Pete Bellotte—down through the years: the absolute freedom of not having to fret about directing each session musician on what or how to play, so that he could concentrate solely on the tasks of composing the melodies and recording his vocals. "I'd gotten disillusioned," John told the *Hollywood Reporter* in 2013, "but in the twilight of my career, here's someone whom I feel as excited about as when I first met Gus Dudgeon. He's gotten my love of recording back. I thought I'd lost that."

For Burnett, assuming such delimited responsibilities necessitates no small amount of trust between himself and the recording artist—a skill he has proven uniquely adept at through a range of musical and cinematic projects. In applying those responsibilities while working with an artist of the caliber of Elton John, the sense of trust is even more intense. "I just try and make him feel comfortable," Burnett told *Rolling Stone* in 2016. "He's an artist like Dylan—you just try and point him in the direction he was already going."

In a 2010 HBO documentary on the making of *The Union*, Burnett further explained, "When you're producing a record, you have to vibe with everybody. It's all vibe. So I just went in and paid attention. That's my job—to pay really close attention. You're the proxy for the audience, so you have a responsibility to them. If you're going to listen to it and record it, then it has to be great and it has to be something that's going to be worth their time."

Albums produced

- *The Union* (2010)
- *The Diving Board* (2013)
- *Wonderful Crazy Night* (2016, co-produced with Elton John)

9

When Are You Going to Land?

Themes of Escapism in *Goodbye Yellow Brick Road*

Awaiting the imminent release of his latest LP, *Don't Shoot Me I'm Only the Piano Player*, Elton John was already eager to commence work on his next album. Unfortunately, the Château d'Hérouville was, for the foreseeable future, unavailable, so he would need to choose another studio in which to record what would become his first double album, *Goodbye Yellow Brick Road*. Having grown accustomed to making records in a facility where everyone could concentrate on the task at hand in relative seclusion, John fancied finding another location with comparable accommodations.

However, his choice—Dynamic Sounds Studio in Kingston, Jamaica—would prove a most dreadful one.

Come On Jamaica

The notion of rich, successful rock 'n' roll musicians jet-setting around the world to work on their next projects in exotic, often tropical destinations was nothing new, dating back at least to when the Beatles opted to shoot parts of their 1965 motion picture *Help!* in the Bahamas. As far as Elton John knew, Jamaica sounded like paradise. Besides, the Rolling Stones had by all accounts enjoyed their recent rendezvous in Kingston, where they made *Goats Head Soup* at Dynamic Sounds, culminating in such future hits as "Angie" and "Doo Doo Doo Doo Doo (Heartbreaker)."

What could go wrong?

Arriving in Kingston on January 23, 1973, one day after the city had hosted George Foreman's historic title bout with Joe Frazier—Foreman triumphed in a dizzying second-round knockout to assume the world heavyweight championship—the Elton John entourage encountered a foreboding vibe in the air, the first sign of problems. Reluctant to leave his hotel room, John thus hunkered down with a batch of Taupin's latest lyrics, composing twenty-one songs in a three-day span.

"All the lyrics were written before we went to Jamaica," Taupin told author Victor Bockris and Liz Derringer, in a 1976 conversation for *Interview* magazine that was republished in 2015. "I wrote the songs up in Lincolnshire where I had a cottage. I just took a week out, went up there and spent the week writing the songs. It was a particularly productive time. I couldn't stop writing. I was just churning them out and then I gave them to [Elton] and he wrote the music in Kingston while he was waiting for the studio to be put together. In fact, the studio had barbed wire fence around it and a guard with a machine gun."

Producer Gus Dudgeon had actually traveled to Kingston on his own, before the band's arrival, to assess the amenities at Dynamic Sounds, and gave the facility his blessing. Once the musicians convened there for their scheduled recording sessions, however, the studio's dilapidated conditions (run-down and cockroach-infested equipment, a severe lack of recording-studio infrastructure) became extraordinarily apparent to all. After one too many frustrations and calamities, everyone decided to count their losses and return to the chateau in France, where sessions resumed in a shared ambiance of relief and singular productivity.

Forget Us, We'll Have Gone Very Soon

Goodbye Yellow Brick Road has been described as a concept album and, more accurately, a cinematic album. But a closer look at the songs reveals a common theme of escapism—the compulsion to abandon day-to-day reality, if only for the duration of a three-minute pop song. Moments like

Goodbye Yellow Brick Road, released on October 5, 1973, was John's third consecutive US #1 album, and includes such evergreen classics as "Candle in the Wind" and "Bennie and the Jets."   *Author's collection*

"Roy Rogers," for example, deliver the listener to specific scenes among specific characters—sitting before a television alone and away from the monotonies and regrets that come from growing older, fascinated by the titular western hero on the small screen—much as a reader would embrace distinct settings and characters in a compelling work of fiction. With the exception of "Harmony," which ends the double album like a coda with its nameless narrator, constructed as it is on a feeling more than a physical space, the lyrics throughout the album are for the most part written from a third-person perspective. These are character sketches, and all of these characters want (in some way) to transcend the doldrums of their current surroundings and circumstances.

Every song is a vicarious experience, from the narrator who longs to surrender his celebrity trappings and get back to his roots in the title track, to the hard-scrabbled roughneck aching to break up the boredom of yet another endless night out while causing some drunken trouble on the weekend in "Saturday Night's Alright for Fighting." Whether the song is an ode to the ladies of the night ("Sweet Painted Lady") or a lament over the unforgiving lethality and loneliness of fame ("Candle in the Wind"), either ecstasy or danger awaits in the aftermath of the escape.

"A lot of the songs began when I came across a great first line," Taupin said in 2014, to *Rolling Stone*. "The perfect example is 'The Ballad of Danny Bailey.'" Even moments of surrealistic eccentricity, like "Bennie and the Jets," offer an alternative to the mundane mortal plane. "I saw Bennie and the Jets as a sort of proto-sci-fi punk band, fronted by an androgynous woman, who looks like something out of a Helmut Newton photograph," Taupin said in the same interview.

By 1973, John and Taupin had found their collective voice as songwriters, and that voice could produce all manner of perspectives. Their partnership, at this point, simply proved too prolific to be inhibited.

"By the time we got to making *Goodbye Yellow Brick Road*, the machine was so well-oiled within the four musicians and the producer, Gus Dudgeon, it was perfection," John says in the 2014 video commentary on the classic album's fortieth anniversary. "It was the height of our powers."

10

Dirt in My Toes, Dirt up My Nose

The Caribou Sessions

In little more than five years, having made the same number of albums at a handful of recording studios—Dick James Studios on Oxford Street in London, Trident Studios in Soho, Château d'Hérouville in the South of France (not to mention the soon aborted *Goodbye Yellow Brick Road* recording sessions at Dynamic Studios in Kingston, Jamaica)—Elton John sought yet another change of scene.

In most of the previous circumstances to this point, he had recognized how well his band and crew worked together when sequestered for extended lengths of time in an environment that was conducive to both professional and personal necessities, rather than everyone recording in a studio like the ones in Los Angeles or New York, which for the most part afforded intermittent, on-the-clock sessions. Other bands had adopted a similar approach around the same time, from Led Zeppelin at Headley Grange to the Rolling Stones at the aforementioned Villa Nellcôte in France. Rather than choosing a studio based on its unique acoustics or economic incentives or what part of the world could (in theory, at least) offer the best vacation locale, however, John opted for one that could yield the sonic distinctions and energy of the music he most enjoyed at the time. Music by Dan Fogelberg, Rick Derringer, and Joe Walsh's post–James Gang band, Barnstorm—all of it was recorded at Caribou Ranch.

Meanwhile, in making what would emerge as his next three studio albums—*Caribou, Captain Fantastic and the Brown Dirt Cowboy*, and *Rock of the Westies*—John and his professional entourage wrestled with increasingly higher expectations (along with increasingly higher sales, which then amped up expectations further) while creating some of the most successful music of his career to date. Not altogether unlike Château d'Hérouville, Caribou Ranch's bucolic seclusion served the existential pursuit of one's artistic muse along with the often-solitary acts of composition and then rehearsal, while others availed themselves to the more illicit proclivities such isolation proffered on this sprawling, custom-built home on the range.

I Can Hear Crickets Singing in the Evening

In the foothills of the Rocky Mountains—or, to be precise, in the small town of Nederland, Colorado, just outside of Boulder—Caribou Ranch's recording studio was the idea of producer Jim Guercio, who had previously worked with such bands as the Buckinghams, Chicago, and Blood, Sweat, and Tears. Conceived as a pastoral retreat from the countless distractions artists encountered when recording in main hub of Los Angeles, when John decided to decamp his band to Caribou Ranch to make his own forthcoming album, it was most renowned for being the studio where "Rocky Mountain Way" (composed by Joe Walsh and bassist Kenny Passarelli) was recorded.

While such a change in scene proved rewarding in some moments, as the songs on *Caribou* demonstrated, it also proved challenging in others.

Too Late to Save Myself from Falling

John's career had been on an intrepid rise, his critical and popular success a snowballing phenomenon since "Your Song" introduced him to the masses in 1970. His songwriting partnership with Bernie Taupin had strengthened as well, the pair reaching a relative peak with the 1973 double album, *Goodbye Yellow Brick Road*, a veritable best-of collection (if not a greatest-hits one) in its own right. As a follow-up, *Caribou* paled in comparison.

Not that the album—hastily recorded over a nine-day period so that the band could embark on a Japanese tour—lacks redemptive moments altogether. One of its most popular and enduring songs, "Don't Let the Sun Go Down on Me" (#2 US, #16 UK), which in its Phil Spector–like Wall of Sound arrangement features Carl Wilson and Bruce Johnston of the Beach Boys on backing vocals, unquestionably stood alongside John's most emotive, compelling ballads on record to date. Conversely, "The Bitch Is Back," which features both John Lennon (on tambourine) and Dusty Springfield (on backing vocals), picked up where the testosterone-fueled aggression of "Saturday Night's Alright for Fighting" left off on the previous album, its balls-to-the-wall rambunctiousness hurling it to #4 in the States (and #15 in the UK).

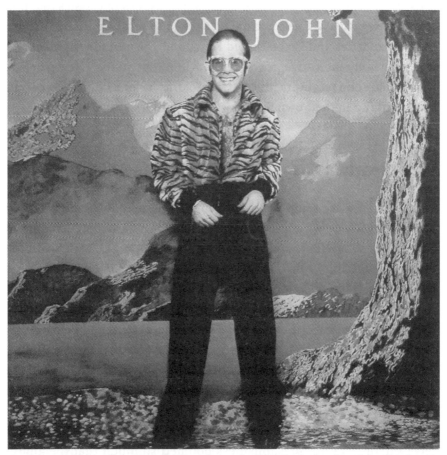

Caribou, released on June 28, 1974, features a pair of US #2 singles, "Don't Let the Sun Go Down on Me" and "The Bitch Is Back," which peaked at #16 and #15 in the UK, respectively.

Author's collection

The side-one label of John's *Captain Fantastic and the Brown Dirt Cowboy*, which was released on May 19, 1975, and became the first album to debut at #1 on the *Billboard* 200 US album charts.   *Author's collection*

The sentiment has been echoed by other members of the band over the years since. "I didn't see it coming. At all," Olsson told *Music Radar* in 2011. "To this day, I don't know why he let us go. His excuse in the press was that he wanted to change the sound of the band. He tried, but I don't think he did. It was just the same songs played by different people."

In what would amount to a rite of passage for incoming band members, the first gig for this new lineup was a monster: headlining a sold-out Wembley Stadium for what was dubbed the Mid-Summer Music Festival, which also featured Rufus with Chaka Khan, the Eagles, and the Beach Boys.

The side-two label of John's *Captain Fantastic and the Brown Dirt Cowboy*.   *Author's collection*

You're in the Band

As one of the new recruits, Denver native Kenny Passarelli was chosen not only for the quality of music he had already made but also what John foresaw him contributing to his music in the future. Not unlike how Miles Davis recruited new musicians for his various bands, John didn't so much audition assortments of possible players as scope out singular talents. But Passarelli didn't know as much at the time. "Elton, I think, subconsciously he wanted to go in that direction," he says. "And he got it. He understood it. Because when I was with Walsh and Stephen Stills, prior to that, those were the kind of records we made."

Having made his decision, John phoned Passarelli to invite him onboard, as the bass player recalls:

> They arranged for me to fly to New York, and I met Elton at TWA International terminal there. That's where we met for the first time. He was there with his assistant, and we flew to Paris. The thing was [to] go to Paris, and the new band organizes there at the chateau. Then we work on the Davey Johnstone solo record, and that'll be the first time [with] this group of people—which was Ray Cooper, Caleb Quaye, Roger Pope—and I was the new guy. Originally David Foster was supposed to play keyboards, but he backed out or he was charging too much money. He was just starting to get on a roll.

After flying with John and his assistant to Paris, then shuttling to Château d'Hérouville to familiarize himself with the rest of the band and crew, Passarelli joined them for a month of rehearsals in Amsterdam.

> So, I met Elton at the airport. We talked for a few minutes. He was very shy. It was a whole other world. I'd been around the block already. I'd been with Stephen [Stills] at a pretty high level, and the rock 'n' roll stuff that I'd done. So I wasn't really intimidated, but this is an international star. And at this time he was definitely the biggest guy on the planet. I was respectful, but I wasn't intimidated. I obviously was thinking, *I'm flying all the way over to Paris. When are we going to audition?* So, we get off the plane, we go to the chateau, it's morning—we flew overnight—and I'm thinking to myself, *Are we auditioning?*

John excused himself to sleep through his jet lag, at which point guitarist and bandleader Davey Johnstone pulled Passarelli aside. "You've got the gig, man," he remembers Johnstone telling him. "You wouldn't be here if you didn't have the gig. You don't have to audition. We'll play tomorrow. Elton knows your work. We came to Caribou because of stuff that you were on. He's well aware of what you've done. He's a huge fan of Crosby, Stills, and Nash; and of Stephen [as a solo artist]. So, if anything, he's a bit intimidated by *your* past."

From that point, the wheels were set in motion, a new beginning on the horizon. "It went from there to rehearsals [in Amsterdam] to Wembley Stadium," says Passarelli. "And then after Wembley Stadium we went to Colorado and did *Rock of the Westies*."

Making News Just Being Around

Having recorded his preceding two albums (*Caribou* and *Captain Fantastic and the Brown Dirt Cowboy*) at Caribou Ranch, John didn't so much seek a change of scene this time around as a change of sound altogether. In other words, a change of band, as Passarelli recalls:

> Here I'm working with a new artist. I wasn't a major Elton John fan when I got the gig, but I realized once I was in the middle of working with these guys first of all what an incredible songwriting team they were. And to see him sit with the lyrics, and work melodies and having some melodic ideas and having them work with the lyrics and not really sit there and scratch words out and redo [them]. He maybe moved them around a little bit, but it was basically what Bernie sent him, he worked with. So, I saw that. I saw him do that. And I think that drew me into being a little closer to the material when it was time to record.

The memories of making the album still stick with the band members, particularly Passarelli. "I saw him write at least half of the record, just hanging out in the big cabin at Caribou Ranch."

After rehearsing for a week together at the ranch, the band was ready to record the album. "It was James, Roger, Ray, Elton, and myself and Davey all in the same room," says Passarelli. "We were a *band*. We were fucking smoking, man. We had some bad reviews on *Rock of the Westies*, but when you listen to that record, that's a live-sounding, kick-ass record."

Having previously recorded at Caribou Ranch with Joe Walsh, Stephen Stills, and Dan Fogelberg, Passarelli had grown accustomed to making albums in this fashion. "To me, that was the way to do it," he says. "Basically, before I played with Elton, overdubbing bass was just occasionally. But mainly, when we cut, it was drums, bass, guitar, keyboard, or whatever . . . that was the way I grew up in the recording studio, that type of work."

Among the album's standouts, "I Feel Like a Bullet (In the Gun of Robert Ford)" recalls the western lyrical themes expressed on 1971's *Tumbleweed Connection*. "It's a fantastic song," says Passarelli. "It's a great-sounding song. That's overdubbed bass. That's one of my favorites. Great lyric, *incredible* lyric. Bernie's brilliant.

"*Rock of the Westies* really is live except for the bass—there may be some guitar overdubs," he continues. "'Street Kids,' 'Hard Luck Story,' 'Feed Me'—those are the three songs, if you listen closely, that's a fretless

Rock of the Westies, released on October 24, 1975, followed *Captain Fantastic and the Brown Dirt Cowboy* to become John's second consecutive LP to debut at #1 on the *Billboard* 200.

Author's collection

bass. Those were live, that's not overdubbed. That was from the live takes that we did."

The results, Passarelli contends, speak for themselves. "It was energy driven," he says. "It was a new group of people, like, all of a sudden the formula had changed."

While the musicians were keen to embark upon this new direction, producer Gus Dudgeon allegedly clung to his most familiar habits when it came to recording, Passarelli remembers:

> We're doing, like, two takes, walking out of there, like, "Let's party. We killed it." And Gus pulled me aside after the very last set and said, "I didn't get a good sound on the bass." I wanted to hit him over the head with a bottle of Jack. I just couldn't believe it. I said, "What?" He said, "You're going to have to redo . . . you're going to have to overdub the bass parts." I said, "All I have is fretless basses, man." He said, "No, I can't get a sound on those basses."
>
> I went to Jimmy Guercio, the owner at Caribou, who was a bass player; he was like my big brother. I said, "What am I going to do?" He said, "Well, McCartney gave me a Höfner, and I've got a couple other basses here. Take a look and see if you can get a sound." Well, what does he do? He picks the McCartney Höfner that had the worst action. It was like torture.
>
> In his eulogy, when he passed away, I told the story. I said, "I was wrong." My sound is unbelievable. My bass is so predominant and so powerful that I had to say, "He had a vision. I just didn't quite see it." When I listen to "Feed Me" and stuff like that, those are really badass tracks. He just had a system, and my thing wasn't going to quite work out with him then. So the rebellion started there. And it wasn't necessarily with me. I had something to do with it because I was pissed about having to redo the bass parts.

And We're About to Abandon Our Plans for the Day

In part blowing off steam and in part embracing the in-the-middle-of-nowhere atmosphere they were enjoying with living part-time at Caribou

Ranch, extracurricular activities abounded among the members of the band.

"Everything was crazy," recalls Passarelli. "We were partying, but nothing like . . . I remember Bernie said something stupid in an interview that he didn't even remember making *Rock of the Westies*. Nobody was that. . . . These guys were amateurs compared to what I'd seen. They were doing shitty drugs, coke . . . I'd been around Stephen Stills. Come on."

Also out of control during this time—though it was not a new phenomenon, by any means—was Elton John's competitive streak, which manifested itself in everything from playing soccer with the band before the Dodger Stadium performances—"He popped me in the face!" Passarelli recalls. "He almost broke my nose!"—or shooting pool in the dressing rooms. "If you beat him at something in the studio," Passarelli says, "he would just be pissed off at you for a couple days. He's the ultimate competitive monster talent. What can you say? No wonder he is what he is."

Caleb Quaye's recollections of the *Rock of the Westies* sessions are a bit more philosophical, though not mollified by any means. "Obviously we were aware of Elton and Bernie's personal problems, things like that," he says, "but it was like those [things] were separate. When we got in the studio to record, that's a whole other thing. The personal problems, they're outside. When we were in the studio, making the music, they were precious times. No question about it. I have great memories . . . we were thoroughly enjoying ourselves."

Rock of the Westies became John's second (and final) LP to debut at #1 on the *Billboard* 200 chart, where it spent three weeks; it peaked at #5 in the UK. "Island Girl," its lead single, topped the *Billboard* Hot 100 singles chart in the US for three weeks while peaking at #14 on the UK singles chart.

"The music was sensational," recalls Passarelli. "The music was sensational in terms of the recording process that created the ability for other participants to be involved in co-writing. It was a real magic time."

For now, at least, nothing could curtail Elton John's dominance on the charts and in the popular culture at large.

"It was a giant dream," says Passarelli. "It was just beyond me. There I was, in Colorado, my own familiar Caribou, up there recording with Elton. [*Rock of the Westies*] was the only record I did with Elton in Caribou. Then we did the *Rock of the Westies* tour, which was all West Coast. It was pretty cush—our own jet, blah blah blah. I played in my hometown, Denver. Number one record: "Island Girl." Number one, the album. I mean, it went by pretty quick. It was phenomenal."

11

Well, They're Packed Pretty Tight in Here Tonight

Notable Live Performances

Lights out. An aching bell tolls in ominous alarm, dry ice and synthesizers suffusing the darkness in a billowing whirlwind. The sound of fanfare spirals high and ever higher out of the din, as if heralding a regal coronation. From an imposing grand piano comes a melody in the dark, brooding yet solemn in the quintessential prelude. "Funeral for a Friend" then spits and sputters into "Love Lies Bleeding," exploding like a clarion call, encapsulating the majesty and mayhem to come.
Welcome to Elton John, live.

"He's an animal," says bassist Kenny Passarelli. "I can't believe how hard he works, but he always was that way. His work ethic is ridiculous."

Indeed, the concert stage is where Elton John has summoned his most extravagant and fulfilling self, a rock 'n' roll idol behind some of the past half century's most indelibly beloved songs. At least since his star-making set at the Troubadour in 1970 (see chapter 6), John has cultivated a sterling reputation as an incomparable live performer.

In this chapter, we survey some of Elton John's most notable concert appearances.

Hollywood Bowl (September 7, 1973)

How had John progressed as a live performer since Chris Charlesworth first saw him at the Krumlin Festival, only three years prior? "Oh, he'd gotten better and better," says the former *Melody Maker* journalist and editor, who attended this performance. "He'd also added Davey Johnstone on guitar by that time, so there was a much fatter sound altogether. The show was getting longer and longer. Acts like Elton, once you've had a lot of hits, you've more or less got to play them all, haven't you? So he'd reached that point. It was all part of stagemanship and showmanship."

Setlist

- "Elderberry Wine / Your Song"
- "High Flying Bird"
- "Honky Cat"
- "Goodbye Yellow Brick Road"
- "Hercules"
- "Rocket Man (I Think It's Going to Be a Long, Long Time)"
- "Madman Across the Water"
- "Teacher I Need You"
- "Have Mercy on the Criminal"
- "All the Girls Love Alice"
- "Daniel"
- "Funeral for a Friend / Love Lies Bleeding"
- "Crocodile Rock"
- "Saturday Night's Alright for Fighting"
- "Honky Tonk Women"

Madison Square Garden (November 28, 1974)

On Thanksgiving night, the first night of a two-night stand at Madison Square Garden, John Lennon honored a promise he had made with John months earlier: that if "Whatever Gets You Thru the Night," the first single from his current LP, *Walls and Bridges*, reached #1 on the *Billboard* singles charts, he would perform the song with John. To the former Beatle's absolute surprise (and horror, considering he had not played live since his One to One concert at the same venue in 1972, and was not looking forward to the prospect), the song topped the charts, eclipsing Bachman–Turner Overdrive's "You Ain't Seen Nothing Yet."

The performance ended up being Lennon's last ever concert performance.

Setlist

- "Funeral for a Friend / Love Lies Bleeding"
- "Candle in the Wind"
- "Grimsby"
- "Rocket Man (I Think It's Going to Be a Long, Long Time)"
- "Take Me to the Pilot"
- "Bennie and the Jets"
- "Daniel"
- "Grey Seal"

Elton John Live at Madison Square Garden, a fan club–only release.   *Author's collection*

- "Goodbye Yellow Brick Road"
- "Burn Down the Mission"
- "You're So Static"
- "Whatever Gets You Thru the Night" (with John Lennon)
- "Lucy in the Sky with Diamonds" (with John Lennon)
- "I Saw Her Standing There" (with John Lennon)
- "Don't Let the Sun Go Down on Me"
- "All the Girls Love Alice"
- "Saturday Night's Alright for Fighting"

Encore
- "Crocodile Rock"
- "The Bitch Is Back"
- "Your Song"

Mid-Summer Music Festival, Wembley Stadium (June 21, 1975)

As *Captain Fantastic and the Brown Dirt Cowboy* became the first album in history to debut atop the *Billboard* chart, Elton John sought to celebrate his achievement before a sold-out Wembley Stadium before an estimated one hundred thousand people, topping a bill that also included Rocket Records act Stackridge along with Rufus (featuring Chaka Khan), the Beach Boys, Joe Walsh, and the group whose ranks Walsh would soon join, the Eagles.

Whereas the other acts mostly (and, considering the expanse of the audience on hand, wisely) focused on their respective hits, John played his new album in full, which resulted not only in countless blank stares and disoriented fans in the seats but in anxiety on the stage. Onstage with John was his (almost) new band: bassist Kenny Passarelli, guitarist Caleb Quaye, along with other Rocket Records labelmates guitarist Jeff "Skunk" Baxter (of the Doobie Brothers and Steely Dan) and backing vocalists Donny Gerrard and Brian and Brenda Russell.

"Wembley Stadium, for us, was a major deal because that was the famous English soccer stadium—an historic place we all grew up with," says guitarist Caleb Quaye. "And for all of a sudden we're the first rock band ever to play at Wembley Stadium with our names on the scoreboards and everything, it was just a surreal moment.

"We played what we were expected to play, and we loved it," he continues. "We enjoyed the music. We loved it. So it didn't . . . We didn't feel like we were selling out or selling ourselves short or anything like that. No, not at all. We loved it. We just went after it and played it as best we could."

Bassist Kenny Passarelli, whose gig this was his first in the band, has harsher recollections.

> It was very difficult. It was a huge mistake. By the time we started, people were already looking at leaving.
>
> Elton is not crazy about rehearsals, so we were in Amsterdam, and Davey was really the main thing. I hadn't learned all the *Captain Fantastic* [songs] . . . it was very awkward. And, I'll be honest with you, I wasn't a huge, huge fan. So until we got to the hits, by the time we got to the encores, whoever was left of a hundred thousand people, we killed it. The rest of it was, like, everybody was looking at us, like, *Duh*. It was a bold move that only somebody on that level could make. I think it was a mistake . . . I remember I went to the after party and I met [Paul] McCartney and he probably thought I stunk.

The musicians—including some, like Quaye and Pope, who went back a ways with John—nevertheless summoned their professionalism as best they could. Quaye recalls:

> The most major adjustment was just [to] the size and the scope of everything. Musically, the guys in the band—there were a bunch of us: myself, Elton, Davey Johnstone, Roger Pope—we were friends for a long time. So there was a nucleus of both friendship and musicality that held everything together very well. So, in those terms, it wasn't such a major adjustment. I knew the music. I knew where it came from. I knew what was required of me and having Roger in there was just a great anchor to everything. And so musically it wasn't a great adjustment. It was everything else. It was the size and the scope of everything else. Now all of a sudden instead of playing in clubs I'm playing on stadium stages with

tons of room and umpteen-thousand screaming people. *That* was different.

Still, Passarelli adds, "In many ways, that's a ballsy move, playing a record nobody had ever even heard."

Setlist

- "Funeral for a Friend / Love Lies Bleeding"
- "Rocket Man (I Think It's Going to Be a Long, Long Time)"
- "Candle in the Wind"
- "The Bitch Is Back"
- "Dixie Lily"
- "Philadelphia Freedom"
- "Chameleon"
- "Bennie and the Jets"
- "Lucy in the Sky with Diamonds"
- "I Saw Her Standing There"
- "Captain Fantastic and the Brown Dirt Cowboy"
- "Tower of Babel"
- "Bitter Fingers"
- "Tell Me When the Whistle Blows"
- "Someone Saved My Life Tonight"
- "(Gotta Get a) Meal Ticket"
- "Better Off Dead"
- "Writing"
- "We All Fall in Love Sometimes"
- "Curtains"
- "Pinball Wizard"
- "Saturday Night's Alright for Fighting"

Dodger Stadium (October 25 and 26, 1975)

"Dodger Stadium might have been one of the most perfect gigs I think I ever played in my life," says Kenny Passarelli. "It was phenomenal."

In the days before this pair of historic performances, Hollywood observed "Elton John Week," including a ceremony during which John received a star on the Walk of Fame on Hollywood Boulevard. The main event, of course, lay ahead inside the hallowed grounds of Dodger Stadium—the first concerts allowed at the hallowed baseball stadium since the Beatles had unwittingly incited a modest riot nine years earlier—with Emmylou Harris and Passarelli's pal Joe Walsh (just before joining the Eagles) opening.

Beginning with a solo rendition of "Your Song," before his now road-tested band joined him in full throes, John steered clear of the problems that plagued his Mid-Summer Music Festival set at Wembley Stadium back in June, delivering a three-hour-plus performance chock full of crowd-pleasing hits and a reasonably digestible portion of album cuts and covers.

"Dodger Stadium, I don't think anything compares to that in my career," says Passarelli. "I've done a lot of stuff, but that? They were like two perfect gigs. We were perfect, played perfect. We were just *on*. It was weird, because when you look at what was going on with Elton and his personal life, he was crumbling. But, man, when we got onstage, it didn't really matter. He came through, and we played great."

"The Dodgers may not have made it even to the playoffs this year," Robert Hilburn wrote in his October 27 *Los Angeles Times* review, "but Dodger Stadium got its World Series after all. At least, it did for the 110,000 rock fans."

As John recalled in a 2017 interview with BBC Radio 2's Johnnie Walker, "I was beginning to reach the pinnacle of my success, and that was just an endorsement of how big we were becoming."

Setlist (same for both performances)

- "Your Song"
- "I Need You to Turn To"
- "Border Song"
- "Take Me to the Pilot"
- "Dan Dare (Pilot of the Future)"
- "Country Comfort"

- "Levon"
- "Rocket Man (I Think It's Going to Be a Long, Long Time)"
- "Hercules"
- "Empty Sky"
- "Funeral for a Friend / Love Lies Bleeding"
- "Goodbye Yellow Brick Road"
- "Bennie and the Jets"
- "Harmony"
- "Dixie Lily"
- "Captain Fantastic and the Brown Dirt Cowboy"
- "Bitter Fingers"
- "Someone Saved My Life Tonight"
- "The Bitch Is Back"
- "Don't Let the Sun Go Down on Me"
- "(Gotta Get a) Meal Ticket"
- "Lucy in the Sky with Diamonds"
- "I Saw Her Standing There"
- "Island Girl"
- "Philadelphia Freedom"
- "We All Fall in Love Sometimes"
- "Curtains"

Encore
- "Tell Me When the Whistle Blows"
- "Saturday Night's Alright for Fighting"
- "Pinball Wizard"

Madison Square Garden (August 10–13 and 15–17, 1976)

"When we finished at Madison Square Garden, nobody could touch us," says Passarelli. "We were *that* good. Elton was incredible, and we were, too—a badass band."

John's new album, *Blue Moves*—his second double album in three years—wouldn't be in record shops for a couple of weeks yet, but the buzz surrounding his seven-night stand at Madison Square Garden was palpable. He'd just given *Rolling Stone* magazine the scoop of his career to date, conceding (not so much confessing) to journalist Cliff Jahr that he was bisexual. However, with a sixth straight sold-out audience waiting for the world's most famous pop star to take the stage at the world's most famous arena—and with a seventh sold-out performance to follow the next night—Elton John broke up his band.

For the band, getting sacked as they stood in the wings, ready to hit the stage, didn't exactly boost morale. "But that's the way it was," says Quaye, "That's the way it went."

Nevertheless, says Passarelli, "You couldn't have gotten any better than '75 and '76. You couldn't have gotten any better than that. It was magic. Nobody could touch us. We blew everybody off [the stage]. Freddie Mercury, all those guys would come and see us. Freddie Mercury was incredible, but . . . I ran into Roger and John, those guys used to come—the rhythm section of Queen—and they were blown away by how great of a band we were and how phenomenal Elton was. He was incredible. The guy was flawless."

Setlist (August 17, 1976)

- "Grow Some Funk of Your Own"
- "Goodbye Yellow Brick Road"
- "Island Girl"
- "Rocket Man (I Think It's Going to Be a Long, Long Time)"
- "Hercules"
- "Bennie and the Jets"
- "Funeral for a Friend / Love Lies Bleeding"
- "Love Song"
- "Lucy in the Sky with Diamonds"
- "Don't Let the Sun Go Down on Me"
- "Empty Sky"
- "Someone Saved My Life Tonight"
- "Don't Go Breaking My Heart" (with Kiki Dee)
- "I've Got the Music in Me" (Kiki Dee)

- "Philadelphia Freedom"
- "We All Fall in Love Sometimes"
- "Curtains"
- "Tell Me When the Whistle Blows"
- "Saturday Night's Alright for Fighting"
- "Your Song"
- "Pinball Wizard"

Wembley Arena (November 3, 1977)

For this benefit concert in support of the Royal Variety Club and Goaldiggers (which supplied football accommodations for underprivileged children), John needed a band, having effectively fired his last one backstage at Madison Square Garden in August, before the release of *Blue Moves*. He recruited China, which included a few friendly faces—guitarist Davey Johnstone, keyboardist James Newton Howard, and percussionist Ray Cooper—along with guitarist Jo Partridge, bassist John "Cooker" LoPresti, and drummer Dennis Conway.

As Gary Osborne, who was singing backup alongside Kiki Dee and Chris Thompson (of Manfred Mann) that night, reflects:

> And then on the day itself he was in such a bad mood. Something put him in a terrible mood. And when he got onto the stage, he looked just like a gorilla. He had a leather jacket and he had a beret on. He looked like a gay version of Che Guevara—Che Gayvara—and he comes to a point where he says, "A lot of people have been wondering whether I And I thought, *This is it. This is where he says* ... Then he says,'m going to go back on the road." "Well, I'm *not*. I'm never going to tour again." I couldn't believe it. I was standing onstage. I was fired up by the news I'd only gotten the day before.

It had to feel like a certain kind of déjà vu for Howard, Cooper, and Johnstone in particular, hearing John announce shortly before the end of the performance that he was retiring altogether. Mitigating the shock a bit, he escorted surprise guest Stevie Wonder to the stage and, with the Motown icon seated next to him at the piano, rumbled through an extended version of "Bite Your Lip (Get Up and Dance!)" to end the show and, ostensibly, his career.

"Can you imagine what it felt like for me?" says Osborne. "I mean, I get to be on the stage with Davey and Ray and Kiki and Elton and Chris Thompson *and* Stevie fucking Wonder?"

Indeed, while noodling through the opening bars of "Sorry Seems to Be the Hardest Word," John upped and Ziggy Stardust'd the whole thing. "I've made a decision tonight. This will be the last show," he announced. "There's a lot more to me than playing on the road."

Setlist

- "Better Off Dead"
- "Daniel"
- "Roy Rogers"
- "The Goaldigger's Song"
- "Where to Now, St. Peter?"
- "Shine on Through"
- "Tonight"
- "I Heard It Through the Grapevine"
- "Island Girl"
- "Candle in the Wind"
- "One Horse Town"
- "Bennie and the Jets"
- "Sorry Seems to Be the Hardest Word"
- "Philadelphia Freedom"
- "Funeral for a Friend / Love Lies Bleeding"
- "Rocket Man (I Think It's Going to Be a Long, Long Time)"
- "(Gotta Get a) Meal Ticket"
- "Your Song"
- "Don't Go Breaking My Heart" (with Kiki Dee)
- "Bite Your Lip (Get Up and Dance!)"

Central Park, New York City (September 13, 1980)

Before what was reported at the time to be four hundred thousand people gathered on the Great Lawn of New York City's Central Park (more recent and accurate methods of crowd counting have suggested the exact number was far smaller), Elton John performed to his biggest live audience to date, dwarfing the size of his fabled 1975 Dodger Stadium crowds by more than three times. The free concert, sponsored by Calvin Klein jeans and WNEW-FM and benefiting the city's parks projects, saw the superstar back with a full band, his fashion statements as colorfully loud and outlandish as ever. The Donald Duck costume, which he wore to close out the concert, was designed by fashion icon Bob Mackie (see chapter 14), who besides having dressed the likes of Cher and Diana Ross in the seventies, also fitted John with his sequined Dodgers uniform for his historic 1975 performances at Dodger Stadium in Los Angeles.

"He kept the outfit that he was going to wear a secret," says Gary Osborne, "so it was as much a shock to the band, and I was standing in the wings. It was as much a shock to us. His PA [Bob Halley] knew, but when he came on dressed as Donald Duck, you could've blown us down with a feather."

In support of his current album at the time, *21 at 33*, the performance

An officially sanctioned bobble-head commemorating John's September 1980 performance at New York City's Central Park.   *Author's collection*

featured more hits than obscurities—taking too many chances with the setlist in front of such a massive crowd would not have been wise.

Gary Osborne recalls, "I remember his big disappointment that day was he had very much hoped that Lennon would turned up, because, let's face it, it's Central Park, it's only across the road from where Lennon lived. And they had been very close. But Lennon was in his reclusive stage and he didn't turn up. And Elton was a bit disappointed. I remember Elton saying, 'Maybe John will come,' and I thought that'd be great, because I hadn't met him."

Unbeknown to the general public and even most in the music industry at the time, Lennon was busy across town at the Hit Factory, recording his first album in five years, *Double Fantasy*—a fact John let slip in his introduction to "Imagine," most likely the last time that song was performed by anyone so famous without it being intended as a posthumous tribute. Lennon would be dead in less than three months.

The concert brought John back together with drummer Nigel Olsson and bassist Dee Murray of the original Elton John Band, this time augmented by percussionist Ray Cooper, keyboardist James Newton Howard, and guitarist Tim Renwick.

Setlist

- "Funeral for a Friend / Love Lies Bleeding"
- "Tiny Dancer"
- "Goodbye Yellow Brick Road"
- "All the Girls Love Alice"
- "Rocket Man (I Think It's Going to Be a Long, Long Time)"
- "Sartorial Eloquence"
- "Philadelphia Freedom"
- "Sorry Seems to Be the Hardest Word"
- "Saturday Night" (Nigel Olsson)
- "All I Want Is You" (Nigel Olsson)
- "Saturday Night's Alright for Fighting"
- "Harmony"
- "White Lady White Powder"
- "Little Jeannie"

- "Bennie and the Jets"
- "Imagine"
- "Ego"
- "Have Mercy on the Criminal"
- "Someone Saved My Life Tonight"

Encore
- "Your Song"
- "Bite Your Lip! (Get Up and Dance!)"
- "Good Golly Miss Molly!"

Wembley Stadium (June 30, 1984)

The Rocket Man was once again on the ascent, thanks to the breakout success of his two most recent studio albums, *Too Low for Zero* and *Breaking Hearts*, along with the full-time reconvening of his songwriting partnership with Bernie Taupin. Headlining the mighty Wembley Stadium for the first time since his perplexing 1975 performance, during which he performed the entire *Captain Fantastic* album front to back, John made a point this time not to disappoint.

Recorded for broadcast on the Showtime cable channel (which was by no means a household entertainment venue at that point) as the *Night and Day Concert* (and released on VHS thereafter with the same title), the show reflected a back-to-basics approach for John, who augmented his original Elton John Band mates Nigel Olsson (drums) and Dee Murray (bass) with only keyboardist Fred Mandel and evergreen guitarist Davey Johnstone.

Setlist

- "Tiny Dancer"
- "Hercules"
- "Rocket Man (I Think It's Going to Be a Long, Long Time)"
- "Daniel"
- "Restless"

- "Candle in the Wind"
- "The Bitch Is Back"
- "Don't Let the Sun Go Down on Me"
- "Sad Songs (Say So Much)"
- "Bennie and the Jets"
- "Sorry Seems to Be the Hardest Word"
- "Philadelphia Freedom"
- Medley: "Blue Eyes / I Guess That's Why They Call It the Blues"
- "Kiss the Bride"
- "One More Arrow"
- "Too Low for Zero"
- "I'm Still Standing"
- "Your Song"
- "Saturday Night's Alright for Fighting"
- "Goodbye Yellow Brick Road"
- "Crocodile Rock"
- Medley: "Whole Lotta Shakin' Goin' On / I Saw Her Standing There / Twist and Shout"

Live Aid (July 13, 1985)

Before a colossal audience crammed inside Wembley Stadium, John took the stage looking, as Freddie Mercury had teased him, like the Queen Mother.

Setlist

- "I'm Still Standing"
- "Bennie and the Jets"
- "Rocket Man (I Think It's Going to Be a Long, Long Time)"
- "Don't Go Breaking My Heart" (with Kiki Dee)
- "Don't Let the Sun Go Down on Me" (with Wham!)
- "Can I Get a Witness"

Freddie Mercury Tribute Concert (April 20, 1992)

Five months after Freddie Mercury succumbed to AIDS-related pneumonia, the iconic Queen front man was feted with a massive tribute concert. John performed a jolting version of "The Show Must Go On," the prophetic *Innuendo* track becoming a staple of his concert tour in support of his current album at the time, *The One*. He ended with the biggest Queen song of them all, performing "Bohemian Rhapsody" with Axl Rose.

Concert for Diana (July 1, 2007)

Onstage at the newly rebuilt Wembley before an audience of sixty-three thousand (quite less than the old Wembley Stadium), including Princes William and Harry, more than two dozen musicians marked the tenth anniversary of Princess Diana's tragic death in Paris. Younger stars like James Morrison and Joss Stone traded the spotlight with such veterans as Rod Stewart and Tom Jones, performing their most recognized and beloved hits. In his prime-time slot, John eschewed any semblance of solemnity in favor of mostly upbeat classics, turning what could have been a somber affair into a giant party.

Setlist

- "Your Song"
- "Saturday Night's Alright for Fighting"
- "Tiny Dancer"
- "Are You Ready for Love?"

12

Everything Crumbles Sooner or Later

Blue Moves, Breakdowns, and Goodbyes

The writing may not have been written on the wall, but it was suggested by the songs. For the most part, the music John and Taupin had by this point written didn't reveal explicit narrative details. It wasn't obvious or otherwise common knowledge what, say, "Daniel" or "Tiny Dancer" were about—if they were even about anything at all. Unless one of them revealed a song's specific inspiration or meaning to a journalist in an interview, that song's meaning remained obscure, and thus amenable to interpretation. Even with the previous year's LP, *Captain Fantastic and the Brown Dirt Cowboy*—which was, as John and Taupin had proclaimed, an autobiographical album about the early days of their songwriting partnership—the songs contained enough lyrical abstractions so as to maintain a sense of mystery about their inspirations or explicit meanings.

By 1976, though, a barrage of intimate and professional pressures had mounted for both John and Taupin, causing severe fissures in the colossal hit-making machine that had yielded unparalleled success, including seven consecutive #1 albums, along with equally unparalleled expectations that neither man could live up to any longer.

"I know what it did to me," Taupin concedes in the 1991 documentary, *Two Rooms: Celebrating the Songs of Elton John and Bernie Taupin*, "and what it did to me was scary and I had to run away from it because I was frightened to keep going because I was frightened of failure."

Issued on October 22, 1976, as the inaugural release on John's own label, Rocket Records, *Blue Moves* couldn't help but flagrantly reflect the overriding insecurities, anger, and disillusionment that inspired many of

Blue Moves, released on October 22, 1976, features the Top 20 single "Sorry Seems to Be the Hardest Word," which peaked at #6 in the US and #11 in the UK. *Author's collection*

its songs, yet the album's emotional transparency allowed for a refreshed and sophisticated sense of musicality.

"It was a serious time," says bassist Kenny Passarelli. "You had a marriage breaking up. You had a partnership breaking up. You had a relationship between Elton John and [his manager] John Reid [breaking up]. Everything was crazy."

Nevertheless, five months after concluding his West of the Rockies US tour with two ecstatic performances at Dodger Stadium, John reconvened with his touring band at Eastern Sound in Toronto to record his eleventh studio album. As the inaugural Rocket Records release—and with the unprecedented success of both *Captain Fantastic and the Brown Dirt Cowboy* and *Rock of the Westies* still gleaming in the proverbial rearview mirror, both LPs having debuted atop the *Billboard* 200 albums chart— the stakes could not have been higher.

"We had tried to change with every album up to that point, but *Blue Moves* was the most drastic," John recalls in the liner notes of 1990's *To Be*

Continued . . . boxed set. "I was aware that we had been at the peak of our careers, and that that was going to level off."

Having revealed his bisexuality in *Rolling Stone*, in the issue dated October 7, 1976, John faced a swift backlash that contributed to *Blue Moves*, which was released on October 22, not reaching the top of the charts—it peaked at #3 on the *Billboard* 200. Unless an album is a "sleeper" hit (the term used for the phenomenon of motion pictures taking an extended period to become a box-office smash), most reach #1 based on a mixture of enthusiasm carried over from the previous album and anticipation for the new one. In the case of *Blue Moves*, John had received some negative reviews for his previous album, *Rock of the Westies*, and, with the news of his bisexuality stirring up controversy, particularly in the States, his latest effort could only stand to suffer.

"Bernie was writing sad lyrics—his marriage was over with," says Passarelli. "Elton and John Reid were breaking up as a couple. Everything was fucked up. The drugs were just starting to enter the picture. It wasn't crazy at all before with Elton. Elton was nowhere near where he ended up at that point. The guy was very straight, I thought anyways, compared to what I'd been around. He never drank or did anything before he played. He never made a mistake in those years. We worked three-hour concerts. The guy was flawless."

In spite of the sovereignty that comes from being a solo artist, in the studio, John demonstrated an eagerness to collaborate with his band, ensuring that his talent never eclipsed whatever ideas or inspirations arose from their efforts.

"We would be standing around the piano watching him play, and we would instinctively know kind of what he wanted," says guitarist Caleb Quaye. "That's where musicianship comes in. It was fun. We loved it. It was great. And plus Elton, he'd come up with the bare-bones thing, but he trusted us as well. He trusted us to come up with parts. He knew we were going to come up with the right parts, and we knew it as well. It was very comfortable in that respect."

In recalling the open, collaborative atmosphere that infused the sessions, Quaye recalls how a song he'd written, "Your Starter For . . . ," ended up on the album. "One of the days we were in the studio and he said, 'You know what? I want the album to start out instrumentally. Does anybody have any ideas for an instrumental thing?' So I piped up. I said, 'You know, I've got this little piece,' which I'd written months earlier, and I'd written it just as an exercise, a practice piece for my acoustic guitar playing.

"So I just played it down for him in the studio," he adds, "and him and the guys went, 'Yeah, that's great. Let's do that.' So I taught it to him, and we did it."

The song not only ended up opening *Blue Moves* but also served as its thematic template. "I was not that aware of what the theme was going to be, or how it might fit thematically," says Quaye. "So I can only assume that [Elton] had that in mind as to what was going to come after it. But he loved it right from the get-go."

In spite of how relatively briefly these musicians had played together by this point, some of them shared similar histories, dating back to John's earliest endeavors at Dick James Music. Drummer Roger Pope and guitarist Caleb Quaye, for instance, had played together in Hookfoot, the band that backed John on his earliest studio albums. Such shared history and the chemistry it forged no doubt galvanized both the touring band and the *Blue Moves* sessions.

"We all grew up with the same musical influences," says Quaye. "So Elton could say, 'I want it to sound like *this*,' and we all knew exactly what he was talking about and could go there."

In short, the musicians knew their abilities and potential, and they felt compelled to prove their mettle with the material at hand. "Myself and Roger are primarily rock-groove-funk players," says Quaye, "but we also have a huge appreciation for classical stuff as well. And there was a lot of that kind of influence on the album as well."

To that end, keyboardist James Newton Howard proved indispensable through both his contributions on the first polyphonic Moog synthesizer and select string arrangements, most notably on "Tonight" and "Sorry Seems to Be the Hardest Word," instilling the album with both grandeur and sensitive grace. "Elton was the first to be aware of James's genius," says Passarelli. "He gave James the Excalibur. He made James's career."

In the case of "Someone Saved My Life Tonight," John told the *New York Times* in 2002 that he "pinched" the opening chord from the Beach Boys' "God Only Knows," his concession making all the more sense when one considers the profound influence Brian Wilson has long exerted on John's melodic-rich songwriting.

"We knew it was going to be different," says Quaye.

> It was different for a bunch of different reasons, actually. One was, at the time, Elton was . . . there was a lot of personal stress in his life. And on the other hand, the band had become really tight. So it was no longer a piano trio kind of a sound. It was a bigger sound with some very accomplished musicians in there. It was a different scope. The whole thing musically was at a different level. What a lot of people don't realize is that most of that album was actually recorded live in the studio. It was very minimal overdubs except obviously with an orchestra and stuff like that. But the basic tracks, a lot of the guitar solo stuff, it was cut live in the studio.

Passarelli adds, "It was a really together group of musicians, and Elton was totally in it. He felt real comfortable with what we were doing."

I See the Storm Approaching

If any tension seeped into the sessions at all, though, it pertained to Gus Dudgeon's alleged preference for overdubbing. This was a seasoned, tight, and hungry band—and the chemistry they nurtured in the *Rock of the Westies* sessions had only gotten stronger on the subsequent West of the Rockies tour of North America, as Passarelli recalls:

> When we got to Toronto, there was a mutiny and Gus had to do what *we* wanted to do. Caleb, I must say, was a ringleader. We pushed [Gus] around a bit, and that record turned out to be a lot less . . . there was a lot less overdubbing on those basic tracks— fucking killer, man. There was no overdubbing. That was me and Elton playing "Sorry Seems to Be the Hardest Word," "Idol"—that's all live. I overdubbed a couple notes here and there. On top of everything, I was so pissed off at Gus, I went and bought the most expensive bass there was. It was a $4,000 Olympic bass,

fretted. And I stopped playing fretless bass because of that situation. Which was really sad, because that really was my sound. So there's no fretless on that record. But . . . musically, I think it's a killer record.

No matter how much emotional chaos informed or even underscored the *Blue Moves* sessions, John capably summoned his experience and expertise to focus on the task at hand, rallying his musicians in mutual pursuit. Such discipline hearkens back to the cutthroat Tin Pan Alley environment where he and several of his bandmates first plied their trade. "We learned our craft back in the old analog world," says Quaye. "There were no fancy effects or gizmos like they have today. It wasn't about pushing buttons and stuff. It was about whether or not you could sing and play your instrument. So we were trained to come up with it on the spot."

With the lyrics already written, the music John composed in the studio evoked fresh nuance and melodic sophistication, complementing deft jazz and classical elements with some of the most emphatically mature lyrics Taupin had written to date. In fact, *Blue Moves* marked the first time that John outright refused to set some of Taupin's lyrics to music. "It was seventy-six and we were exhausted, and drugs had set in," John told Q magazine in 1995. "And he was going through a very angry stage in his life as far as personal relationships were concerned, and I just couldn't sing them."

It's a Sad, Sad Situation

"All this shit was going on, and it was all covert, but subconsciously it was coming through the music," says Passarelli. "All you've got to do is look at the lyrics. It says everybody's story."

Just as individual tensions prevailed through the group, a more ominous undercurrent influenced the sessions.

"The dramatic part of the *Blue Moves* [sessions] was the basic consciousness of the end of an era," says Passarelli. "Things were dissolving.

Things were breaking up. And there was a sadness in all the lyrics, pretty heavy shit. 'Someone's Final Song,' come on. That's like a suicide note."

Passarelli recalls of the tension, "It permeated, but not in any sort of confrontational way, as it was all subconscious, happening within the music, [which was] brilliant . . . Elton's singing on that record is unbelievable."

It speaks to the sheer professionalism of the musicians, however, that such stresses and mounting interpersonal conflicts—no matter how pervasive or debilitating—didn't hinder their progress in the studio. Nobody threw a punch.

Passarelli recalls:

> The poor guys like Caleb and his wife, Roger and his wife, and Ray [Cooper], they were all kind of like just part of the audience. All the drama was going on with these other folks. It's almost like this huge soup of emotion and personal drama is going on, all undercurrent, while this record is being made, and the pressure Elton was under, with this being the first record on Rocket, it was intense. It really was. It wasn't a joyous time. I'll have to say that. *Rock of the Westies* was pure joy. *Blue Moves* was exactly what it was—blue moves.
>
> It was painful. There's a lot of pain there. There's a lot of covert . . . there's a lot of shit going on. I really think that everybody suffers, and there's a lot of pain. But there was never any *confrontational* stuff, other than maybe some stuff with Gus, like Caleb and everybody going, "Fuck you, Gus. We're doing it our way." But, really, nothing with Elton. He was moody. There was definitely some mood stuff going on, but no scream-outs among band members or anything. Elton didn't come up to me and say, "What the fuck is going on?" It was all undercurrent.

Some of the retrospective disappointment surrounding this album centers on the fact that it yielded only one hit single, "Sorry Seems to Be the Hardest Word." On the other hand, from the beginning of his career, John had proven himself as an album-oriented artist. Sure, some albums yielded more radio-friendly singles than others, but the songs themselves were part and parcel of a greater whole. *Blue Moves* was an *album* from start to finish, and arguably an even more thematically and musically cohesive one than John's previous double album, *Goodbye Yellow Brick Road*. Critics have warmed to it in the years since, and today *Blue Moves* merits nearly as much appreciation as any of John's most esteemed recordings—something with which Passarelli agrees:

> It got poor reviews, and to this day, that is one of the best records I think he ever made. It's way stretched out, everything from "Tonight" to "Your Starter For . . ."—he was really experimenting in hard rock; the disco thing was just starting and they released more of a Stones, kick-ass [song in] "Bite Your Lip"; but the only hit off that record was "Sorry Seems to Be the Hardest Word," and it kind of got shelved as a failure, and then the band broke up.
>
> We were a cooking band. It was a great band. There was nothing in the air that he was going to stop, so when we were doing *Blue Moves*, it was like, *This thing's going on forever*.

Blue Moves was the first Elton John album since *Madman Across the Water* to not reach the top of the *Billboard* 200 chart, peaking at #3 in both the US and the UK, while yielding one US Top 10 single, "Sorry Seems to Be the Hardest Word."

The album's failure to reach the top of the charts arguably had more to do with the public's slackening enthusiasm for Elton John in general, however, than it did with the specific quality of his latest songs.

But Don't Pretend That It Won't End

"It was an incredible time," says Passarelli.

> We ended up in August of '76 with seven nights sold out at Madison Square Garden, and nobody had ever done that; a choir behind us for the encore, everybody's just rocking out. We're all making a lot of money. When Elton pulled us aside on the second-to-the-last night, crying—and again part of that was him being freaked out about being gay and not being able to show it. Add the pressure of that, add the pressure of nonstop working, two albums

a year because of a shit-ass contract with Dick James [who] was a monster—sticky fingers. Here [Elton] is, knocking out records, number-one guy in the world, gay but can't show it, just starting to do drugs, just starting to head down that disastrous trail. It was like he was having a meltdown. Nobody expected it. He took us aside after the second-to-the-last night, after the gig, and he said, "I can't do this anymore." He was crying. He said, "I've got to take some time off, I'm going to break the band up." Roger Pope never got over it. He died never getting over it—*floored.*

Caleb Quaye concurs. "It spoiled a good thing," he says. "It was a rough time."

"Six years, from 1970 to 1976, was a lot of product out—a lot of albums and a lot of hard work—[which] drained me to the point where I never wanted to see a piano again," John told journalist and friend Paul Gambaccini in an August 1980 interview for the BBC. "The main reason for coming off the road, apart from the fact that I was growing stale, I felt musically, was the fact that I was very unhappy and I was thirty years of age and I couldn't do anything on my own without being afraid to do so."

Working at the time as the US correspondent at *Melody Maker*, veteran journalist Chris Charlesworth, who interviewed John extensively throughout the seventies, recalls, "I think I could have made more of it at the time: 'Elton: I'm retiring.' Big headline, you know what I mean? But I don't think I did. I think I maybe missed the trick there, because he was really opening up to me there."

Nearly two years would pass before John released another studio album—one that he would create, for the first time since hitting it big, without the services of his closest collaborators, none more conspicuous than Bernie Taupin.

"I think it got out of hand, to tell you the truth," says Charlesworth. "I think he overworked himself up to about '75, '76. He overdid it, and of course he was drinking and taking a lot of drugs as well, which everybody was. He was wearing himself out. He had to step back, which is what he did."

Or, as Kenny Passarelli puts it, "Things were starting to crumble."

13

And It Feels So Good to Hurt So Bad

The Soul Man

Like so many of his compatriots who arrived with the initial wave of the British Invasion not even a decade before his earliest success, Elton John has long been enthralled with American rhythm and blues. Just as the primordial explosions of early rock 'n' roll, from Jerry Lee Lewis to Elvis Presley, offered a stark raving alternative to the mainstream mediocrity of fifties pop fare like "How Much Is That Doggie in the Window?," rhythm and blues—informed as much by the church as the cotton fields—proffered a richer, decidedly more adult perspective. For a shy only child coming of age in Pinner, England, with music in his bones, it was as though these strange, primal sounds emanated from another world altogether.

By the time he was playing in Bluesology as a teenager, John was already well versed in all kinds of music, especially R&B and blues.

It was the culmination of every hour he'd sat transfixed in front of his bedroom record player, basking in the gutbucket brilliance of Ray Charles or the imperial finesse of Nina Simone; to Bluesology gigs backing the likes of Major Lance and Patti LaBelle and the Bluebelles. "I feel an affinity for black music like no other," he told *Rolling Stone* in 2011, "and I feel sometimes when I'm playing it that I'm channeling something. Like Eric Clapton, or when Mick [Jagger] sings the blues. Black music was our gospel."

One of the first public indications that John's music belied a whopping amount of soul empathy was, in 1972, when Aretha Franklin recorded a version of "Border Song" for her LP, *Young, Gifted, and Black*. As the closing track on an album teeming with future classics like "Rock Steady," "Oh Me Oh My (I'm a Fool for You Baby)," and "Daydreaming," the John–Taupin composition fit right in with its gospel rave-up and thematic subtext of racial equality. "Up to that point," John recalled in a 2001 *Rolling Stone* interview, "that was the biggest highlight of our career." Indeed, John wrote the lyrics to the song's final verse, which actually is attuned more to gospel themes—"There's a man over there, what's his color I don't care / He's my brother, let us live in peace"—than the ones which it proceeds.

In 1989, John collaborated with Franklin on the #16 *Billboard* hit single "Through the Storm" (written by Diane Warren), the title track and best song of the Queen of Soul's then-latest album. In 1993, Franklin and John (who, incidentally, shared the same birthday, March 25) sang on the same stage, performing "Border Song" for Lady Soul's *Duets* television special.

John and Taupin have experienced the honor and thrill of seeing songs they'd written top the R&B charts, often with John singing lead. It's a trend that would surface, in various forms, throughout his career.

Something Leaves Me Speechless: "Bennie and the Jets" Becomes an Unlikely #1 R&B Hit

In February 1974, the phones were ringing off the hook at Detroit's leading R&B/soul station, WJLB. Program director (and future radio and television personality) Donnie "The Love Bug" Simpson couldn't shake his liking to "Bennie and the Jets," introducing it as an album cut into regular rotation—a move that made it the most requested song in the station's history. Other urban stations around the US and Canada followed suit, generating a buzz for "Bennie" that virtually nobody saw coming—especially Elton John.

"It took me to a whole new audience," John said in a 2014 interview with *Clash* magazine. "I love black music more than any other music—gospel music, soul music and blues music, so to have that [#1] was just an essential for me. It did me a lot of good confidence-wise, to be accepted by that area of people buying records, and it was a huge boost for me on the radio in America."

Actually, John had wanted "Candle in the Wind" to be the third single released from *Goodbye Yellow Brick Road*—as his British record label had already done in the UK, putting "Bennie" on the B-side—but MCA Records recognized the national potential for "Bennie" as an R&B smash and beseeched John to change his mind. Confronted with (and flabbergasted by) a groundswell of crossover success, he ultimately conceded.

Once officially issued as a single in the States, "Bennie and the Jets" peaked at #15 on the *Billboard* Soul Singles chart, spending a total of eighteen weeks on the Hot 100. "Never in a million years, being a white boy from Pinner, did I ever think I was going to have a black record in the charts," John says in the 2001 *Classic Albums* documentary. "And then that was the first time I topped the R&B charts."

"Philadelphia Freedom" Salutes a Sports Champion and the City of Brotherly Love

One of the few instances when Elton John asked Bernie Taupin to compose a song with a title already in mind, "Philadelphia Freedom" occupies a singular origin in John's storied catalogue. "Billie Jean King, a friend of mine, she had the team the Philadelphia Freedom at the start of World Team Tennis," he reflects, in the liner notes to the *To Be Continued . . .* boxed set. "I said, 'I shall write a song for you.'"

While the song's title honored Billie Jean King and her tennis team, musically the song paid tribute the soul masterpieces coming out of the City of Brotherly Love, particularly the music produced by Kenneth Gamble and Leon Huff and Philadelphia International Records. Graced with an orchestral accompaniment courtesy of producer/arranger Gene Page, whose intoxicating symphonic treatments sweetened songs for the likes of Barry White, Diana Ross, and Marvin Gaye, "Philadelphia Freedom" ascended to the top of the charts, becoming an anthem of its era and the second major crossover hit of John's career. This time, John was not reluctant to supplicate the R&B marketplace—he actively sought it, and, with its enormous success, he stepped into history by appearing on one of pop culture's most defining television programs, *Soul Train*.

Hey Kids, Shake It Loose Together: The *Soul Train* Appearance

Over its record-breaking thirty-five-year run (1971–2006), *Soul Train* signified far more than a syndicated weekly television show. In matters of black culture, politics, fashion, dance, and the hippest vernacular, it served as a generational nexus for young people across the nation. Of course, its *main* course was music, and particularly in the program's first decade on the air, some of the era's most renowned and significant R&B artists—from Marvin Gaye to Aretha Franklin to the O'Jays—performed on its stage.

While John had at first resisted his record label's pleas to release "Bennie and the Jets" as a single in 1974 only to see it top the US singles chart and (most improbably) climb to #15 on the *Billboard* Soul chart, he proved far more sympathetic to the possibilities of "Philadelphia Freedom" a year later. Incidentally, Gamble and Huff had also composed the program's theme song, "TSOP"—short for "The Sound of

The *Soul Train* logo.   *Author's collection*

Philadelphia"—which, reflecting their combined talent and consummate success at the time, also became a sizable radio hit on its own.

In this light, it likely seemed appropriate at the time (even as it appeared most improbable) that John should promote the song on *Soul Train*. In fact, as the program's creator and executive producer, Don Cornelius, recalled in an interview taped for the 2010 VH1 documentary, *Soul Train: The Hippest Trip in America*, John himself—or at least his management—requested the much-coveted appearance. Cornelius immediately obliged, and at the taping on March 22, 1975, which also featured Barry White and the Love Unlimited Orchestra, he welcomed John, who performed live-to-tape versions of "Philadelphia Freedom" in one segment followed by "Bennie and the Jets" in another, as select *Soul Train* dancers boogied behind his see-through glass piano.

It's also worth noting that while Elton John was not the first white artist to appear on *Soul Train*—that distinction goes to Dennis Coffey and the Detroit Guitar Band—his appearance was nevertheless a watershed pop-culture event. In the United States, especially, John owned 1975 much like the Beatles had owned 1964; his music and likeness saturated radio, television, and print publications. "The episode was an important moment for cultural relations," writes Questlove (of the Roots and *The Tonight Show with Jimmy Fallon* fame) in his 2013 book, *Soul Train: The Music, the Dance, and Style of a Generation*. "It stated to me that if your music was quality, you would be embraced by Soul Train. Talent transcends all, no matter what color you are. Elton was a prime example."

As with Coffey and even Oakland's integrated Tower of Power before him, along with artists like David Bowie and Teena Marie after him, John was received with warmth and enthusiasm by the *Soul Train* viewing audience (not to mention its legendary host) because he delivered the goods—and those specific goods were synonymous with the kinds of music they appreciated.

Booking Elton John on *Soul Train* most likely meant as much for Cornelius as it did John—both men, though they would each enjoy long and fruitful runs in their respective fields, were at their commercial peak in 1975.

Wish for Something Special: *The Complete Thom Bell Sessions*

This collaboration seemed like a match made in soul-music heaven: John, an ardent student of R&B, collaborating with a consummate soul-music maestro. After all, Bell had by this time already earned much of his legend as one of those very architects, having written and produced much of what was known as the Philly sound with the likes of the Spinners, the Delfonics, and the Stylistics, among many others.

In retrospect, John has credited Bell with giving him vocal advice that has since served him well, namely how to best utilize and exploit his lower register. By most other accounts, however, clashing egos and

The UK CD single for the 2004 remix of "Are You Ready For Love?" which also features the original version of the song, as included on *The Complete Thom Bell Sessions*.

Author's collection

disparate work ethics doomed the partnership from the start. Still, it wasn't a total wash.

The sessions commenced at Kay Smith Studio in Seattle with the recording of six Gary Osborne originals—Bernie Taupin reportedly wasn't interested in the project, and was busy writing for other artists at the time anyway—including the eventual #9 *Billboard* Hot 100 hit "Mama Can't Buy You Love," which topped the black radio charts. Bell finished up the tracks back in Philadelphia, at Sigma Sound, sprucing up the production and adding various backing vocals, including some by the Spinners. Upon hearing the finished mixes, though, John reportedly expressed dissatisfaction, saying the production was too "saccharine," and, in one instance, taking issue with how what were supposed to have been supplementary Spinners vocals sounded to him like they overshadowed his lead performance.

This may have been one of those occasions, as John has in the past described, where a producer envisions something in a piece of music that the artist may not altogether see, because the six tracks that emerged, eventually, in 1979 proved to be enduring gems. Indeed, a 2002 remix of "Are You Ready for Love," which had for the most part hovered under the radar for decades, shot to the top of the British charts (and hit #1 on US Dance charts) in 2002, and would earn a regular spot in John's live performances in the years ahead.

Come to Your Senses: *Sleeping with the Past*

An album as homage was nothing new. Billy Joel, who would become a familiar figure to John in the years to come, found enormous success with his 1983 LP, *An Innocent Man*, on which he paid tribute to the classic R&B, doo-wop, and soul that inspired him as a kid on Long Island.

For John, not to mention Taupin, constructing a consistently themed pastiche to their favorite soul icons seemed similarly appropriate. John had taught Taupin much about R&B and soul, while Taupin educated John on such lyrical songwriters as Leonard Cohen and Joni Mitchell. For John's final album of the eighties, *Sleeping with the Past*, both songwriters

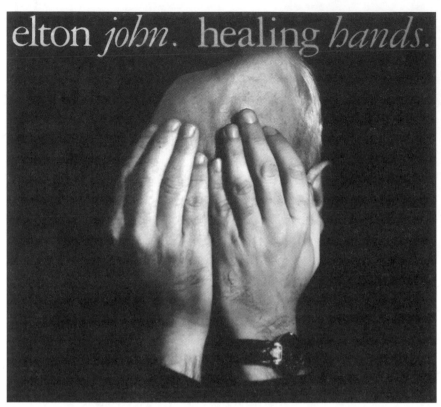

The UK CD single for the 1989 single of "Healing Hands," originally included on John's 1989 LP *Sleeping with the Past*, was written in homage to "Reach Out I'll Be There" by the Four Tops.
Author's collection

sought to make an album that consolidated those influences while leaning heavy on classic soul.

"We came up with this concept of harking back to the songs that really inspired us when we first met," Taupin told BBC Radio 1's Roger Scott in 1989. "I'd take a song like 'Do Right Woman' by Aretha Franklin and I would do my own version of it. It wasn't like copying it. 'Stone's Throw from Hurtin',' I wrote something that I thought would be like a Sam and Dave thing. There's a Ray Charles thing, 'Amazes Me'—it's got that Ray Charles feel; the Drifters thing in 'Club at the End of the Street.' They're not rip-offs. What we did is, we just used [them] as seeds and nurtured them into our own versions of them."

14

Sitting Pretty in the Masquerade

The Fashions

Glamour and extravagance have long inspired Elton John's live performances, which have been distinguished by similarly grandiose fashion statements. Whether his outfits glorify Old Hollywood glamour, parody elements of camp and ironic humor, or echo the cutting edge of high fashion, Captain Fantastic has never hit the stage underdressed.

"When you go onstage, it's very important to dress the part," he said in 2016, during a Sirius XM Town Hall with veteran music journalist David Fricke. "I couldn't come onstage in a T-shirt and jeans, and I don't really like seeing that many bands who do. I like to feel like, 'This is an occasion.'"

In this sentiment, John is no doubt underscoring the incendiary first impressions Little Richard and Elvis Presley, among others, made on him as a child—just from the vibrant, decadent headshots that graced their record sleeves, long before John ever saw their alchemical performances live in person.

While the wistful pop balladry of his signature radio singles suggested his tastes and onstage demeanor were more in line with somber singer/songwriters, John flaunted flamboyance and sartorial excess more often than eloquence. Since donning hot pants and platform boots in front of an unsuspecting audience at the folk music–disposed Troubadour club in West Hollywood during his US debut in August 1970, John has often incorporated an ironic sense of camp and folly in the clothes he wore onstage, from vivid feathered boas and gigantic eyeglasses to suiting up and boogying down in a Bob Mackie–designed Donald Duck costume before a reported four hundred thousand fans on the Great Lawn in New York City's Central Park.

"I do like my rock stars to be a little larger than life," John later told the *Guardian*, in an interview published on September 19, 2004. "I don't mind the earnest ones at all, but I do like a bit of individuality."

As former *Melody Maker* correspondent Chris Charlesworth explains, "A lot of acts around that time that were becoming very popular that were Californian–type acts—the Eagles were typical, let's say—they just shambled on in their jeans and T-shirts and played and didn't put on a show at all. People enjoyed the music. It was the same with Crosby, Stills, and Nash. They were *huge* acts—same with Bob Dylan, for that matter—but Elton was like a throwback to showbiz, a throwback to Liberace. People enjoyed that, I think, for a change, as he came bounding on in his silly outfits."

Principal songwriting collaborator Bernie Taupin has voiced his bemused displeasure with plenty of John's fashion stances over the years. "I shook my head and rolled my eyes," Taupin says in the 2010 BBC documentary, *Madman Across the Water: The Making of Elton John*. "You don't sing 'Your Song' in a Donald Duck outfit in Central Park. It's *beyond* awful, but nobody was really going to tell him no at the time."

Nobody told him he couldn't do it, true, but Taupin was not alone in publicly expressing his abject displeasure that John carried on with such outlandish costumes onstage. Someone else who was nonplussed was Nicky Hopkins, who attended the Royal Academy of Music as an adolescent during some of the same years as John, before earning a sterling reputation as perhaps the most versatile and in-demand session keyboardist in England, playing on sides by everyone from the Beatles and the Rolling Stones to Dusty Springfield, Joe Cocker, and Ella Fitzgerald.

According to author Julian Dawson's 2011 biography, *And On piano . . . NICKY HOPKINS: The Extraordinary Life of Rock's Greatest Session Man*, Hopkins once said of John, "He's a good songwriter, but he put me off so much when I saw him. Someone like Mick can come off very cool, but with Elton it just looks silly. When is he going to grow up? Star-spangled hot pants, six-mile diameter shades with white rims and dyed hair—I just can't get behind all that."

Nevertheless, John conceded long ago—and in retrospect maintains—that he wore many of the over-the-top costumes to compensate for his severe self-consciousness and how it manifested from issues pertaining to his ever-fluctuating weight. The music, he has always affirmed, stands on its own merits.

I Color Life with a Broader Stroke

"Since I'm not your rangy rock idol in skinny leather pants, I wear flamboyant clothes," John told *Time* magazine in 1975. "People shouldn't take the clothes and the dyed hair so seriously. Honestly, it's just a joke. I'm affectionately parodying the rock 'n' roll business by saying, 'Here it is, let's all have a laugh and enjoy ourselves.'"

Many of John's most extravagant style exploits were courtesy of the aforementioned American fashion designer Bob Mackie, whose exotic, often-bejeweled creations have graced a coterie of larger-than-life luminaries (mostly women) including Judy Garland, Barbra Streisand, Carol Burnett, Liza Minnelli, Tina Turner, Cher, Diana Ross, and Marilyn Monroe, for whom he designed the "nude" sequined dress she wore on May 19, 1962, while cooing "Happy Birthday" to President John F. Kennedy during his fortieth birthday party at Madison Square Garden. After seeing Mackie's creations worn by Cher in her CBS debut variety special in 1975 on which he appeared—he performed "Bennie and the Jets" with Cher and "Mockingbird" with Cher and Bette Midler, another famous Mackie client—John beseeched the designer to conceive of some costumes for his own stage shows. Over the ensuing years and indeed decades, Mackie has designed some of John's most iconic fashion statements, including the sequined Los Angeles Dodgers uniform worn at Dodger Stadium in 1975, the Donald Duck costume worn during the encore of the 1980 Central Park performance, and the "Amadeus" ensemble (described by John as being either Chopin or Mozart) worn during his 1986 *Leather Jackets* world tour—most notably during the Tour De Force performances with the Melbourne Symphony Orchestra in Australia.

If Mackie enabled John to exude the boldest, most vivid fashion statements to suit his imagination and talent, Italian fashion designer and close friend Gianni Versace most boldly introduced him to the culture from which it came. Affectionately known to each other as "Bitch," the musician and the fashion icon forged a deep friendship like that of close siblings, laughing one minute and bickering the next. For John's professional expressions, Versace designed not only John's stage clothes but also the stage itself for his world tour in support of the 1992 LP, *The One*, the album's artwork also bearing his audacious aesthetic.

"Initially, it was fun," John said, looking back on his wild costumes in 2007, during an appearance on the British TV talk show *Parkinson*.

A publicity photograph released by MCA Records to promote John's 1987 LP *Live in Australia with the Melbourne Symphony Orchestra*, featuring John in a Bob Mackie–designed costume loosely recalling the styles of classical composers Frédéric Chopin and Wolfgang Amadeus Mozart.

Author's collection

"Initially, it was done on the spur of the moment. But then it got . . . everything had to be bigger and better and glitzier, and it really went too far."

I'm Not the Man They Think I Am at Home

Sartorially speaking, what transpires on the outside often reflects what is going on inside. For Elton John, the glitz, the flash, the Bob Mackie–designed pizazz were in stark and strident reaction to the rules and rigidities that young Reg Dwight was forced to comply with as a child. Sure, it's a little funny for a grown man to appear before thousands of

An officially sanctioned Elton John postcard, illustrating his nineties fashion.   *Author's collection*

people in sequins and feathers and glasses that blink lights with the help of a ten-pound battery supply. Consider it making up for lost time. Hell, consider it revenge, in a sense. Elton John owed no compliance to anybody, and that was the point when stepped into his stage clothes. It was an act of rebellion.

"Being outrageous onstage is part of it for me, I have to," John said in a 1970 interview with *Rolling Stone*, "because ordinarily I'm such a quiet person."

And that quiet person needed to express himself, one way or another. But even though a rock 'n' roll concert can be as cathartic as the most enthralling sex or the most glorious sermon—or any other likewise transcendent experience—it's not therapy. Beyond an audience's adoration and applause, the motive behind the Mohawks and Mackie designs are not always revealed.

"When he first came out in these crazy outfits, Dee and Davey and I would have a good laugh before, saying, 'You're not wearing that, are you?'" drummer Nigel Olsson recalled in 2017, in an interview with the *Yorkshire Evening Post*, "and he [would] say, 'Oh yeah, I am.'"

On the face of it, wearing such loud, glitzy (and, let's be honest, sometimes garish) clothes and costumes seems like an extension of an equally loud, extravagant personality. However, it's closer to the truth that Elton John (at least in his most flamboyant phases) was a profoundly insecure, shy individual who presented such fashions as a means to compensate for those insecurities. It was a coping mechanism, to be blunt, manifested in effervescent feathers and sequins, cartoonish hats, and platform boots.

Picture My Face in Your Hands

Having hit the peak of his popularity during the ribald age of glam, John recognized the significance of image in ways that perhaps only Mick Jagger and David Bowie surpassed at that time, and the visual art of photography abetted his celebrity ascent.

Of the countless photographers who have chronicled his ever-changing styles—from Herb Ritts with his pungent black-and-white portraits (such as the one that graces the cover of John's 1989 LP, *Sleeping with the*

A publicity photograph released by MCA Records to promote John's 1988 LP *Reg Strikes Back*, shot by veteran Elton John photographer Terry O'Neill.   *Author's collection*

Past) to Richard Avedon—none has depicted more iconic images of Elton John than Terry O'Neill.

Most recognizable among them are album covers, including those for *Rock of the Westies* and *A Single Man*, as well as concert shots from John's historic performances in 1975 at Dodger Stadium.

"Terry's photographs are so dignified, loose yet monumental," percussionist Ray Cooper notes in the 2015 book of O'Neill images, *Two Days That Rocked the World: Elton John Live at Dodger Stadium*, "capturing and celebrating the true joyous force of nature that Elton is and the love that was so evident in that Stadium; images masterfully put onto film by a man who completely understands the music, rhythm and composition of the moment."

Having captured the usual musical icons, including the Beatles and the Rolling Stones and David Bowie, O'Neill managed to show Elton John as he wanted to be seen: as dazzling and larger than life, a superhuman with movie-star presence, donning spangled Nudie suits, skintight jumpsuits, and suit coats boasting every color in the rainbow.

"There was this huge Hollywood glamour attached to him that you didn't get with anybody else apart from, perhaps David Bowie, who also understood that way of putting across your music," says Chris Charlesworth. "So that helped him a lot. It set him apart from other rockers at the time. But he always had the music. He was always such a great composer, him and Taupin, and he just got bigger and bigger."

15

Let Me Get Electric, Put a Silk Suit On

But Was Elton John Really Glam?

As his music branched out from the pensive or solemn ponderings of his most beloved ballads to brandish funkier rhythms (performed in ever-funkier outfits), Elton John likewise embraced and reflected the wild and unruly phenomenon of glam rock.

"Glam swept the nation in ways that were at once innocent and morally subversive," author Barney Hoskyns writes in the 2011 anthology, *Glam! Bowie, Bolan, and the Glitter Rock Revolution.* "It called into question received notions of truth and authenticity, especially in the area of sexuality. It blurred the divide between straights and queers, inviting boys and girls to experiment with images and roles in a genderless Utopia of eyeliner and five-inch platform boots."

In his quest to come to terms with the tenets of his own identity, his sexuality, and indeed his own agency as a human being, John personified the creed of glam rock to a tee. Like a precocious child testing the limits of his parents' authority before exceeding them to wage their response, he pushed his art and the artifice with which he played to their own limits, testing the possibilities of pop music and fashion in new and unprecedented ways. His act was part rebellion, part regalia; subversive yet innately soulful at the same time. Almost as if he was actively disobeying his father with every new and outlandish display, John seemed to exhibit his own sense of inflammatory defiance—an attitude his young fan base all too eagerly subscribed to, imitated, and wanted to emulate. He seemed to be simultaneously asking himself, "Can I get away with this?" and saying, "I can get away with anything!" in the same precocious breath.

"This is probably something that's more UK than American," says Chris Charlesworth, who chronicled John's early-to-mid-seventies ascent at *Melody Maker* magazine as closely as (if not more than) any other journalist of the era, "but because of the clothes he wore—the glittery clothes, the headdresses, the unusual spectacles he wore, the big boots with the stacked heels, all that silver stuff—he was lumped in with the glam-rock movement, which of course was more or less led by David Bowie at that point, but also included Elton and also included T. Rex—Marc Bolan's group—and a group called Slade; and we're sort of moving down the league stable of these acts, if you like, and then there was the Sweet, and then there were a few also-rounds who jumped on the bandwagon."

A *Captain Fantastic* miniature memorabilia-inspired statue, recalling John's seventies glam fashion.   *Author's collection*

Rather than following the latest trends, though, John (and, in tandem, Taupin, too) pursued whatever musical styles piqued his curiosity—and, more to the point, whichever style suited the song at hand. Considering his musical bedrock, thanks to the broad spectrum of styles and eclectic artists he was exposed to from early age to adolescence in particular, such curiosities were similarly varied. If certain songs fell into certain genres, it was more by chance—the manifestation of well-rounded talent than of deliberate design. And so, whether it was the earnest singer/songwriter balladry of "Your Song" and "Tiny Dancer," or the rich R&B affinities displayed by "Bennie and the Jets" and "Philadelphia Freedom," such ventures pointed to John's interests and influences, not to what was popular at the time. That a song like "Bennie and the Jets" could simultaneously be embraced not only by mainstream pop listeners but also by glam-rock and hardcore R&B aficionados was preposterous. In other words, Elton John didn't need to try to sound or look glam. Glam tried to be Elton John.

It Kind of Makes Me Feel Like a Rock 'n' Roll Star

Elton John is a singer/songwriter who doesn't write the words to his own songs. In that sense, every song, to him at least, is a fantasy. Here he was, a gay man singing songs written by a straight man, whose lyrics often were about women he neither knew nor loved, imparted with the emotion that conveyed the very opposite.

In an infamous *Melody Maker* cover story dated January 22, 1972, David Bowie, on the verge of revealing his gender-bending alter ego, Ziggy Stardust, heralded his supposed homosexuality—"I'm gay," he said to journalist Michael Watts, "and always have been, even when I was David Jones"—but did so to stir publicity, to court controversy. As he so seamlessly espoused, if you act like a star, you'll be treated like one—and one day you'll be one. When John told journalist Cliff Jahr he was bisexual in *Rolling Stone* in 1976, it was a confession, laced with no ulterior motive other than declaring his truth, perhaps in the hope of gaining some peace of mind at the culmination of a hectic period in his life.

"I grew up out of that British variety, music hall, pantomime era," John told the *Telegraph* in 2004. "We were all larger than life. The first one was Marc Bolan, who was a dear friend; he was completely from another planet. I do like my rock stars to be a little larger than life. I don't mind the earnest ones at all, but I do like a bit of individuality."

Unlike singer/songwriters like Bruce Springsteen or Joni Mitchell or even John Lennon, Elton John doesn't chronicle his day-to-day life in the songs he writes. Bernie Taupin (or Gary Osborne or Tom Robinson or Tim Rice) may well be doing that to some extent in the lyrics they write for John, but always in some oblique fashion—because nothing is explicated in either lyrics or liner notes—but John's compositional proprietorship of those lyrics effectively transcends and removes such contexts. Such stories are no longer the lyricist's own. They once and for all belong to Elton John, and, by default, to anyone who finds some singular significance to a moment or melody or chord sequence in that song. Such elements or distinctions are impersonal on face value, yet they resonate in the most visceral ways.

There's a detachment in this sense—a separation between artist and art that may, in some instances, allow listeners to construct an emotional narrative out of certain phrases they hear. In other instances, lyrical mysteries abound—sometimes even to the songwriters themselves.

"Elton was certainly part of the glam-rock movement," says Charlesworth, "though he transcended it, of course, just as David Bowie did.

"Elton's background as a trained keyboard player," he adds, "and all the experience he'd had before, with Bluesology—all that experience put him in good stead for lasting the course."

16

But I Know What I Feel

Captain Fantastic Comes Out

By any possible perspective, Elton John was living an extravagant life in the mid-seventies. Considered an overnight sensation in the United States following his triumphant debut at the Troubadour in 1970, in truth John had by August 1976 spent the better part of fifteen years on the road playing music. The trajectory of his career—including a streak of seven #1 albums in America, extending back to 1972's *Honky Château*—had placed John among the decade's most successful artists and given him the sort of fame and pop culture significance achieved only by the likes of the Beatles and Elvis Presley before him.

But having grown up in a repressive, authoritative household where even the most general mentions of sex were implicitly prohibited, he had learned to be cautious about who he let into his most private spaces. The flash, the fashions, the over-the-top flamboyance, all of it masked an insecure and confused human being beneath. Rumors had flown for years, but the truth of John's sexuality was unknown to the public at large. His record company had wanted it that way, and who was he to rock the boat—especially when the boat was worth millions of dollars?

Not that those closest to him, either family or friends or members of his band, didn't know the truth. When bassist Kenny Passarelli joined the band just prior to the Mid-Summer Music Festival at Wembley Stadium in 1975, he recalls being apprised of the situation by guitarist Davey Johnstone at the Château d'Hérouville. "'Listen, Elton's homosexual,'" he recalls Johnstone saying. "'That's his manager, John Reid, and they're a couple. And he's got a little entourage, but it's very quiet, because his audience is twelve, thirteen, fourte, fifteen-year-old girls. He has a huge audience amongst other people our age [too], but MCA does not want to disclose his homosexuality.'"

By the fall of 1976, however, too many pressures had built up. Elton John was no longer under the thumb of Dick James Music—he was releasing his own albums on Rocket Records, his own label—and he was feeling the need to come clean across the board. He was almost thirty years old, he had just broken up his band and announced his retirement to the shock not only of fans around the world but of his band, and after almost seven years of unprecedented success, John wanted out. Out of obligations, out of the hustle and hectic pace of being Elton John.

In the October 7, 1976, issue of *Rolling Stone*, John addressed the one topic that garnered the most whispers and innuendo from the media—the subject other journalists had yet to broach in any sort of serious or direct fashion. Once and for all, he would put questions about his sexuality to rest.

And Now I Shall Be Free

Cloistered in his suite at the Sherry-Netherland Hotel in Manhattan, the day after the last performance of a six-night stand at Madison Square Garden, John eased into a lengthy and ultimately revelatory conversation with *Rolling Stone*'s Cliff Jahr, at first about a range of fleeting conversational topics—bickering with David Bowie, partying with drag queen Divine—before delving into some decidedly forthright and intimate subjects.

"Can we get personal?" Jahr asked John. The journalist sought to get John on the record, addressing his sexuality—the topic had cropped up in prior interviews in other publications, but John had never clarified once and for all—but Jahr did not want to offend or ambush John with his inquiries. Besides, the interview was ostensibly intended to promote John's forthcoming album, *Blue Moves*—his first double album since 1973's *Goodbye Yellow Brick Road*, and his debut release on his own label, Rocket Records—but the conversation seldom ventured toward mentions of music.

In Jahr, John recognized an interested, empathetic listener—the journalist, who was openly gay, had even offered to shut off his voice recorder, lest John not wish to address his sexuality on the record—and rather than dodge the topic altogether, he opened up as if confiding in a friend. Speaking with Jahr about suffering from bouts of depression and severe loneliness, John (perhaps subconsciously) steered the conversation to the inevitable question of his sexual orientation.

"I haven't met anybody that I would like to settle down with—of either sex," said John. "There's nothing wrong with going to bed with somebody of your own sex."

As the conversation wound down, John confided, cutting to the universal crux of his sexual anxiety, "I'm afraid of getting hurt. I was hurt so

A mid-eighties publicity photograph released by MCA Records.   *Author's collection*

much as a kid. I'm afraid of plunging into something that's going to fuck me up."

The interview proved so personally revealing, in fact, that *Rolling Stone* editor-in-chief Jann Wenner, whose own homosexuality was still a well-guarded secret at the time, called John to verify his consent in publishing the piece.

Whatever fear he harbored in admitting his sexuality, in truth John endured far more turmoil in coming to terms with his sexual orientation (and embracing his sexuality in general) than he did with what others thought about it all. Still, the news didn't sit well with some of the general public. "There was no way it was not going to have an effect," says Passarelli.

Many among John's audience were adolescents, who at least since the onslaught of the Beatles have possessed unprecedented and exorbitant amounts of expendable cash with which to spend on records and concert tickets. "That was the audience that the record company was afraid he was going to lose," says Passarelli. "And when he came out and said he was bisexual, I just laughed. I was going, 'He's not bisexual! He's gay!' It was ridiculous."

John's friend and part-time lyricist Gary Osborne saw matters a bit differently. "Although the coasts of America were hip enough not to care, in the middle of America, the sales just went down the toilet," he says. "I always thought it was very brave of him to do it."

This Boy's Too Young to Be Singing the Blues

"I just assumed that people knew, because all my friends knew, obviously," John says in the 2007 documentary, *Me, Myself, and I.* "I didn't really think twice about it."

While John is known to have engaged in intimate physical relationships with at least two women—Linda Hannon, who almost became his wife and was immortalized in part in the 1975 hit single, "Someone Saved My Life Tonight," and recording engineer Renate Blauel, to whom he was married from 1984 to 1988—John has since publicly conceded that he is in fact not bisexual, but, rather, homosexual. Why, then, as John was asked in a 1995 interview with Q magazine, didn't he just admit he was gay in the 1976 *Rolling Stone* interview, rather than bisexual? "Because I was probably scared," he replied. "It was easier to say. I suppose it was a cop-out, but at the time I thought, *Well, let's be diplomatic about it.*"

Besides, he knew he wasn't the first to make such a public claim. David Bowie, despite having proclaimed himself to be gay in a 1972 *Melody Maker* interview, further blurred the lines of his identity by later announcing that he was in fact bisexual, but his admission amounted more to a publicity stunt than to an intimate confession. Further, Bowie thrived as an avant-garde artist who flirted on the edge of societal tastes and taboos, and his persona (even in the relatively early stage of his career in 1972) was accordingly rebellious. Elton John, for all his sartorial flamboyance and onstage camp and theatricality, was a mainstream pop star whose fan base included parents and children. Bowie boasted far more leverage from which to expound upon on his chameleonic identity and sexual predilections than John ever would.

In contrast to Bowie and other contemporaries like Rod Stewart and Mick Jagger, for whom sex had progressed from being a mischievous curiosity at a young age into a carnal, lustful pursuit as virile young men, John didn't seem to acknowledge sex as anything so rewarding, let alone comforting. "The first time I masturbated I was in pain. I was so horrified," he told Neil Tennant of the Pet Shop Boys, in a 1998 *Interview* magazine feature. "And my parents found out because I'd used all my pajamas. And then I got completely and utterly ripped apart for doing it. Sex was completely frightening."

His thoughts on sex becoming more and more confused, his identity a nagging question, John contended with his own self-consciousness and emotional chaos for years, well into his first years as a world-famous celebrity.

"I didn't sleep with anyone until I was twenty-three," he told NPR's Terry Gross in 2016. "I didn't really know what I was until I came to America and I had sex [for the first time] in San Francisco in 1970. It was with someone of my own sex. I suspected my homosexuality, but I had never acted out on it because I was afraid of sex. It was awful to be afraid of sex, but that's what the fifties did to people. It was, 'Sex is disgusting, it shouldn't be talked about; nudity is disgusting; we just don't talk about those kinds of things.'"

Whatever emotional turmoil or confusion he may have faced in figuring out his sexuality, his feelings about what others would think of him could not have been any more indifferent.

Having ultimately come to terms with his sexuality and his self-esteem, John looked back on the moment he confessed the most pressing issue of his life, save for his music, with a rational mind. "A few radio stations were a bit upset and people burnt my records," he told *Mojo* magazine in 2006. "But you know what? It was a very small price to pay for the freedom that it gave me."

17

Like Freedom Fields While Wild Horses Run

The Football Fanatic

Coming of age in a culture where one typically pledges allegiance as a child to the English football club whose stadium is nearest his or her family home, Elton John was born a Watford fan.

"You have to understand that my dad used to take me to Watford when I was about six years old," John states in the 2007 documentary, *Me, Myself, and I*, "and they've always been my team."

While any number of American sports, from basketball to baseball, attract their own respective and passionate followers, in Britain, football commands an insatiable national enthusiasm. "You grow up watching football, you grow up following a team," says lyricist Gary Osborne. "You get excited whether they go up in the league or down in the league, whether they win this game or that game. People identify with a club, a certain club usually."

In 1973, John purchased shares in the team, and was duly bestowed with the honorary title of Vice President. John's support of the club only grew as he invested more time and money into the venture. The following year, he was asked to join the board of directors.

After purchasing a majority stake in the club's shareholdings, John assumed the role of chairman in the summer of 1976—a role he relished even more once he abruptly stepped away from the concert stage following a six-night stand in August 1976 at New York's Madison Square Garden.

In an era when John's omnipresence on the radio and *Billboard* charts was only superseded by his sartorial extravagance and whispers about his sexual preferences, the music superstar understood a far more modest and regimented protocol must be followed in the hallowed world of football. To be taken seriously as a representative of his beloved and long-suffering hometown team—no matter in what symbolic or official capacity—he'd have to ditch the luminous feather boas and sequined ensembles in favor of a conservative suit and tie, not to mention a whole heap of humility.

"Watford has brought me back down to earth," John told *Time* magazine in 1975. "I love it as much as music itself, and that's a lot to say."

Under John's impassioned direction, the club ascended from the fourth tier to the second in the span of six years—a rare and rewarding feat for a relatively modest football team. He hired Graham Taylor as the team's manager, forging a relationship that saw the once-modest club rise through the ranks, ultimately placing as runners-up (behind Liverpool) in the First Division in the 1982–1983 season, and reaching

The logo for Watford Football Club also known as the Hornets, of which John maintained varying degrees of official association from 1973 through 1998. As a child growing up in Pinner, he often accompanied his father to matches, forging a lifelong passion for his hometown team.   *Author's collection*

the 1984 FA Cup Final at Wembley Stadium—the site of his cousin Roy Dwight's finest hour as a football player, and, not least of all, several of John's own milestone concert memories.

Taylor departed the team in 1990, and John likewise sold his majority shareholding in the club, at which point he became the club's life president. When Taylor returned to his old stomping grounds as manager in 1997, so did John as chairman, with the team's overall good fortunes repeating themselves for a mere three years before both men departed from the organization once again.

A new grandstand was commemorated in John's honor in 2004, for which John attended Vicarage Road stadium to behold and celebrate. More than a hobby, John's association with Watford also served as a formidable check on his outrageousness and coping mechanisms for his own private despondency. John's respect for the sport and for those who ran and played for the organization was so profound, he dialed down (if not abstaining altogether) from his most self-destructive behavior, particularly when it came to certain beverages and substances.

Graham Taylor died January 12, 2017, at age seventy-two, inspiring an avalanche of condolences and tributes from both fans and colleagues, none more prestigious (or, arguably, appropriate) than the statement John inscribed for his old friend that was read aloud at the manager's memorial.

"He was like a brother to me," John wrote. "We went on an incredible journey together. He took my beloved Watford from the depths of the lower leagues to uncharted territory and into Europe. We have become a leading English club because of his managerial wisdom and genius. This is a sad and dark day for Watford. The club and the town. We will cherish Graham and drown our sorrows in the many brilliant memories he gave us. I love you Graham. I will miss you very much."

18

I've Got a Line or Two to Use on You

Composing with Other Lyricists

The Elton John legend was forged with Bernie Taupin, but beginning in the late seventies, John sought out other lyricists with whom to write. Rather than sabotaging a proven and successful (not to mention lucrative) formula, he found such experiments broadened the template and expectations of his own capabilities.

There are plenty of instances wherein certain musicians are given a writing credit—such as James Newton Howard and Davey Johnstone, to cite two of the most prominent examples—but as far as the bare-bones composition of words and music, John has composed with a precious relative few.

Gary Osborne

As co-composer, lyricist Gary Osborne wrote more than thirty songs with Elton John, beginning with "Shine on Through," which was among the highlights of John's 1978 LP, *A Single Man*, for which Osborne wrote all of the lyrics. Writing together at a time when John and Bernie Taupin were pursuing outside projects for the first time in their collective history, Osborne and John created a mini-catalogue of hits like "Blue Eyes," "Chloe," and "Little Jeannie," spanning close to a decade of albums.

"Memory of Love," from John's lackluster 1986 LP, *Leather Jackets*, marks the final appearance on an album of one of their songs, their songwriting collaboration effectively over. But was their split acrimonious?

"There was nothing to be acrimonious about," says Osborne. "I didn't feel that I had that gig as a right . . . I think it was a little bit of a bereavement for me, but it was something I had to get used to and get over."

Tim Rice

Long before they composed the music for a trio of stage-and-screen blockbusters—*The Lion King*, *Aida*, and *The Road to El Dorado*—John and lyricist Tim Rice collaborated on "Legal Boys," from 1982's *Jump Back!*

Prior to this, Rice had forged an immensely successful collaboration with Andrew Lloyd Webber, composing songs for such indelible seventies musicals as *Joseph and the Amazing Technicolor Dreamcoat*, *Jesus Christ Superstar*, and *Evita*. The pair split at the dawn of the eighties, when Lloyd Webber branched out with other collaborators and subsequent productions like *Cats* and *Phantom of the Opera*, leaving Rice open to new opportunities that often diverged from the dramatic whims of musical theater.

Tom Robinson

Robinson contributed only two songs to Elton John's vast catalogue, but in "Elton's Song," which features on *The Fox*, he conjured one of the most stirring, topically provocative love songs he has recorded to date; and in "Sartorial Eloquence," from *21 at 33*, a soulful pop gem. Prior to his association with John, Robinson had written an anthem of sorts, "Glad to be Gay," a UK hit in 1978. Another Robinson ballad, "Reach Out to Me," was rewritten for John's 1980 duet with French vocalist France Gall, "Les Aveux," with "Donner Pour Donner" on the B-side.

Leon Russell

Russell's career saw him recording with everyone from Frank Sinatra and Elvis Presley to Joe Cocker and the Beach Boys; he wrote songs that the most in-demand, elite artists rushed to record. He continued to play the live circuit, appearing at out-of-the-way venues like Jannus Landing in St. Petersburg, Florida, where the scattered throngs gathered to dance to "Lady Blue" and "Delta Lady." He'd sign autographs afterward from his seat on the tour bus.

The fans loved him, obviously, but life proved increasingly difficult for Russell as his star-power faded. John hadn't seen or heard from his idol since the seventies, when Russell caught one of John's torrid 1970 performances at the Troubadour in Hollywood, and their subsequent tour dates soon after. On safari in Africa with his partner and future husband, David Furnish, John broke down in tears upon hearing, seemingly for the first time in forever, some of Russell's classic recordings playing on the couple's iPod. Compelled to check in with Russell, John contacted him, ultimately inviting him to co-write and record a new album with him. He asked T Bone Burnett to produce it, and *The Union* was born. John composed some of the songs with Bernie Taupin, while Russell wrote a few on his own. In fact, the only song credited to both John *and* Russell as composers is "A Dream Came True," a fitting title from John's perspective, considering the high regard in which he had held Russell since his own career's earliest days.

The album was a critical and commercial triumph, but in a more poignant context it not only restored Russell's career but also refreshed his life. Then, on November 13, 2016, after a series of health setbacks, the self-proclaimed Master of Space and Time slipped away.

"My darling Leon Russell passed away last night," John said in a statement. "He was a mentor, inspiration and so kind to me. Thank God we caught up with each other and made *The Union*. He got his reputation back and felt fulfilled. I loved him and always will."

19

These Independent Moves I Make

A Timeout from Taupin—*A Single Man* and *Victim of Love*

A brazen new breed threatened the old guard, its snarling contempt at the mainstream music scene infecting attitudes throughout the UK and US in the mid-to-late seventies. Heralded as punks, they prided themselves on stomping out the most bloated, blandest bands of the era, including pop and rock dinosaurs likes the Rolling Stones and Led Zeppelin, Fleetwood Mac and the Eagles, Rod Stewart and Elton John.

The decade's most successful solo artist—a brazen character in his own right, with his decadent fashion statements and fiercer spirit of independence—had taken his platform-heeled foot off the gas as far as making music was concerned, having announced his retirement in 1976 in order to serve as chairman of the Watford Football Club. The problem was that when he wasn't supervising the kicks on the field, John was kicking around his spacious Woodside mansion, oftentimes just lying in bed with nothing much to do.

"When I saw the Sex Pistols slagging me off on television," John told the *New Yorker*, in its issue dated August 26, 1996, "I thought, Yes you *are* a lazy fat cunt."

What more could he say (even to himself) in response, really? John hadn't written (much less recorded) any new music since *Blue Moves*, and any plans in the pipeline to make anything new lay dormant on the horizon.

"He had retired," says lyricist Gary Osborne. "It may seem a long time ago, and it doesn't seem important, but he actually quit. He didn't make an album for two years. He didn't do a tour. He concentrated on Watford."

Being preternaturally talented while retired, however, is a tough distinction to reconcile oneself with at any age, never mind when your talent has made you a multimillionaire before the age of twenty-five, attracting a loyal audience around the world. If such circumstances had made Elton John at all restless, they made his manager, John Reid, outright apoplectic.

"Now, the worst thing you can do if you're a manager is to manage an act that's retired," says Osborne. "You're better off managing an act that's dead. People don't suddenly go mad buying Elton John records because he says he's retired. They probably don't believe him anyway."

Reid recognized that he needed to jumpstart John's creative juices before there was nothing left to jumpstart at all.

Bereft of the familiar faces he had come to count on—without a band on retainer with which to record or tour, without Gus Dudgeon on hand to produce, and most conspicuously without Bernie Taupin available to write any lyrics—John faced the most obscure future since he signed on with Dick James Music as a staff songwriter more than a decade before. In so doing, he entered one of the most challenging yet underrated phases of his career, recording music and embarking on select solo tours—including his historic first performances in the Soviet Union—that, if nothing else, revealed his penchant for taking artistic risks remained as vibrant as ever. For a superstar who had shattered records that had previously seemed unfathomable, John still believed he had much more to prove.

Nevertheless, with each subsequent project, he sought to absolve the role he was to play in the studio—until he relegated himself to being, exclusively, a vocalist singing someone else's song, someone else's production. In the space of just two years, he would record three projects, each one proving distinctive in its own right while at the same time as analogous to the others as *Empty Sky* had been to *Tumbleweed Connection* and *Goodbye Yellow Brick Road*. First, though, he needed to find another lyricist with whom to write—a move that would change his whole way of working.

You Found a Different Way to Get Your Kicks

Gary Osborne had seen Bluesology back in the sixties, playing clubs like the Speakeasy and the Cromwellian. He and John weren't friends back then, but rather passing acquaintances who moved in the same social circles. It was in the seventies, after they worked indirectly with each other on various projects for John's Rocket Records label, that their friendship took root.

"We'd hang out together," says Osborne. "We'd go to his house, he'd come to our house. We spent the Queen's Jubilee together in 1977, and we just became really good chums. We used to play cards, we used to play backgammon. I used to go to Watford with him."

Still, the prospect of John and Osborne collaborating together in a formal sense seemed, at least to Osborne, far-fetched. Besides, he had his own commitments, namely as lyricist to the popular Jeff Wayne musical version of *The War of the Worlds*. "It's really weird," says Osborne in retrospect. "I always thought I'd be remembered as the guy who wasn't quite as good as Taupin. But it turns out I'll be remembered as the guy who wrote the words of *The War of the Worlds*, which is odd."

John had a melody he had created—a practice he was not all that used to. "What really was the difference was that Elton had spent the last five years putting music to Bernie's thoughts," says Osborne. "Five years of Elton not writing a song until Bernie had given him some words. But every creative composer will occasionally have a tune pop into his head, and *that's* what happened."

In the meantime, Reid was searching for a means to lure John back into the recording studio. The incentives were clear, and were right in front of him.

"Here's Elton hanging out with Gary Osborne on a weekly basis," says Osborne. "He's with me and my wife, and he's godfather to my kid. And I got on very well with John, and he's thinking, *If I can just encourage a bit of writing* .... This is exactly what happened."

Having written an instrumental piece that he had been tinkering with for a brief time, John broke the ice.

"He plays the tune," Osborne recalls. "I casually say, 'I'll give it a try.' He leaves about four in the morning. And, of course, it was mostly written by six. I couldn't wait for the asshole to get out of there so I could start work on the thing."

Osborne and John's working styles varied drastically. "For me, a lyric takes anywhere from a minimum of a day," Osborne says, "but mostly a week, two weeks, or a month, whereas his tunes are coming out in fifteen-minute intervals."

It took Osborne a while to come to terms with the discrepancies in the ways the two men approach their craft.

> Because he's so quick, because everything comes to him so quick musically, and the whole thing about lyrics is that they take a long time because you've got to craft, you've got to work out: put this line in the first verse or the second verse? And maybe, now that I've written a second verse, that first verse doesn't work so well. Maybe I could move that line to the end, or maybe I should just start again. It's a much more painstaking . . . you get flashes of inspiration, but for him, the whole tune was a flash of inspiration. He'd get an idea or he'd get a chord sequence or he'd get Bernie's lyric, and he'd get a flash of inspiration and it would be done.

Just as Taupin would never second-guess John's results once he set his lyrics to music, John, in turn, never second-guessed Osborne's lyrics once he applied them to his own pre-written tunes—a rare thing, Osborne notes.

> When I would give him lyrics—he'd give me the tune, I'd give him the lyric—he never asked me to change anything. That's very rare. All the tune writers I've ever worked with, when you give it to them, they say, "I'm not sure that that line," or "Could you change that word?" or you have an argument, you have a negotiation—they win, you lose, or you win, they lose, or some kind of compromise is struck. I never got that with Elton. I was always expecting him to say, "Hmm, that's okay, but I'm not mad about the third verse." Christ, I would've done anything for him. I would stand my

ground, but I wouldn't argue with him, because it's going to be on his album, remember, so, you know, he had to have the final say.

Much like John's smattering of lyrical contributions to songs like "Border Song" and "Don't Go Breaking My Heart," Osborne also contributed fragments of musical ideas to John's compositions.

There are little tiny bits of these tunes that I've actually written bits of. I wrote the chorus of that song "Return to Paradise" from the *Single Man* album, because the chorus he'd written was very much like another song. While I was writing the lyric, I noticed the similarity to the other song. So I did the lyric to the tune as he

A Single Man, released on October 16, 1978, was the first of John's solo albums not to include lyrics written by Bernie Taupin, and instead featured lyrics written by Gary Osborne.
Author's collection

wrote it, but then I wrote another tune over the chords and said, "Look, here's your lyric as it stands, but I think that's kind of a nick off, a steal off of this song. But I do have an alternative tune." Can you imagine the fucking nerve of me? I've hardly had any success at all and I'm rewriting Elton John's tunes and he's letting me!

The predominant revelation, though, was that John had discovered a new way of working for the first time in over a decade. "What he found," says Osborne, "was that he didn't *need* a piece of paper with the words on it. He could just delve into his head and write a tune. He described it at the time like a cork coming out of a bottle and all these tunes that have been lying around inside him just all of a sudden came out."

As Osborne concedes, though, he also served a primary purpose in getting John back on the treadmill of working again.

The great use that I was, was to get him writing so that he would go in the studio and if he went in the studio then he would have recordings. Then if he had recordings he would have to promote them. Then if he promoted them he would have to go back out on the road. And back on the road, you're once again a functioning act.

I would go with that dummy lyric and try to keep some of it because what I thought I was doing—what I *was* doing in certain instances, certainly what I *felt* I was doing—was I was finally putting Elton's thoughts into Elton's songs. Elton had been singing Bernie's feelings, Bernie's thoughts, Bernie's obsessions, Bernie's passions, Bernie's heartaches . . . he'd been singing Bernie's life story, if you like. Now this was an opportunity to put some of his self into it.

Toward the end of the sessions, John asked engineer Clive Franks to start recording, and he played a spare, melancholy instrumental track on the keyboard. This time, he did not ask Osborne to write a lyric. ("Can you imagine how disappointing that was for me?" Osborne says, with a tinge of good-natured sarcasm, recalling the enormous success the song enjoyed.) The following day, John learned that Guy Burchett, a seventeen-year-old studio runner, had been killed the day before, while delivering some Elton John items to the BBC. In tribute, John christened the instrumental, which closes *A Single Man*, "Song for Guy."

"The surprise was that it was an actual hit here," says Osborne, noting the tune's success in the UK, where it peaked at #4 (it reached #110 in the US). "It's a very simple little instrumental. And then he did that fantastic little lyrical thing at the end, 'Life isn't everything / Isn't everything life.' I loved that, because it turned around on itself so that if you listened to it from a certain point of view, he's saying 'life isn't everything' or 'isn't everything life.' So 'life isn't everything' becomes 'isn't everything life.' I don't even think he did that consciously."

All in all, *A Single Man* not only generated a couple of surefire hits to sustain what had been his stagnant recording career, it also inspired John to continue working on additional songs, additional projects.

"What had happened was exactly what John Reid had hoped for," says Osborne. "He had gone back in the studio just to demo and produce more songs to demo, so therefore he suddenly had three or four songs. And he said, 'Well, let's go in and record these songs.' And while we're recording *those* songs, here's another tune, here's another tune, here's another tune. We went in to record three or four songs, and ended up with twenty songs. We were still using tracks from those sessions as B-sides. He was still using them after we'd stopped working together."

What a Fool You've Made of Me

Sometimes, reaching for the right thing sends one down the wrong path. With 1979's *Victim of Love*, Elton John sought out the full services of Pete Bellotte—to write the lyrics and produce the record, albeit unfortunately in a disco vein. Of course, John was not the only pop star or rocker to indulge the late-seventies disco phenomenon. Yet it seemed that for every rock act that succeeded on the dance charts—from Rod Stewart's "Do Ya Think I'm Sexy" to the Rolling Stones' "Miss You"—another act faltered.

It's not like John wasn't suited to the disco style. The genre was essentially a souped-up offshoot of the same sort of soul and R&B he had appreciated and performed since his adolescence, so neither the vibe nor the sped-up tempos of disco were foreign to him—a point he had already

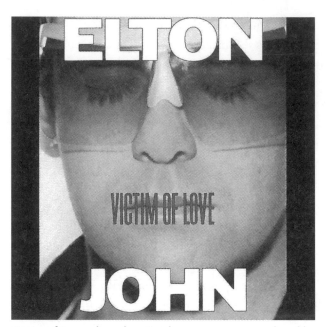

Victim of Love, released on October 13, 1979, was produced by disco producer Pete Bellotte. The experimental album strove to capitalize on the waning disco craze, but it ultimately found John mired in mundane dance clichés.   *Author's collection*

made clear with far stronger, groovier songs in the form of "Bennie and the Jets" and, more emblematic of the sonic root of the issue, "Philadelphia Freedom." On top of that, his collaboration with Thom Bell on "Mama Can't Buy You Love" far surpassed the quality of any of his disco experiments with Bellotte—and the song didn't sound out of place on the radio alongside disco hardliners like Donna Summer or KC and the Sunshine Band. But nothing on *Victim of Love* rivaled such credibility or quality.

"It was a good idea," John told *Rolling Stone* in 2016, defending the album, "except that disco had finished by then. It was just too late."

20

Me and You, We're All We've Got

Ten Best Duets

Much as with the rarity of his covers of other artists' songs, Elton John has not recorded too many duets over the past half-century. When he has done so, however, it as usually been with artists he admires, not fleeting, flavor-of-the-month novelty acts that would benefit from any such association with him.

Of course, in 1993, John released an entire album, *Duets*, comprised of nothing *but* duets (save for its closing song, aptly titled "Duets for One"), but while some of its recordings still withstand time and critical scrutiny, not all of them made the cut for this list of his ten best duets.

10. "Snowed in at Wheeler Street" with Kate Bush (*50 Words for Snow*, 2011)

British singer/songwriter Kate Bush has long credited Elton John as one of her few adolescent musical idols, and the influence of his songs and their orchestral, cinematic arrangements abounds in her earliest works. The admiration is mutual, as John has, beyond heralding her best music, credited her siren-like vocal on "Don't Give Up," her 1986 duet with Peter Gabriel, with pulling him through some of the darkest moments of his life, particularly when in the throes of substance addiction in the late eighties.

For the 1991 tribute album, *Two Rooms: Celebrating the Songs of Elton John and Bernie Taupin*, Bush recorded a cosmic version of "Rocket Man," drawing out the song's themes of loneliness while summoning one of the collection's most audacious performances. As a single, it even reached #12 in the UK. Twenty years later, on her *50 Words for Snow*, the Rocket Man himself returned the favor, singing with Bush on her own "Snowed in on Wheeler Street," a harrowing tale of unconsummated passion.

"The idea is that there are two lovers, two souls who keep on meeting up in different periods of time," Bush said in a 2011 interview with the *Quietus*. "So they meet in Ancient Rome, and then they meet again walking through time. But each time something happens to tear them apart."

9. "Rock This House" with B.B. King (*80*, 2005)

Barnstorming through this raucous boogie-woogie blues, John may have been just one of many guests—the album is credited to "B.B. King and Friends"—on hand to celebrate the King of the Blues' eightieth birthday, but he was having the most fun. Raving up the keys on his piano like he surely did during Bluesology's most boisterous gigs in the sixties, John complemented King's volcanic delivery and guitar stabs note for note. This one does just what it says on the tin.

8. "Runaway Train" with Eric Clapton (*The One*, 1992)

Slowhand and the Rocket Man came together with mutual venom on this scorcher, which was released as the third single from John's 1992 LP, *The One*—reaching #10 on the *Billboard* Mainstream Rock chart—while also featuring on the official soundtrack to the motion picture *Lethal Weapon 3*. Both men had recently survived their own versions of personal hell, with John having spent six weeks in a Chicago rehabilitation facility in 1990 to confront his longstanding substance addictions and eating disorder, and with Clapton having contended with the unimaginable grief of losing his four-year-old son, Conor, who perished in 1991 after falling out of an open, forty-fifth-floor New York City window. When together they sing, almost growling, "I'm trying to get a grip on my life again," the subtext resounds, loud and ferociously clear. Whatever Bernie Taupin intended the lyrics to mean, in John and Clapton's hands this song is a

The UK CD single for the 1993 duet between Elton John and Eric Clapton, "Runaway Train," which was originally included on the former's album from the previous year, *The One*.

Author's collection

rock 'n' roll catharsis, two virtuosos channeling their anguish and rage into raw, exquisite musicianship.

7. "Through the Storm" with Aretha Franklin (*Through the Storm*, 1989)

Suggesting the template for making an album packed with all-star duet partners a decade before Santana reveled in the glory of *Supernatural*, Aretha Franklin recruited a handful of friends and legends for 1989's *Through the Storm*. The results were mixed—Whitney Houston couldn't muster the necessary bravado at that point to sing toe-to-toe with the

Queen of Soul on "It Isn't, It Wasn't, It Ain't Ever Gonna Be," and Franklin's saccharine remake of "Think" pales in comparison to her anthemic 1968 original—yet on the title track, written by proven hit-maker Diane Warren, Franklin and Elton John inspired the best out of each other.

The prospect of these two superstars joining forces on the same track must have originated when Franklin recorded John's classic "Border Song" on her 1972 LP, *Young, Gifted, and Black*. She clearly appreciated John and Bernie Taupin's songwriting, and they clearly adored her soul-drenched vocal mastery. The opportunity for these two artists to work together proved irresistible. Released as a single, "Through the Storm" reached the Top 20, peaking at #16 on the *Billboard* Hot 100 chart.

6. "Written in the Stars" with LeAnn Rimes (*Elton John and Tim Rice's Aida*, 1999)

Unrequited love is a tough fate to accept, but as "Written in the Stars" illustrates so well, to have loved and lost may be an even more bittersweet pill to swallow. As featured on the official soundtrack to the Tony Award–winning Broadway musical, *Aida*, John's duet with crossover artist LeAnn Rimes, with its crescendoing, rhapsodic chorus complementing its bittersweet lyric, may well be the most romantic duet of John's career. The song proved to be John's fifty-seventh—and to date final—Top 40 single, ending a streak of at least one Top 40 hit per year since "Your Song" in 1970. Not a bad way to say goodbye.

5. "Never Too Old (to Hold Somebody)" with Leon Russell (*The Union*, 2010)

Having rekindled their musical friendship with *The Union*, Elton John and Leon Russell demonstrated that old habits—like writing warm, affectionate songs—die hard. This song, more than any other on what remains a sensational album, illustrates the best of both artists: Russell's southern gospel musicality, John's melancholic bliss. And, together, they blend

A CD single for "Written in the Stars," a duet between Elton John and LeeAnn Rimes, which was originally included on the 2000 soundtrack to the Broadway musical *Aida*, and found John co-writing with *The Lion King* lyricist Tim Rice. It ended up being John's last Top 40 single to date, ending a thirty-year streak during which he achieved at least one Top 40 hit per year.   *Author's collection*

those distinctions like sacraments, luring the listener in with a love song of hope.

4. "Sorry Seems to Be the Hardest Word" with Ray Charles (*Genius Loves Company*, 2004)

Recording the original during the making of the 1976 double album, *Blue Moves*, proved a trying, emotional experience for all involved in its creation, considering the despondent circumstances its lyrics suggest, the prevailing sense of intimate drama permeating the sessions during which it was recorded (see chapter 12). For Elton John, in revisiting "Sorry Seems to Be the Hardest Word" as a duet with Ray Charles, for what would end up as the latter's posthumous album, *Genius Loves Company*, it was crying time again.

Having already recorded duets with such artists as Norah Jones ("Here We Go Again"), B.B. King ("Sinner's Prayer"), and Willie Nelson ("It Was a Very Good Year"), Charles was near death by the time he and John recorded "Sorry Seems to Be the Hardest Word," and the fragility of his once herculean voice imbued this heart-wrenching performance. For John, standing mere feet from one of his undisputed idols, beholding his struggle to sing a song he and Bernie Taupin had composed nearly three decades prior, was enough to bring tears to his eyes. It turned out to the final recording of Charles's iconic life; he succumbed to liver cancer on June 10, 2004. On February 13, 2005, at the 47th Annual Grammy Awards, this version of "Sorry Seems to Be the Hardest Word" earned a Grammy nomination for "Best Pop Collaboration with Vocal," losing to Charles and Jones's version of "Here We Go Again."

3. "A Woman's Needs" with Tammy Wynette (*Duets*, 1993)

On an album that for the most part showcases Elton John singing with select special guests on revamped versions of such vintage pop and R&B classics as "I'm Your Puppet" and "Ain't Nothing Like the Real Thing" (not to mention a few hits culled from his own back catalogue), his duet with Wynette on "A Woman's Needs" towers above them all. Written by John and Taupin, and exuding all the heartbreak and lovesick poignancy of every rose-colored Nashville masterpiece, the song may as well have belonged to Wynette, who, in delivering its fragile laments and ultimatums, evokes the same damaged yet graceful despair as whenever she performed "'Til I Can Make It on My Own" and "D-I-V-O-R-C-E." "I've been shortchanged and cheated *so* many times," she sings in the second verse, nailing the crux of her suffering in one bleak inflection, the chances of her finding lasting, redemptive love sounding about as likely as mending her tired, tortured soul.

2. "Don't Go Breaking My Heart" with Kiki Dee (Non-Album Single, 1976)

Maybe the prevailing mood had grown too dour for his taste at the time, for in late 1975, Elton John asked Bernie Taupin if between the two of them they could come up with an up-tempo, lighthearted song. They'd been spending their Christmas vacation in Barbados, writing the songs that would comprise the forthcoming double album, *Blue Moves*—songs that, in certain instances, would characterize Taupin's unraveling relationship with his first wife, Maxine. According to author David Buckley's stellar *Elton: The Biography*, some of the lyrics were even supplied by John himself. In fact, the whole song took no more than ten minutes for John and Taupin to compose.

By the time John, Taupin, producer Gus Dudgeon, the band, and the crew had convened at Eastern Sound studios in Toronto for the *Blue Moves* sessions, the song had evolved somewhat, its influence now shifting from its disco-based dance origins to reflect some of the vanguard duets recorded at Motown by the likes of Marvin Gaye and Tammi Terrell—songs like "Ain't No Mountain High Enough" and "You're All I Need to Get By." It was also now a duet between John and Kiki Dee, who, besides having sung backup on a number of albums by John and others, like Dusty Springfield, had scored hit singles with the English-language version of "Amoureuse" (featuring lyrics by Gary Osborne) and "I've Got the Music in Me." John recorded the full song with the band in Toronto, singing Dee's lines in a high register to distinguish them from his own; Dee recorded her vocals later, in London. Their distance notwithstanding, their chemistry—and above all, the song—worked like pop-music magic. Released as a non-album single (with another non-album track, "Snow Queen," on the B-side), "Don't Go Breaking My Heart" rocketed to #1 for four weeks in the US, while in the UK it topped the charts for six weeks, giving John his first-ever #1 in his homeland. He wouldn't achieve his first solo #1 single there until 1990, when "Sacrifice" topped the UK singles chart.

1. "Don't Let the Sun Go Down on Me" with George Michael (Non-Album Single, 1991)

George Michael maintained such a mercurial vision about how best to pursue his career that his decisions often rankled with the executives at his record label. Consider, for instance, his 1991 Cover to Cover tour, which, instead of serving as a proper promotional jaunt for his current LP, *Listen Without Prejudice Vol. 1*, instead featured Michael for the most part performing hits by some of his favorite singers and songwriters. Only four years after the release of his solo debut, *Faith*, the standard operating procedure would have warranted a tour explicitly in support of his latest album of original material, not a celebration of material by *other* artists.

In addition to performing songs by the likes of David Bowie ("Fame"), Stevie Wonder ("Superstition"), and the Temptations ("Papa was a Rollin' Stone"), not to mention a smattering of Wham! and solo selections, Michael sang two Elton John songs, "Tonight" and "Don't Let the Sun Go Down on Me." A recording of the former, taken from Michael's performance at the Rock in Rio Festival, was released in October 1991 on the various-artists LP, *Two Rooms: Celebrating the Songs of Elton John and Bernie Taupin*.

As for the latter, Michael had invited Elton John to his performance at Wembley Arena on March 23, 1991, to sing the song with him, reprising their momentous duet six years prior at Live Aid. John was returning to the live stage for the first time since his six-week stint in a Chicago rehabilitation facility, and his surprise appearance with Michael succeeded so well that Michael sought to release the performance as a single. Even John thought it was a bad idea, not believing a song that had been a hit back in 1974 could be resurrected and further redeemed. Michael persisted, however, and his live duet with John on "Don't Let the Sun Go Down on Me," released in November 1991, topped the *Billboard* Hot 100 for one week and spent two weeks at #1 the UK.

21

Something Tells Me You're Not Satisfied

Uneven in the Eighties

E lton John was not the only veteran rock 'n' roll artist who at times seemed out of place in the age of Day-Glo, breakdancing, and parachute pants. Aging troubadours like Bob Dylan, Neil Young, and even Paul McCartney sometimes resembled musical relics, struggling to find their footing in a decade besieged by new wave and hair metal, wherein superficiality and flash too often superseded the simple genius of great songwriting.

Though he wasn't churning out two albums per year like he did in the early to mid-seventies, pursuant to his 1970–1976 contract with Dick James Music, John nevertheless released nine studio albums between 1980 and 1989, not to mention live sets (*Live in Australia with the Melbourne Symphony Orchestra*) and greatest-hits compilations (*Elton John's Greatest Hits Volume III*).

His prolificacy during these years didn't always translate to quality, however—at least not the sort of quality that called to mind his most inveterate seventies classics. Such inconsistency—along with numerous distractions, personal misfortunes, and the cumulative toll of his inner demons—at times overshadowed some genuinely inspired efforts.

One such reason for these inconsistencies was the fact that since John began writing with lyricist Gary Osborne prior to the release of *A Single Man* in 1978, he had branched out to compose with even more lyricists—a decision that not only divvied up the credits on his albums to reflect an increasing number of co-writers, but also (perhaps unwittingly) encouraged a sense of rivalry among them, as Osborne recalls.

On the three albums that Bernie and I did about half each, most of the singles were mine, and even though they weren't big hits off of *The Fox*, "Nobody Wins" was mine, "Chloe" was also a single. I tended to do quite well. People forget that. It's not a competition, but when we were head-to-head, I think I held my own. You see, I was never going to win that competition, because if you were an Elton John fan, you weren't really going to take kindly to this new guy, because Bernie's part of the legend as I was just the new guy. If you were an Elton John fan—if you were a died-in-the-wool Elton John fan—you would have a little resistance to me and I understood that whereas if you were not an Elton John fan then I was a very useful stick with which to beat him.

What followed throughout the decade were nine studio albums that, while each to different degrees yielding at least a hit single or otherwise redeemable moment, varied wildly in terms of their overall quality.

21 at 33 (1980)

Ten years after his self-titled album and breakthrough performances at the Troubadour put him on the map, John stepped into the new decade as a fully fledged veteran artist, boasting one of the most enviable back catalogues in popular music. Still, he had more to prove. Having in the previous few years dabbled in sonic experiments that for better (*The Complete Thom Bell Sessions*) or worse (*Victim of Love*) relied less on his compositional talents than on the prevailing sonic fads of the moment, John could only improve with his first album of the eighties. With *21 at 33*, he returned to both co-writing the songs and playing the piano, composing music that reflected and indeed reaffirmed his perennial talents.

Despite teeming with four lyricists—Bernie Taupin, Gary Osborne, Tom Robinson, and newcomer Judy Tzuke—the album is John's most cohesive effort since *Blue Moves*, sweeping between moments of sharp, new-wave pop ("Two Rooms at the End of the World") and soul-disposed balladry ("Dear God"). Recorded at Superbear Studios in Nice, France, *21 at 33* should have been a bigger hit than it was, reaching #13 in the US and #12 in the UK.

"Little Jeannie," with lyrics by Osborne, stands as the best of the bunch, earning John his biggest hit single since "Don't Go Breaking My Heart" four years earlier, reaching #3 in the US (but peaking at only #33 in the UK). Though composed for the most part in the music-first dynamic of the John–Osborne collaboration, the song actually took its shape from John supplying a few key lines, including the song's title and its most conspicuous couplet—"I want you to be my acrobat / I want you to be my lover"—around which Osborne then wrote further lyrics to accommodate.

"I could not understand what the line meant or why he was singing it," Osborne says, "because it was literally the first thing that came into his head." As the song progresses, saxophonist Jim Horn—whose credentials include everything from the Concert for Bangladesh to the Rolling Stones' *Goat's Head Soup* and Stevie Wonder's *Songs in the Key of Life*—provides exquisite counterpart throughout. "The sweetest bit is the vamp at the end," Osborne adds. "He sings so great over it, and if you listen to the end he sings fantastic ad-libs over it, just *beautiful* ad-libs over it."

Also contributing to the lyrics was singer/songwriter Judy Tzuke, who, on the strength of such hits like "Stay with Me 'Till Dawn," earned a spot on the Rocket Records roster and an opening slot on John's 1980 tour, including his historic Central Park performance. Her collaboration with John, "Give Me the Love," is actually among the album's more soulful moments. Other highlights include "Sartorial Eloquence," with lyrics written by Robinson. While John's subsequent albums of the eighties would vary between two extremes—mainstream pop and R&B-disposed balladry—*21 at 33* established the basic template they would follow going forward.

The Fox (1981)

The songs on *The Fox* are largely holdovers from the sessions for *21 at 33*, which was for a short time being considered for double-album treatment. The album marks the first appearance on an Elton John record by producer Chris Thomas, whose credentials included albums by the Sex Pistols, Paul McCartney, and the Pretenders, and who would occupy an extended presence on John's albums over the next two decades, ultimately eclipsing Gus Dudgeon for total number of Elton John albums produced. Clive Franks and John produced some of the tracks as well. The album reached #21 in the US while peaking at #12 in the UK, heralding John's debut on Geffen Records, which by this time could also boast the signing of John Lennon (and would, in a few years, sign Neil Young, creating far more problems for the label than it would prized hits).

Having entered the golden age of music video (sparked by the cosmic clip that accompanied Queen's bombastic "Bohemian Rhapsody" in 1975), John sanctioned videos for each of the album's nine songs. None of them made any impact whatsoever, and now, even with hindsight, offer little but a nostalgic look at an album that, overall, missed the mark. Not that it lacked any highlights whatsoever. In fact, the album's most moving and enduring moment comes with "Elton's Song," a rapturous ode to young, unrequited love, featuring lyrics written by Tom Robinson. John still plays it live to this day in his solo performances.

Another standout, the instrumental "Carla/Etude," was composed for producer and engineer Clive Franks's wedding to his bride, Carla.

Jump Up! (1982)

On the strength of "Blue Eyes" and "Empty Garden (Hey, Hey Johnny)"—the latter of which John and Taupin wrote in tribute to John Lennon in the aftermath of his murder in 1980—*Jump Up!* reached

Jump Up!, released on April 9, 1982, includes the US #13 hit "Empty Garden Hey, Hey Johnny," which John and Bernie Taupin composed in memory of John Lennon.   *Author's collection*

#17 in the US and #13 in the UK. The album was recorded in Montserrat, at AIR Studios, owned by former Beatles producer George Martin. Pete Townshend, who at the time was forging his own solo career, played acoustic guitar on "Ball and Chain." "To have Pete on that was lovely," says Gary Osborne.

Lyricist Tim Rice, who would forge a triumphant team with John with the *Lion King* phenomenon in the nineties, contributed one song, "Legal Boys," to the affair. Unfortunately, the album lacks in quality what it achieves in compositional diversity. "I think one of the worst albums we ever made, though it does have one of our best songs on there, is Jump Up!" Bernie Taupin told *Rolling Stone* in 2013. "It does have 'Empty Garden,' but the rest of it is just junk." A bit harsh, but in the ballpark.

Too Low for Zero (1983)

This is Elton John hitting his stride in a decade built on greed and decadence. "It was the first time I'd written on synthesizer," he told music journalist and friend Paul Gambaccini in 1984. "It's very hard to write three-chord songs on the piano. I can write ballads and complex songs, but the fast songs I've written I've never been entirely happy with. They've either been too fast [or] too slow, and they've never been what I wanted. So I get this synthesizer, which sounds like a guitar in some parts, and then I can write three-chord songs all of a sudden."

The album's success was bolstered by the music videos for "I Guess That's Why They Call It the Blues" and "I'm Still Standing," directed by Russell Mulcahy, who had also directed the videos that accompanied the release of *The Fox*. The videos, particularly "I'm Still Standing," portray John not as some washed-up relic from the Troubadour's golden age of singer/songwriters but as a vital artist who could hang with the big shots of the day, like Michael Jackson and Duran Duran.

Whether or not he was intent on recapturing the sound and success of his seventies glory days, John couldn't help but conjure that impression when he welcomed producer Gus Dudgeon, bassist Dee Murray, and drummer Nigel Olsson back into the fray. With Taupin also on board for

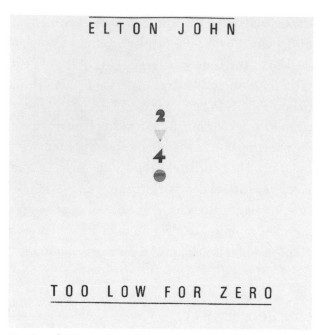

Too Low for Zero, released on May 30, 1983, featured the hit singles "I Guess That's Why They Call It the Blues" #4 US / #5 UK and "I'm Still Standing" #12 US / #4 UK. For the first time since *Blue Moves* in 1976, the lyrics to all of the songs were written by Bernie Taupin.   *Author's collection*

the album's entirety for the first time since *Blue Moves*, *Too Low for Zero* bore all the makings of another classic—and it delivered.

One of the most distinctive elements of "I Guess That's Why They Call It the Blues"—Stevie Wonder's harmonica solo—almost didn't happen. The idea for a harmonica solo at all came from producer Chris Thomas, who had a difficult time convincing John it would work in the song. Once John heard Wonder playing the riff, however, he warmed to the idea wholeheartedly.

Breaking Hearts (1984)

Reaching #20 on the *Billboard* album chart and yielding the massive single "Sad Songs (Say so Much)," *Breaking Hearts* is a continuation of what *Too Low for Zero* established. Recorded as well at AIR Studios in

Montserrat, it brought back the old band (bassist Dee Murray, guitarist Davey Johnstone, drummer Nigel Olsson), producer Chris Tomas once again returned to shape the sound, and Bernie Taupin wrote all the lyrics. While not as much of a runaway smash as its predecessor, *Breaking Hearts* nevertheless achieved its own preeminence. Sweeping ballads like "In Neon" and "Burning Buildings" could sit alongside classic album tracks like "Blues for Baby and Me," while "Who Wears These Shoes" foreshadows the R&B inflections that would surface with greater distinction later in the decade.

Ice on Fire (1985)

Marking the first time Gus Dudgeon produced an Elton John album since *Blue Moves* in 1976, *Ice on Fire* has aged better than its initial critical reception may have suggested. The album's biggest single, "Nikita," reached #7 in the US and #3 in the UK, and kept John in the Top 20 pantheon he'd forced his way into fifteen years before. However, for all the success of the lead single, the album suffered a slow decline on the charts. (A subsequent cut, "Wrap Her Up," a campy duet with George Michael—still in his Wham! days—didn't fare nearly as well.) Besides Michael, the album features such guests as bassist John Deacon and drummer Roger Taylor of Queen, but even with Dudgeon back on board, there just wasn't enough solid material to give the album the distinction it deserved.

Leather Jackets (1986)

The last Elton John album produced by Gus Dudgeon, *Leather Jackets* represents a creative nadir in a decade of inconsistencies. Reaching only #91 on the *Billboard* album chart, it also marked the end of his tenure on Geffen Records.

"It was done under the worst possible circumstances," Dudgeon reflected in a 2002 interview with *Hercules: The Elton John Fan Club* magazine, just three months before his death. "There were a few leftover tracks from the previous album [*Ice on Fire*] for a start. [Elton] was only going to

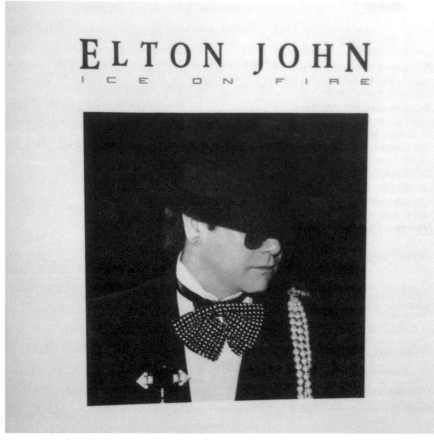

Ice on Fire, released on November 4, 1985, features the Top 10 hit "Nikita" #7 US / #3 UK.
Author's collection

be available for something like ten days because he was going to be off to the wedding [to Renate Blauel]. To me, that was the height of it, the coke thing really went mad."

The album's lead single, "Heartache All Over the World," stalled at #55 on the US chart, marking the first time since *Tumbleweed Connection* (from which no single was released) that one of John's albums didn't yield a Top 40 hit.

"Slow Rivers," a duet with Cliff Richard, is a pleasant enough ballad, but much of what fills out the album is just that—filler. If the album led to anything worthwhile, it was a historic tour of Australia with the Melbourne Symphony Orchestra, which of course then led to one of the greatest and most gripping live albums of John's career. He wouldn't be the first major artist to release an album that served mostly as an excuse to tour. "*Leather Jackets* has a lot of awful songs on it," John told *GQ* in 2001, "and there's some very uneven work in the eighties and nineties due to the fact that I wasn't concentrating on what I was doing. And because of the drugs, of course."

Reg Strikes Back (1988)

The album's cover tells the tale—Elton John sought a clean slate. Hoards of old costumes, frothy feather boas, gigantic eyeglasses, the Donald Duck costume from the 1980 Central Park concert—all of it in a heap, as if dumped out in the trash. He had auctioned off his old sartorial trappings in search of a new beginning. The problem was he was still very much the same man, still ingesting as much cocaine and alcohol as he ever did.

Miraculously, his talent remained intact (along with his throat, now surgically repaired), and, given the right lyrics, he could still bring a bit of magic to bear. With producer Chris Thomas behind the glass once more, *Reg Strikes Back* generated a #2 hit single in the R&B stomper "I Don't Want to Go on with You Like That," but underrated songs such as "A Word in Spanish" (which reached #19 in the US) and "Japanese Hands" enriched the album with some of John's most soulful moments of the decade. Guest appearances by Pete Townshend (who adds acoustic guitar to "Town of Plenty") and Beach Boys alumni Carl Wilson and Bruce Johnston (who sing backup on "Since God Invented Girls") don't add much distinction, and though John still wasn't creating anything as cohesive as *Honky Château* or *Goodbye Yellow Brick Road*, the strongest moments on *Reg Strikes Back* rival his best of the decade overall.

Sleeping with the Past (1989)

Dissatisfied with the disconnected quality and styles of his previous albums, and recently divorced, Elton John sought a tonic for his sadness. After a hectic decade in which his albums were often as uneven in quality

elton *john.*

MCAD-6321

sleep*ing with the past.*

Sleeping with the Past, released on August 29, 1989, pays homage to John and Taupin's forma-tive soul and rhythm-and-blues influences, including Ray Charles, Aretha Franklin, and the Drifters.   *Author's collection*

as they were inconsistent in musical style, John and lyricist Bernie Taupin wanted their last album of the eighties to reflect a unifying theme and mood. Recorded over six months at Puk Recording Studios in Denmark, *Sleeping with the Past* succeeded in reflecting the thematic consistency, not to mention the chemistry, John had with his band at the time.

"First he would put his idea down on the song with the keys, just to make sure that he was together on what he wanted to play," said bass-ist Romeo Williams, who played in the band at the time. "Then we all got together and started playing." The songs that emerged—hit singles "Club at the End of the Street," "Healing Hands," and "Sacrifice" among them—not only reflect the stylistic consistency John had striven for but also a renewed sense of creative vitality. "We were making history with him," Williams added. "With Elton, he's such a prolific writer. It's always such a pleasure to play with somebody that's innovative, that's different, that doesn't follow the norm. And that was him."

He'd no doubt written a modern classic in "Sacrifice," which earned him his first ever solo #1 single in Great Britain—his only previous UK chart-topper was his 1976 duet with Kiki Dee, "Don't Go Breaking My Heart"—and helped him close out the eighties on a well-earned artistic high.

22

Do They Know What It's Like to Have a Graveyard as a Friend?

Grief, Tragedy, and the Untimely Deaths of Famous Friends

As Elton John has demonstrated over the arc of his career, the more famous one gets, the more famous one's friends become. Similarly, when a famous friend dies, particularly in untimely or otherwise tragic circumstances, one often must grieve and express private pain in public. One parallel quote that comes to mind is from Pete Townshend, reflecting during the 1995 multi-part series, *The History of Rock and Roll*, "Look at my life, look at my generation. How did that work? Jimi Hendrix, Brian Jones, Janis Joplin, Keith Moon, the list is fucking endless. They're dead people, my life is full of dead people, my friends are dead—my friends! They might be your fucking icons, they're my fucking friends! They're dead!" Replace some of the names with those of other such icons, throw in a few fates of more violent demise, and the sentiment (not to mention the underlying stories) remains much the same.

Millions around the world reacted with abject shock and overpowering sadness at the untimely and sudden deaths of John Lennon and Princess Diana, to cite but two of the most conspicuous deaths of the past half-century. For John, however, he also mourned the loss of two dear, close friends.

Sadly, in mourning so many famous friends, John has endured grief attached to some truly heinous murders—a trend that revels in the underbelly of celebrity culture. "I would give everything I own and go back to starting again," he told ABC's Barbara Walters in 1997, after the recent deaths of Gianni Versace and Princess Diana, "if I could have my friends back."

Marc Bolan (Died: September 16, 1977)

Untamed youth blessed with luminous charisma, Marc Bolan exuded glam rock in all its decadent ecstasies. Far more successful and influential in his native Great Britain than in America, Bolan's mighty T. Rex inspired worshipful adulation from an army of ardent fans through an early seventies deluge of hit singles—"Children of the Revolution," "Get It On," and "20th Century Boy" among them—and enthralling live performances. Even as contemporaneous hits from David Bowie, Slade, the Sweet, and, yes, Elton John, cascaded around in his rarefied orbit with sequins to spare, Bolan remained glam rock's prettiest and for a time most popular star, a veritable icon of his era. John, who had performed (or mimed) "Get It On" along with his most cosmic friend during the December 27, 1971, episode of *Top of the Pops*, had paid homage to Bolan on "I'm Gonna Be a Teenage Idol," from his 1973 LP, *Don't Shoot Me I'm Only the Piano Player*, the same year he appeared along with mutual friend Ringo Starr, who directed a biographical film of Bolan's life, *Born to Boogie*.

Beneath the blue-hot haze of his own hero worship, though, Bolan contemplated more mortal concerns. Born Marc Feld, he had retreated from the spotlight, having witnessed his stardom falling as glam faded from acute public fascination. By the mid-seventies, Bowie had long since manifested into his "Plastic Soul" persona of *Young Americans*; Elton John was flying around the world on Led Zeppelin's airplane and selling out baseball stadiums along the way; both men had transcended their glitter rock flirtations as so many lesser artists descended into oblivion's ether. After three years spent in America as a tax exile, however, Bolan stood ready to reassert his singular talent and imagination back home. By the fall of 1977, he had taped an episode of his short-lived TV show, *Marc*, featuring Bowie and designed to reacquaint himself with his audience.

His ambitions would never flourish. On September 16, 1977, while en route to his Richmond home around 5:00 in the morning after spending the evening at a club called Morton's in London's Berkley Square, Bolan was the passenger in a purple Austin Mini 1275 GT driven by his girl-friend (and the mother of his only child, twenty-month-old Rolan Bolan), American soul singer Gloria Jones ("Tainted Love"). While driving over a bridge near Barnes rail station, less than a mile from their destination, Jones lost control, the Mini careening into a fence before colliding into a sycamore tree. Bolan, aged twenty-nine, died instantly; Jones survived, sustaining serious injuries including a broken jaw. Neither had been wearing a seatbelt. While hospitalized, she was told of Bolan's death on the day of his funeral at Golders Green Crematorium—attendants included Rod Stewart, David Bowie, and producer Tony Visconti—which occurred just four days after the accident, in keeping with the tenets of Bolan's Jewish heritage. Elton John, unable to attend, sent a bouquet.

John paid tribute to Bolan during his set at Live 8 in 2005, performing "Children of the Revolution" with Babyshambles lead singer Pete Doherty, the latter's ragged performance garnering scathing reviews and ironi-cally reaffirming how time had not extinguished the public's insatiable fascination with glam's greatest guru.

John Lennon (Died: December 8, 1980)

Only the most notorious political assassinations of the sixties, from JFK to MLK to RFK, rivaled the murder of John Lennon in terms of sheer newsworthiness and social impact. For Elton John, though, the severe grief felt by millions the world over following the breaking news of December 8, 1980—"The death of a man who sang and played the guitar overshadows the news from Poland, Iran, and Washington tonight," said Walter Cronkite as he opened the *CBS Evening News* the following night—was surpassed by the profound loss of a dear and beloved friend. Like so many others who remember exactly where they were when they first heard the news, his memory has remained strikingly clear.

"I was on a plane going from Brisbane to Melbourne, in Australia," John recalls in the 2007 documentary, *Me, Myself, and I*, "and when we

John Lennon Strawberry Fields mosaic   The Strawberry Fields memorial mosaic for John Lennon in
Central Park, New York City.   *Photo by Donald Gibson, Author's collection*

arrived in Melbourne, my manager, John Reid, came onto the plane. And someone made the announcement, 'Will all the Elton John party please stay onboard?' No one could believe it. It was a horrible, horrible moment, just one of disbelief—especially to be murdered."

Though he has performed it many times on many stages throughout the world, John summons a unique poignancy whenever he sings "Empty Garden (Hey, Hey Johnny)" in Madison Square Garden, not only recalling Lennon's last concert performance along with him on Thanksgiving of 1974 in that venue but also in memory of the life that was lost on that cold, December New York night.

Freddie Mercury (Died: November 24, 1991)

They shared similar tastes and eccentric compulsions, from drink to drugs to shopping. They shared the same manager, John Reid, for three years. They also shared a fondness for promiscuous sex in an era that proved lethal with the epidemic onset of AIDS.

Though he was one of the most irreverent, flamboyant front men in rock 'n' roll, Queen's Freddie Mercury fiercely guarded his privacy outside of his immediate social circle. In fact, he didn't publicly admit that he was battling AIDS until the day before his death at age forty-five on November 24, 1991, but he had confided in John when he was diagnosed in 1987. "I was devastated," John writes in his 2012 memoir, *Love Is the Cure: On Life, Loss, and the End of AIDS*. "I'd seen what the disease had done to so many of my other friends. I knew exactly what it was going to do to Freddie. As did he. He knew death, agonizing death, was coming."

Reflecting years later in a YouTube video, John not only recalled the many episodes of public extravagance and the ultra-macho stage persona that Mercury personified as if graced with the indomitable bombast of the gods, but also reminisced about the selflessness his friend exhibited in the throes of his own horrific demise. "He was still spending money and buying things at auction right up to the point that he died, which I thought was hilarious and probably the kind of thing I probably would do. But that Christmas just shortly after he died, I got a present delivered to me in a sheet. And I collect Henry Scott Tuke paintings. And it was a painting by Henry Scott Tuke from Freddie, saying, 'Dear Sharon, Hope you love this. Love, Melina.' I just completely broke down."

On April 20, 1992, less than five months after Mercury's death, John appeared at the Freddie Mercury Tribute Concert for AIDS Awareness before an estimated audience of seventy-two thousand people at Wembley Stadium. Festooned with all the outsized pomp and circumstance the late front man would have relished if not required for such an occasion, John joined the surviving members of Queen along with an avalanche of icons—David Bowie, Roger Daltrey, George Michael, Annie Lennox, and Robert Plant, to name but a few—to sing his praises, and his songs. Arm in arm with Axl Rose, John performed "Bohemian Rhapsody" before delivering a solo, stunning version of "The Show Must Go On," the latter of which also found a place on the setlist for John's extensive world tour in support of his 1992 LP, *The One*. Both performances provided a fitting prologue to a most rewarding friendship.

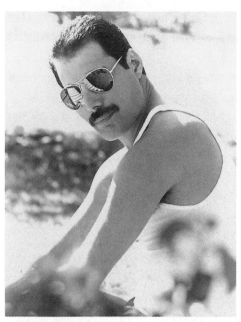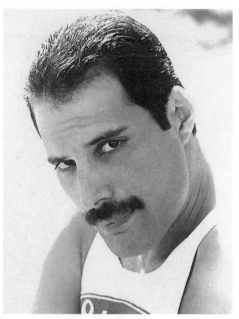

Publicity photographs of Queen front man Freddie Mercury. Among Mercury's closest friends, John was one of the few people to whom he confided his fatal diagnosis of HIV/AIDS in 1987. After a four-year battle, Mercury succumbed to AIDS-related pneumonia on November 24, 1991, aged forty-five. John celebrated his friend at the Freddie Mercury Tribute Concert at London's Wembley Stadium, singing "The Show Must Go On" and "Bohemian Rhapsody" with Axl Rose in his honor.

Author's collection

Gianni Versace (Died: July 15, 1997)

At the intersection of rock 'n' roll and fashion, Gianni Versace stood alone, towering above all rivals who dared step foot on his turf. Brandishing a vibrant confluence of rich culture and clothing flaunted by the era's preeminent supermodels—from Cindy Crawford to Christy Turlington to Naomi Campbell—the Italian fashion designer instigated provocative responses with his incendiary ideas and bold imagination. Along the way, he befriended Elton John, who in some respects had unwittingly personified much of what Versace had always envisioned for his own aesthetic—to integrate the seemingly stark and respective realms of popular music and high fashion.

The obvious parallels between Versace and Lennon's murders—and the manner in which John learned about both—were all too eerily similar for him not to acknowledge. "I got a phone call from John Reid, my manager, who also told me about John Lennon's death," John told the Pet Shop Boys' Neil Tennant, in a 1998 *Interview* magazine feature. "And as with Lennon, I just didn't believe it. I could not believe it. Gianni was such a huge part of my life. Two of my best creative friends have been murdered outside their fuckin' houses in America—Gianni and John."

In a scene grimly reminiscent of John Lennon's assassination at the entrance to his home at the Dakota building on Manhattan's Upper West Side, Italian fashion designer Gianni Versace was gunned down on the front steps of his Miami Beach mansion. Serial killer Andrew Cunanan, who had slayed four people on a murderous rampage before Versace, committed suicide on a houseboat shortly after. Versace had only recently survived a bout with a rare form of cancer of the inner ear.

In a press statement released in the immediate aftermath of the murder, John said, "I am devastated to have lost one of my closest friends, who I loved so much and who I had been so looking forward to seeing again on holiday very soon. We were so very close that it's like a large part of my life has died with him. I'm in deep shock at the news—it really hasn't sunk in yet. I feel so sorry for all of Gianni's family. The world has lost a wonderful creative genius, and I have lost a very dear friend." John dedicated *The Big Picture*, released later the same year, to Versace's memory.

At Versace's public memorial service on July 22, at Gothic Roman Catholic cathedral in Milan, John sat inconsolable in the pew, his partner, David Furnish, to his left; to his right sat Princess Diana, who in five weeks would herself be dead in a tragic incident, her life and spirit mourned the world over.

Princess Diana (Died: August 31, 1997)

From receiving a knighthood to performing in concert at Buckingham Palace, Elton John is no stranger to British royalty. However, in Princess Diana he found a genuine friend. The two met at Prince Andrew's birthday party in 1981, where they danced the Charleston (John, ever the shy boy from a council house in Pinner, reluctantly so), the princess and the rock star forging an unlikely yet enviable bond that more or less endured for nearly two decades. (Though they had fallen out briefly in the months before the murder of mutual friend Gianni Versace, Diana comforted a distraught Elton John at the fashion designer's memorial service.)

Arguably the paparazzi's top target to photograph, whether at public functions or in private getaways, Princess Diana had grown accustomed to (though not comfortable with) the rogue media attention that trailed her every move. Cash compensations for her photographs, depending on their location and context, had increased exponentially after Diana's divorce from Prince Charles was formalized on August 28, 1996, especially when photographers captured her with a potential (or even acknowledged) paramour.

Just over a year after the divorce, on August 31, 1997, the cost of Diana's fame proved lethal. Upon leaving the Hôtel Ritz Paris after previous attempts to dodge swarming paparazzi proved logistically problematic, Diana and her companion, Dodi Fayed, and bodyguard Trevor Rees-Jones were whisked away in a black Mercedes S280 driven by Henri Paul, the hotel's deputy head of security. Multiple contributing factors—the fact that Paul was intoxicated three-and-a-half times the legal limit in France, that he was speeding to evade encroaching photographers, that neither Diana nor Fayed were wearing seatbelts in the back seat—came to a head in the Pont de l'Alma tunnel, wherein, at 12:23 a.m., Paul lost control of the car, plowing head-on into a pillar. Fayed and Paul perished at the scene; Princess Diana died at 4:00 a.m. at the Pitié-Salpêtrière hospital, aged thirty-six.

On September 6, 1997, John was called on to console a reeling British nation and untold grieving millions around the world in the wake of Diana's tragic death. Tasked with singing a revised version of "Candle in the Wind," which Bernie Taupin wrote to eschew any mention of Marilyn Monroe in the song, lest it seem improper under the circumstances, John performed alone at piano during the memorial service at Westminster Abbey. Before a live audience of two thousand people in the cathedral—which included Queen Elizabeth II, Luciano Pavarotti, and George Michael—and a viewing audience of an estimated two billion worldwide, John sang one of his most familiar songs with a last-minute, mostly unfamiliar lyric, using a teleprompter to ensure he didn't mistakenly sing the original words out of habit.

Following the church service, John proceeded to Townhouse Studios in West London, where, with George Martin producing, he recorded a studio version of "Candle in the Wind 1997," which soon became the most successful single in British music history, and the second most successful single worldwide (Bing Crosby's "White Christmas" holds the top spot). It has sold thirty-three million copies to date, with proceeds for those sales going to various charities supported by Princess Diana.

George Michael (Died: December 25, 2016)

"I am in deep shock," John wrote in a statement posted online. "I have lost a beloved friend—the kindest, most generous soul and a brilliant artist."

John had followed Michael's musical career since the latter's earliest days in Wham!, even joining Michael and Andrew Ridgeley during the duo's final live concert at Wembley Stadium in 1986. The year prior, both men joined John for "Don't Let the Sun Go Down on Me" at Live Aid, in one of the most emotionally resonant moments of the benefit show.

Michael had been a massive fan of Elton John for most of his life, buying copies of such albums as *Blue Moves* on their day of release. His affinity for that album in particular emerged in two stunning live performances, the first from 1991, as witnessed at the Rock in Rio festival, in which Michael sang "Tonight," wrenching out its implicit desperation with each haunted verse, the performance later being chosen to close out the 1991 tribute LP, *Two Rooms: Celebrating the Songs of Elton John and Bernie Taupin*. The second performance, included on Michael's 2014 album, *Symphonica*, was "Idol," John's lament for a megastar falling out of fashion and, indeed, falling apart (in 1976, it was most likely Elvis Presley), rendered with uncanny empathy, and, as it turned out less than two years later, chilling prescience.

In John's first live performance since Michael's death, at Caesar's Palace in Las Vegas, he lamented the loss of his friend. "It was the most awful news because he was on the road back, supposedly, to good health," he said. "But apart from the music, which is outstanding, and for those of you who don't know his music go and listen to it. It stands up so brilliantly. What a singer. What a songwriter. But more than anything, as a human being, he was one of the kindest, sweetest, most generous people I've ever met."

Fresh with grief and fighting back tears, John suitably dedicated his next song, "Don't Let the Sun Go Down on Me," to the memory of Michael, adding, "I only wish he were here to sing it with me."

23

It's a Human Sign When Things Go Wrong

Demons and Addictions

S ad songs say so much, which is one reason why Elton John loves them more than happy, uplifting ones. His deep empathy for melancholy is no doubt connected to his own struggles through the years, including substance abuse and suicide attempts. Understanding these struggles through the lens of his songs (and without judgment) may perhaps shed light unto some of the music he has made, from somber moments to sardonic ones.

"Miserable songs are so great to write," John confided to *Noisey* in 2015. "I love writing them. It's much harder for me to write an up-tempo song than a misery song. We're all afraid to admit that part of our soul: that we want to fall in love with someone and we hate having our heart broken. It's a very masculine thing to soldier on in the face of adversity. But at the end of the day, it's like, 'Oh, I'm human, I do want to be loved, I do want to get well, I do want a happy life.' And music has carried that through."

There Were Times I Was Crazy, Couldn't Handle My Life

John first endured (or, perhaps, "enjoyed" is the more apt description, considering his willingness at the time) the charged effects of cocaine during an early trip to America in August of 1970, although he didn't realize it at the time. Attending a dinner at Three Dog Night's Danny Hutton's house in Laurel Canyon, along with the mercurial singer/songwriter Van

Dyke Parks, John stayed up until the following morning, seemingly with no problem—not knowing that Hutton had spiked his food. It would be nearly another four years before John would dabble (then drown) in cocaine by his own enthusiastic accord.

John snorted cocaine, he has said, not necessarily for the unvarnished rush or the energy jolt it generally gives users, but rather as an aphrodisiac with intimate partners. Nevertheless, even that purpose lost its appeal as his exorbitant use spiraled further out of control.

What a Scandal If I Died

John's two most publicized suicide attempts include an incident from 1968, when he shared a residence in Furlong Road with his fiancé, Linda Ann Woodrow, and Bernie Taupin. Overwhelmed by his impending nuptials, he placed a pillow in an open oven and switched on the gas, like Sylvia Plath—except he'd left the windows open wide. Taupin discovered him and laughed at the predicament.

His other well-known attempt came when he swallowed a bottle of sleeping pills and dived into a hotel swimming pool. His grandmother reportedly scoffed, "Well, I guess we can go home now." (Brits aren't known for weeping sentimentality or melodrama.) He was rescued and escorted to the hospital, where his stomach was pumped, and the next day he performed before fifty-five thousand people at his inaugural concert at Dodger Stadium. "I Think I'm Gonna Kill Myself" seems ironically prescient in retrospect, while "Someone Saved My Life Tonight" now cuts an all-the-more compassionate tone.

In an echo of his conflicted childhood, John didn't possess the perspective or necessary tools to cope with or make sense of his most troubling emotions. Indeed, the catalyst for changing his own life first emerged when he reached out to help someone else.

24

I'm Strangled by Your Haunted Social Scene

The Philanthropist

Elton John is arguably the world's most prominent, visible advocate for HIV/AIDS research, prevention, and potential cure. Aware of and concerned by the HIV/AIDS epidemic arguably sooner than most other celebrities—though, as he has conceded, not soon enough for his own liking, in retrospect—John over the past thirty years has evolved from participating in select humanitarian acts and events to embracing a more personal and immediate approach. As the founder of the Elton John AIDS Foundation, he has sought to mitigate the crisis not just by raising money for and awareness of the calamitous autoimmune disease, but by providing practical day-to-day support to those it most affects.

John's prime-time appearance at Live Aid in 1985 wasn't directly related to HIV/AIDS awareness at the time, but the power of celebrity-driven philanthropy must have nonetheless resonated with him, the event underscoring the interconnectedness of the world's citizens, regardless of social or economic distinctions. His involvement in the benefit single "That's What Friends Are For" (along with Dionne Warwick, Gladys Knight, and Stevie Wonder) was a harbinger of things to come, including the establishment of the Elton John AIDS Foundation (which would benefit, in part, from the profits from all of John's singles), the annual Elton John AIDS Foundation Academy Awards Viewing Party, and his all-star tennis ("Smash Hits") exhibitions. In the late eighties, John's brief friendship with HIV-infected teenager Ryan White was a prime, public catalyst in his philanthropic efforts to combat the AIDS epidemic.

Live Aid

On July 13, 1985, at Wembley Stadium in London and JFK Stadium in Philadelphia, Live Aid boasted one of the all-time biggest rosters in rock 'n' roll, with proceeds from the benefit concerts—which were organized by former Boomtown Rats front man Bob Geldof and Ultravox's Midge Ure—supporting Ethiopian famine relief. While the Philadelphia assemblage included anticipated appearances by the likes of Madonna, Eric Clapton, and Led Zeppelin (in their first set since drummer John Bonham's death five years prior), very few of the performances lived up to the preshow hype. Most of the magic was happening in the UK, with performances

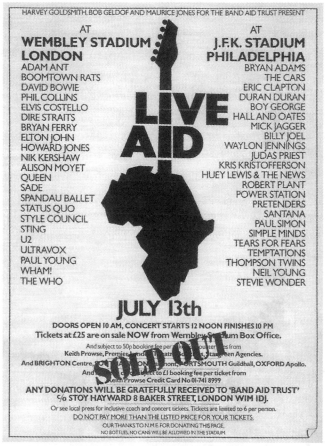

A Live Aid advertisement boasting the scheduled roster of the transatlantic performances on July 13, 1985, at JFK Stadium in Philadelphia and Wembley Stadium in London.   *Author's collection*

by U2, David Bowie, and Dire Straits electrifying the more than seventy thousand fans inside Wembley Stadium, and the nearly two billion more watching on television from home. Queen, in particular, delivered a transcendent and career-defining set, with front man Freddie Mercury summoning breathtaking vocal agility and cocksure irreverence.

By the time John sauntered on, at nearly 9:00 in the evening, wearing a glitzy black-and-red coat with pillbox hat that Freddie Mercury had jokingly said made him look like the Queen Mother, the energy in the stadium was on the wane. Still, John pleased the teeming masses, and, as one of the select few prime-time performers, inspired his fans at home to donate plenty of money to the charitable cause at hand.

In the middle of his world tour in support of *Ice on Fire*, which featured George Michael on both "Nikita" and "Wrap Her Up," John welcomed the Wham! lead singer onstage (Michael in turn brought on his Wham! partner, Andrew Ridgeley, who sang backup) to sing "Don't Let the Sun Go Down on Me," a performance that would prove one of the more memorable of the day, while yielding the most enduring musical moment between the two good friends at center stage.

Honoring the wishes of the concert's creators that each act be a "human jukebox" that delivered the hits, John stuck with what worked in his twenty-minute set: "I'm Still Standing," "Bennie and the Jets," "Rocket Man," "Don't Go Breaking My Heart" (with Kiki Dee), "Don't Let the Sun Go Down on Me," and then, just for fun, or perhaps to underscore the event's more sobering subtext, Marvin Gaye's Motown standard "Can I Get a Witness."

"That's What Friends Are For"

Despite the climate of such philanthropic mid-eighties events as Live Aid and blockbuster benefit singles like "Do They Know It's Christmas?" and "We Are the World," the ever-looming specter and disastrous consequences of AIDS—acquired immune deficiency syndrome—registered barely a blip in the general culture. That a pop song might raise not only awareness about this devastating epidemic but also sorely needed funds as a means to combat its insidious spread seemed like a long shot.

Aside from the song's charitable ambitions, just the lineup had to have struck John as soul-music heaven; the opportunity to sing alongside Dionne Warwick, Gladys Knight, and Stevie Wonder most certainly was a dream come true for the boy from Pinner, who had probably listened to their records in his bedroom as a child.

The song, originally recorded in 1982 by Rod Stewart for the soundtrack to the film, *Night Shift*, found fresh legs when Warwick was working with her old mentor, Burt Bacharach, with whom she had recorded such classic sides as "The Windows of the World," "Alfie," and "I'll Never Fall in Love Again." At first, Warwick considered recording the song as a duet with Stevie Wonder, with whom she'd recorded three songs ("Moments Aren't Moments," "It's You," and "Weakness") for his 1984 soundtrack to the motion picture, *The Woman in Red*. However, once the song's proceeds were repurposed to benefit Elizabeth Taylor's charity AmfAR (the American Foundation for AIDS Research), Bacharach and his co-writer (and wife), Carole Bayer Sager, felt more star power was in order. Gladys Knight proved an appropriate fit, along with—at first, at least—Luther Vandross.

In her 2016 autobiography, *They're Playing Our Song: A Memoir*, Sager hails Vandross as a "great R&B singer, but his vocal [on 'That's What Friends Are For'], though excellent, still left us wanting that cleanup batter to hit it out of the park."

Vandross was accordingly cut from the track, after which Bacharach and Sager consulted Arista Records CEO Clive Davis, who suggested Elton John for the job. John, who also played keyboards on the track (which was recorded at Conway Recording Studios in Hollywood), delivered, Sager writes, "a vocal so undeniably brilliant that on listening back to what would soon be the entire record, [John] said, 'If this record is not a fucking #1 song, I am leaving the business.'"

"That's What Friends Are For," credited to Dionne Warwick and Friends and appearing on Warwick's LP, *Friends*, spent four weeks at #1 on the *Billboard* Hot 100 chart in January 1986, earned over three million dollars for AmfAR, and won twice over at the 29th Annual Grammy Awards: "Best Pop Performance by a Duo or Group with Vocal" and "Song of the Year." For Elton John, whose music had been nominated dozens of times in the most prestigious categories since his eponymous 1970 debut album, these awards for "That's What Friends are For" were his first ever wins.

Elton John AIDS Foundation

By 1985, the biggest problem in Elton John's life was Elton John. Having nursed a nasty drug habit for more than a decade, his music—the one consistent, positive force in his life—suffered as a result. That year, he read a magazine article about a young boy in Kokomo, Indiana, named Ryan White, who was born with hemophilia and later contracted HIV from a treatment of factor VIII. Learning about how White and his family—his mother, Jeanne and his sister, Andrea—were enduring a barrage of small-town bigotry and random acts of violence perpetuated by neighbors who were ignorant of what HIV or AIDS actually meant or entailed, John reached out, feeling compelled to help in any way he could. In his benevolence, John gained insight into his self-destructive troubles as well as a treasured, invaluable friendship. "The Whites were a blue-collar family through and through, much like my own family growing up," he writes in *Love Is the Cure: On Life, Loss, and the End of AIDS,* "which is perhaps why I instantly connected with them when we finally got to know one another."

John had known others who had died from HIV and AIDS, but Ryan White symbolized the cruel scope of the viruses, as well as the compassion that was required in treating those they afflicted. For John, White was more than a friend; he was also the prime catalyst for facing demons John had long needed to address in his own life, as well as the spark behind his creation of the Elton John AIDS Foundation.

Established in 1992 in Atlanta, Georgia, the Elton John AIDS Foundation, a nonprofit organization, was conceived with the idea of helping those who needed it not just through financial means but also through day-to-day assistance like providing food, shelter, and legal and medicinal treatment.

"The mission I decided on," John writes in *Love Is the Cure,* "was to provide funding such basic programs, with the ultimate goal of reducing the incidence of HIV/AIDS, eliminating the stigma and discrimination associated with the disease, and providing direct treatment and care services to HIV-positive people, to allow them to live with dignity."

Another catalyst for his burgeoning need to help bring awareness and compassion to the AIDS epidemic was his own absence in the growing movement up until that point. During a speech at Harvard University on November 6, 2017, following his acceptance of the institution's "Humanitarian of the Year" award, he recalled, "During my addiction in the nineteen eighties, the AIDS epidemic surfaced, and was quite horrific for everyone involved. And I was in such a haze, I didn't do anything. I never marched with them, I never got in touch with them, and I had that shame when I got sober that I had to do something to put things right. I wanted redemption."

"American Triangle"

As the most topically provocative moment on John's stellar 2001 LP, *Songs from the West Coast*, "American Triangle" was written about Matthew Shepard, the gay University of Wyoming student who, on October 12, 1998, at the age of twenty-one, died from injuries sustained five nights earlier in a savage, torturous assault. Rufus Wainwright, also gay, sang backup on the track. The song was later featured in the 2002 NBC television film, *The Matthew Shepard Story*.

On April 3, 2009, John played a benefit concert in Laramie dedicated to Shepard's memory. The song conjures notions of identity along with visual themes of the pastoral American landscape—two distinctions Taupin has explored throughout his lyrics in prevalent ways, ever since *Tumbleweed Connection*. The awareness raised by "American Triangle" through record sales alone—*Songs from the West Coast* has sold upward of three-and-a-half million copies worldwide—cannot be overstated.

25

You Put the Spark to the Flame

Forty Most Underrated Deep Cuts

In the seventies, one couldn't go five minutes without encountering an Elton John song on the radio. Most often, though, such songs were the singles. Hardcore fans, however, scoured the albums for less popular but no less worthwhile fare, dropping the needle on songs John likely wouldn't perform on arena or stadium stages. All such lists are subjective, of course, but in the spirit of debate, this chapter offers this forthcoming list of Elton John's forty most underrated deep cuts.

40. "Japanese Hands" (*Reg Strikes Back*, 1988)

Every new and burgeoning romance begins as a foreign experience until at once it is familiar. One of the underrated highlights of 1988's *Reg Strikes Back*, "Japanese Hands" summons the mystique inherent to the physical mystery of an unfolding intimate affair. Its lyrics suggest consummation in the Far East, each tactile sensation—"Flesh on silk looks different than on a cotton sheet back home"—throwing heated signals between new, eager lovers.

39. "Dark Diamond" (*Songs from the West Coast*, 2001)

Featuring Stevie Wonder on harmonica (marking his third such appearance on a track on which John sings, after "I Guess That's Why They Call It the Blues" and "That's What Friends Are For"), "Dark Diamond" finds John contemplating a series of misfortunes as a good thing stands to finally snap his bad spell. "Spent all of my life trying to get it right," he sings. "I've put it together and it falls apart."

38. "Honey Roll" (*Friends* soundtrack, 1971)

Funky like a Fats Domino ode to New Orleans, this swinging little stand-out from the *Friends* soundtrack would fit right in on *Honky Château* or *Madman Across the Water*—which is the album it was actually destined for in the first place.

37. "Looking Up" (*Wonderful Crazy Night*, 2014)

Having set out to make an upbeat, joyous album that harkened back to his seventies classics, John may have set his sights a bit too high. Yet with this particular song, the man hit the mark, turning out a choo-choo train (à la *Soul Train*) rhythm that alone would be enough to rouse a sleeping beast to boogie down.

36. "Old 67" (*The Captain and the Kid*, 2006)

In the Summer of Love, as *Sgt. Pepper's Lonely Hearts Club Band* blasted from passing cars and opened-wide apartment windows on the suburban streets of England, an untested lyricist from rural Lincolnshire was introduced to a timid keyboardist from suburban Pinner, the latter ultimately changing his name to Elton John. "What a time that was, what a time of innocence," John sang over a barrelhouse blues motif a half-century later, his now-seasoned singing voice brimming with nostalgia for that most decisive year of his life, underscoring the distance he and Taupin have traveled together as co-composers and, ultimately, mutual survivors.

35. "My Elusive Drug" (*Peachtree Road*, 2004)

In what sounds like a reckoning, John recounts his past sins as if to a lover who sees such confessions not as flaws but as senseless insecurities. On an album suffused with Southern imagery and motifs, "My Elusive Drug" simmers like a Stax or Atlantic Records throwback, shrouding its brooding self-reflection in hot-blooded soul.

34. "In Neon" (*Breaking Hearts*, 1984)

In the wake of the huge success of 1983's *Too Low for Zero*, which included such worldwide hit singles as "I Guess That's Why They Call It the Blues" and "I'm Still Standing," John's next LP, *Breaking Hearts*, seemed like a bit of a letdown. Regardless, "In Neon" is as melodically affecting as anything he had composed to date, and Taupin's lyric—telling the story of a woman aching to be noticed and appreciated—holds up among his finest as well.

33. "Stone's Throw from Hurtin'" (*Sleeping with the Past*, 1989)

Patterned after "I Heard It Through the Grapevine"—most likely Marvin Gaye's sinewy, slow-burning masterwork rather than Gladys Knight's more rambunctious rendition—this one finds John whispering the vocal, his upper register forever lowered after throat surgery in 1987. His performance is at once alarming yet indisputably hip, making for a soft soul throwback unlike anything in his catalogue.

32. "Empty Sky" (*Empty Sky*, 1969)

For those paying attention to his debut album, their first impression of Elton John—from the opening track—would likely have been of a psychedelic rocker, not a pianist prone to the subtleties of melodic pop. One of his longest compositions, clocking in at over eight minutes, "Empty Sky" rages and simmers like something Santana or Joe Cocker would have performed at Woodstock.

31. "Wasteland" (*Songs from the West Coast*, 2001)

A piano-pounding, pile-driving blues on which John sounds like he is documenting the aftermath of an apocalyptic hell, "Wasteland" is the product of a stone-cold survivor.

30. "House" (*Made in England*, 1995)

Insecurity compels one to cling to whatever offers a sense of peace of mind. While reciting, almost as a child describing his surroundings, the places he feels most comfortable and safe, John ponders the profoundest of thoughts. "What is my soul?" he sings, further immersing himself in his own room at the top of the world. Complemented by a bare-bones piano-based arrangement, "House" is at turns reassuring and strikingly poignant.

29. "Shine on Through" (*A Single Man*, 1978)

The first song John recorded after retiring from making and performing music in order to focus more on his role at Watford Football Club, "Shine on Through" marked the first time he had collaborated with a lyricist besides Bernie Taupin. With lyrics by Gary Osborne (who would go on to write the words to "Blue Eyes" and "Little Jeannie," among others), the sprawling ballad is among John's most unwavering love songs.

28. "Freaks in Love" (*Peachtree Road*, 2004)

On *Peachtree Road*, John set most of its songs in the South, drawing on gospel and country and rhythm-and-blues motifs, while a windmill of related imagery—porch swings and Elvis, humidity and Sunday church services—shines through. In such a light, "Freaks in Love" is like a Flannery O'Connor short story, as it empathizes with the bond shared between lost souls, resounding like a proud affirmation for all manner of misfits and outcasts.

27. "The Power" (*Duets*, 1993)

Not many moments on *Duets* transcend the initial intrigue of learning how a particular song is performed or how a certain collaboration sounds, but "The Power" is one of them. A full-circle moment if ever there was one, here John trades verses with one of his childhood idols, Little Richard, who instead of singing in the high-pitched holler of "Lucille" and "Good Golly Miss Molly" sings in his natural, guttural tone. Adding to the excitement are the song's gospel resolve and socially conscientious lyrics, culminating in one of John's most captivating nineties performances.

26. "Idol" (*Blue Moves*, 1976)

The toll taken on those who pursue superstardom is sometimes self-destructive, and, all too often, lethal. Elton John—along with his mother, Sheila Farebrother, who had bought her son the 78 of "Hound Dog" that in part ignited his rock 'n' roll fantasies—famously met Elvis Presley before one of the King's concerts in Washington, D.C., in 1976. Both were shocked by Presley's bloated, exhausted condition, his once-ribald eyes sunken in his head. Farebrother predicted that Presley would soon be dead. On "Idol," John laments Presley's declining vigor and significance, while at the same time celebrating his incalculable effect as a rock 'n' roll icon more than twenty years before, expressing with poignancy the sadness of witnessing a larger-than-life falling star.

25. "Burning Buildings" (*Breaking Hearts*, 1984)

What is left to hope for when one's hope runs out? John contemplates such a despondent fate on the impassioned final track from 1984's *Breaking Hearts*, summoning one of his most searing, soulful performances of the decade. Yet in its plea for something genuine—"How long before the pain ends?" John sings, "Tell me when living starts"—"Burning Buildings" offers no resolutions to mitigate such existential duress.

24. "Elton's Song" (*The Fox*, 1981)

A rhapsodic ode to unrequited love (perhaps a first love), this song conjures all the melodramatic insecurity and self-doubt that swirls inside the narrator. "It was very homoerotic," John told *Rolling Stone* in 2013. "I could imagine the boy that I wanted to be, on the parallel bars, swinging with his tight little outfit on and his bare feet. It was the first gay song that I actually recorded as a homosexual song."

23. "Did Anybody Sleep with Joan of Arc?" (B-side to "This Train Don't Stop There Anymore," 2001)

A good storyteller finds innovative ways to tell familiar tales, and with this obscurity from the *Songs from the West Coast* sessions, Taupin demonstrates why he is one. Portraying Joan of Arc almost like a teen idol ("bigger than Elvis in her day") who symbolized virtues and strengths for others, he ponders whether she ever was loved for the human being she was and not what she may have represented. John then married the words to one of his most stirring melodies of recent years, his vocal resonating with the conviction the song deserves.

22. "Chameleon" (*Blue Moves*, 1976)

While hundreds of artists have recorded covers from the John–Taupin songbook, in the seventies the team fielded far more requests to write original songs for other artists. Having resisted such calls after their dissatisfying turn at composing for the likes of Lulu and Engelbert Humperdinck in the fledgling days of their professional partnership, they accepted the Beach Boys' offer in 1975. While composing a melody normally took John no longer than half an hour, "Chameleon" took six months. Perhaps humbled by the specter of writing for Brian Wilson's group, he struggled in painstaking detail, subconsciously striving to please him. Upon presenting the song to the group, however, they declined it. John then recorded his own version, including it on *Blue Moves* the following year.

21. "The North" (*The One*, 1992)

Indefinable and elusive—"There's a North in us all," John sings, "But my North can't hold me anymore"—this song could be about childhood, or perhaps a longstanding burden; some metaphorical origin or the literal place of one's birth. Regardless, the ballad's abstractions lend to its authenticity, giving listeners the opportunity to find meanings beyond what its songwriters may have had in mind.

20. "I Need You to Turn To" (*Elton John*, 1970)

Having graduated from writing lyrics heavy on surrealistic imagery of the late sixties' flower-power era, Bernie Taupin honed the verbosity into concise, chiseled vignettes. With "I Need You to Turn To," he rendered his most honest and direct love song to date. John resurrected it from relative obscurity nearly two decades after it appeared on his 1970 self-titled album, recapturing its subdued production (courtesy of Gus Dudgeon) and orchestral arrangement (courtesy of Paul Buckmaster) on his 1987 tour of Australia with the Melbourne Symphony Orchestra (arranged and conducted by James Newton Howard), where he delivered arguably its definitive version.

19. "Oceans Away" (*The Diving Board*, 2013)

The Diving Board exemplifies John and Taupin reaching a new peak with their craft in their later years, composing songs that come not from a perpetually young rock 'n' roll perspective but rather a distinctly adult one. "Oceans Away" stands out among its most affecting moments, Taupin's lyrics written in tribute to both his late father, who fought in World War II, and the Greatest Generation in general. Altogether, the song celebrates those who so selflessly sacrificed while fighting the ignoble force of fascism in the twentieth century's most crucial conflict.

18. "The Greatest Discovery" (*Elton John*, 1970)

A marvel of both musical craft and lyrical economy, Taupin here conjured in keen detail (as if from a short story) a set of lyrics based on what he experienced as a child when his younger brother spent his first moments at home after he was born. Like the finest writers, he turns a personal story into a profoundly universal one.

17. "Roy Rogers" (*Goodbye Yellow Brick Road*, 1973)

Despite teeming with nostalgia and recollecting a child's wide-eyed fascination with western legends and comic book heroes, "Roy Rogers" is really about adult regret and missed opportunities. As the song suggests, while a television's silver screen may provide an enthralling distraction—a means to recall old glories and memories that once served to thrill one's soul—the remorse still remains.

16. "Hercules" (*Honky Château*, 1972)

Nothing more than a rollicking, swift blast of rock 'n' roll, "Hercules" in a way recalls glam-era David Bowie on "John, I'm Only Dancing," sending teenage girls into a frenzy and blowing off some steam.

15. "Holiday Inn" (*Madman Across the Water*, 1971)

Chronicling the itinerant life of a traveling musician, John sings of the repetitious stops between concert stages, where the cities are a blur and the beds offer but a temporary respite from the circus life. "Slow down, Joe, I'm a rock 'n' roll man," he sings, summoning at once the exhaustion that lies just under the surface, and the resilience that stands to keep him indefinitely on the road.

14. "Never Too Old (to Hold Somebody)" (*The Union*, 2010)

Reminiscent of the mossy, darkly embossed ballads from both John's *Tumbleweed Connection* and Leon Russell's *Will o' the Wisp*, this one could have been a classic, had it been written and released forty years ago. It's still well worth appreciating now, however.

13. "Amoreena" (*Tumbleweed Connection*, 1971)

After the *Elton John* album in 1970, with its austere orchestral arrangements, John and Taupin looked toward America for musical and lyrical influences redolent of its Old West mythology and the emergent country-rock movement, as summoned by the likes of the Band. Named for manager Ray Williams's newborn daughter, "Amoreena" was among the first such fruitions on which John and Taupin (whom Williams named his daughter's godfathers) melded their singular mixtures of country, gospel, and funky-soul traits, culminating in a must-get-back-to-my-baby classic.

12. "A Woman's Needs" (*Duets*, 1993)

If *Duets* as an album didn't quite live up to its fullest potential overall, this specific duet, with Tammy Wynette, more than exceeded it. The country icon delivers her quintessential vulnerability with such unadulterated grace that listening to her sounds like eavesdropping on a relationship disintegrating in real time.

11. "Sugar on the Floor" (B-side to "Island Girl," 1975)

The only song on this list not musically composed by John, "Sugar on the Floor," written by Kiki Dee, was first featured on her 1973 LP, *Loving and Free*, in a country-and-western arrangement that John, guitarist Davey Johnstone, and bassist Dee Murray, among others, pulled off with aplomb. For the B-side to "Island Girl," a single from 1975's *Rock of the Westies*, John rearranged it into a sparse, piano-driven ballad, performing it from an entirely fresh and exhilarating perspective.

10. "Indian Sunset" (*Madman Across the Water*, 1971)

One of Paul Buckmaster's finest achievements as an arranger, this ambitious track illustrates the synthesis of orchestral and pop-music elements that John's music had first proposed on 1970's *Elton John*. An epic melding of the Old West themes introduced on *Tumbleweed Connection* with a sweeping Native American saga, the song was resurrected during John's most recent Las Vegas production, *The Million Dollar Piano*.

9. "Curtains" (*Captain Fantastic and the Brown Dirt Cowboy*, 1975)

On this, the final track on *Captain Fantastic and the Brown Dirt Cowboy*, John relates his and Taupin's shared history as aspirant songwriters in the late sixties—including a nod to "Scarecrow," the first song the pair ever wrote—by calling on universal refrains of nostalgia and the enchantment of children's fairytales. Such thematic parallels are cunning, appropriate, and, in the context of the song, performed with a full, emphatic flourish.

8. "Harmony" (*Goodbye Yellow Brick Road*, 1973)

Closing a double album that deceptively conjures scenes of murder, memorials, and unmitigated violence, "Harmony" almost seems incongruent. As a pop song, though, it's among John's most beloved, and rightfully so.

7. "Ticking" (*Caribou*, 1974)

Inspired by the rise of gun-related violence in America in the mid-seventies, Taupin wrote lyrics describing scenes of everyday nightmares. That the song seems more attuned to the violent climate in the States today—random mass shootings, the political assertions of the National Rifle Association in American civil discourse—is eerily remarkable. That the song still resonates musically is quite simply a testament to great songwriting.

6. "Sixty Years On" (*Elton John*, 1970)

Predicting a grim and harrowingly lonesome old age, "Sixty Years On" speaks of mortality without companionship. "I've no wish to be living," John sings, from a young man's perspective, of the uncounted decades yet to unfold, his voice seething with resentment. On "When I'm Sixty-Four," the Beatles (or, more appropriately, Paul McCartney) sounded relatively assured that the future will turn out fine, that someone will be there to care. In "Sixty Years On," John offers no such illusions.

5. "Have Mercy on the Criminal" (*Don't Shoot Me I'm Only the Piano Player*, 1973)

This riveting performance is galvanized by Paul Buckmaster's indefatigable arrangement, with strings emboldening the dire lyric's unyielding suspense thick in the heat of the hunt. And then there's John's tormented vocal, its bloodcurdling desperation resounding like an eleventh-hour plea from the edge of his own crypt, once and for all sealing the lawless narrator's fate.

4. "Blues for Baby and Me" (*Don't Shoot Me I'm Only the Piano Player*, 1973)

There is more to life than what the narrator and his sweetheart are living for here. With its unmitigated sense of escapism, of a young couple lighting out on their own, leaving their watchful parents' eye in order to lay claim to their own life, "Blues for Baby and Me" is Bruce Springsteen's "Thunder Road," but with a different means of transportation. They've got one last chance to make it real, too, and these young lovers opt for the bus rather than a four-wheeled dream machine, but either way, by the end of the song, they're still pulling out of here to win.

3. "We All Fall in Love Sometimes" (*Captain Fantastic and the Brown Dirt Cowboy*, 1975)

Here, in one of John's most piercing, unflinchingly tender affirmations, he lays his emotions on the line with unaffected solemnity. "I cry when I sing this song," he confided to Cameron Crowe in *Rolling Stone* in 2013, "because I was in love with Bernie, not in a sexual way, but because he was the person I was looking for my entire life, my little soul mate. We'd come so far, and we were still very naïve."

2. "Tonight" (*Blue Moves*, 1976)

Expressing the anguish felt when a relationship collapses before one's eyes, this nearly eight-minute epic is the prime example in Elton John's catalogue of the whole being greater than the sum of its parts. In lyrics written by Taupin during his divorce-doomed estrangement from his first wife, Maxine (with whom John's bassist, Kenny Passarelli, was engaged in a clandestine affair), the song achieves its greatest strength in expressing such human vulnerability. James Newton Howard's orchestral arrangement adds to the already cinematic context, his employment of strings in particular escalating the sense of despondency underscored throughout to unnerving detail. Altogether, "Tonight" is the masterpiece of *Blue Moves*.

1. "Street Kids" (*Rock of the Westies*, 1975)

Corrosive, sandblasting six-strings, a riotous tale of urban gang warfare . . . Dorothy, we have ditched the *Yellow Brick Road*. With the dismissal of bassist Dee Murray and drummer Nigel Olsson in favor of bassist Kenny Passarelli, drummer Roger Pope, and guitarist Caleb Quaye, John sought to achieve a more rock-oriented balance in his band. "Street Kids" is the most resounding manifestation of that desire. "The guitar solo I did on there was cut live," says Quaye. "The whole track was done live."

In fact, prior to the *Rock of the Westies* recording sessions at Caribou Ranch, the band had been on the road, galvanizing their talents into a potent operation. "You can hear the energy on there," says Quaye. "I mean, we're fresh off of the tour. We were on top of the mountain."

26

I'm a Bitch, I'm a Bitch, I'm Better Than You

Infamous Feuds and Fallouts

Elton John's temper first erupted in early childhood, maybe as an emotional consequence of growing up in an often chaotic home disrupted by his parents' constant marital discord. He is so renowned for his colossal mood swings and infuriated outbursts, in fact, that the 1997 documentary, *Tantrums and Tiaras* struck die-hard fans less as a surprise than as a probable and often hilarious corroboration. Indeed, John has pitched such huge hissy fits, raised such holy hell, and instigated such stubborn grudges that few others dare to take him on.

These are the ones that have made the newspapers, providing grist for the tabloid mill—Elton John's most infamous grudges and public feuds.

Keith Richards

"The Beatles want to hold your hand," journalist Tom Wolfe once wrote. "The Stones want to burn your town." From their first snarling riff, the Rolling Stones emanated menace and cockiness, their slightly disheveled appearances and fuck-all insouciance toward authority and establishment figures underscored the band's identity in ways that would never fade, even as the band itself succumbed to mortality, and, on occasion, caricatured monotony. To this day, rhythm guitarist Keith Richards in particular evokes a don't-mess-with-me bravado, his grizzled skin and unkempt gray hair underscoring an implicit subversiveness that, like the man himself, refuses to die.

Of course, rock 'n' roll—at its most fundamental—was subversive, too. Whether it came from Little Richard or Elvis Presley or Jerry Lee Lewis, it challenged the most conservative conventions of sex, gender, and authority with unrivaled irreverence. Assuming the mantle as if it were a generational call to arms, the Rolling Stones continued to set the status quo smack-dab within their line of fire. Times change, most men and women mellow with age, but Richards has remained defiantly anti-establishment. When fellow Stone Mick Jagger was knighted by Queen Elizabeth II in 2002, Richards publicly scoffed at the honor. "I thought it was ludicrous to take one of those gongs from the Establishment," he told *Uncut* magazine, "when they did their very best to throw us in jail."

So, when a reporter asked the guitarist about Elton John having performed a revised version of "Candle in the Wind" at Westminster Abbey during the funeral for Diana, Princess of Wales, Richards didn't mince words. "His writing is limited to songs for dead blondes," he said.

John, bemused, shot back. "I'm glad I've given up drugs and alcohol. It would be awful to be like Keith Richards," he said in sardonic response. "He's pathetic. It's like a monkey with arthritis, trying to go onstage and look young."

Tina Turner

Rehearsals are a time for working out the kinks, for making sure everyone's on the same page and playing the correct parts. However, when "honorary diva" Elton John and Tina Turner hit a snag on the latter's signature rendition of "Proud Mary" during preparations for *VH1 Divas Live '99*, which boasted such superstars as Whitney Houston, Faith Hill, and Cher, at New York City's Beacon Theatre, practice didn't lead to perfect—it led to all-out war. With the two icons already booked for a joint summer tour, their combined performance of "The Bitch Is Back" and "Proud Mary" was to be the show's climactic moment. It almost didn't happen, though.

John and Turner's friendship extended back decades, both icons having appeared in the 1975 film adaptation of the Who's *Tommy*—John singing "Pinball Wizard," Turner singing "Acid Queen"—as well as sharing the stage at the Prince's Trust concert in June 1986; Turner also appeared in the 1991 *Two Rooms* documentary, covering "The Bitch Is Back," as she'd done countless times onstage over the preceding years. In 1999, Turner took part in the all-star soundtrack composed by Tim Rice and Elton John for the Disney animated feature, *Aida*, singing "Easy as Life," with Beninese singer/songwriter Angélique Kidjo singing backup. John and Turner's friendship and working relationship was at its strongest.

"I made a mistake when I needed to show him how to play 'Proud Mary'—the mistake is you don't show Elton John how to play his piano," Turner recalled to Mike Wallace on *60 Minutes*. "He just went into a rage."

"I don't tell you how to sing," John was reported to have said. "You don't tell me how to play piano."

Incensed, John stormed offstage, and Turner soon followed, the two legends allegedly shouting back and forth in a dressing room out of view (but not earshot) of various assembled music journalists, photographers, and members of the television-production crew. They returned to the stage several minutes later, having made at least tentative amends, and the rehearsal—and, most importantly, their performance later that night—proceeded as planned, with nary a hitch. The damage was done, though, as Turner subsequently canceled the planned concert tour, and she hasn't shared a stage with Elton John ever since.

David Bowie

In the early seventies, David Bowie and Elton John reigned as glam-rock icons, their every outburst and outfit landing on the front pages of the music press. Behind the scenes, though, their similar eccentricities and styles overshadowed a fractious relationship.

"David [Bowie] and I were not the best of friends towards the end," John told the *Evening Standard* in 2016, following the British icon's death. "We started out being really good friends. We used to hang out together with Marc Bolan, going to gay clubs, but I think we just drifted apart. He once called me 'rock 'n' roll's token queen' in an interview with *Rolling Stone*, which I thought was a bit snooty."

Bowie also said, "I consider myself responsible for a whole new school of pretensions—they know who they are. Don't you, Elton?"

In a 1976 *Rolling Stone* feature, Bowie expounded to journalist and future filmmaker Cameron Crowe on his belief that rock 'n' roll was inherently (or, at least generally) "the devil's music" and, in response, Crowe asked Bowie if he thought Mick Jagger—Mr. "Sympathy for the Devil" himself—was evil. "Mick himself? Oh Lord no," Bowie replied. "He's not unlike Elton John, who represents the token queen—like Liberace used to. No, I don't think Mick is evil at all."

Bowie's flippant line about John, who at this point had yet to concede his bisexuality, instigated a rift that would endure until the end of the Thin White Duke's life. There would be fleeting hints of reconciliation (or at least cordiality) in the interim decades, such as when the two British

A publicity photograph of David Bowie dated 1977.   *Author's collection*

legends were caught on camera in a seemingly amicable conversation prior to their appearances at the 1992 Freddie Mercury Tribute Concert, but they never reestablished the bond they once shared.

Dolce and Gabbana

When designer Dolce remarked to *Panorama* magazine, "You are born and have a father and a mother. Or at least that's how it should be," John took exception to the comment, while having long advocated for the LGBTQ community to be able to adopt children. John called for a boycott of the designers.

In the same interview, Dolce stated, "What I call children of chemistry, synthetic babies do not convince me. Wombs for hire [are a] choice from a catalogue. And then you have to explain to this child who is the mother. To procreate ought to be an act of love, today not even psychiatrists are ready to confront the effects of these experiments." John and husband, David Furnish, are the parents of two sons, born to the same surrogate. In an Instagram post, John replied, "How dare you refer to my beautiful children as 'synthetic.' And shame on you for wagging your judgmental little fingers at IVF. Your archaic thinking is out of step with the times, just like your fashions. I shall never wear Dolce and Gabbana ever again. #BoycottDolceGabbana"

In the Italian newspaper *Corriere della Sera*, Gabbana replied, "I didn't expect this, coming from someone whom I considered, and I stress 'considered,' an intelligent person like Elton John. I mean, you preach understanding, tolerance, and then you attack others? Only because someone has a different opinion? Is this a democratic or enlightened way of thinking? This is ignorance, because he ignores the fact that others might have a different opinion and that theirs is as worthy of respect as his.

"It's an authoritarian way of seeing the world—agree with me or, if you don't, I'll attack you," he continued. "I even posted the word 'Fascist!' on his Instagram."

Either in response to the vociferous backlash—spearheaded by John yet also including Madonna and Victoria Beckham, among others—or following a change in his own conscience, Dolce atoned. "I am so sorry," he said to *Vogue*, in an interview published on August 14, 2015. "It was not my intention to offend anyone. I've done some soul-searching. . . . I've realised that my words were inappropriate, and I apologise. They are just kids."

In response, John accepted the apology, writing on his official Instagram page, "Big thanks to Stefano and Domenico for the apology over their comments about IVF children. . . . We look forward to wearing their designs once again."

George Michael

The former Wham! superstar had been an Elton John fan since childhood. They had been friends for years as adults. They had performed "Don't Let the Sun Go Down on Me" together at Live Aid in 1985, and in 1991 they reprised the performance, marking John's first public appearance after a much publicized six-week stint in rehab. When Michael's life (at least the life that was chronicled in the tabloid press) seemed to get a bit out of control, however, his old mate voiced his concern. "George is in a strange place," John said in 2004. "He's quite happy just being at home all the time, and I think that's a waste of talent. There appears to be a deep-rooted unhappiness in his life."

Michael didn't appreciate such unsolicited concern and public scrutiny, and he soon issued a statement via an open letter in *Heat* magazine, in which he said, in part:

> To this day, most of what Elton thinks he knows about my life is pretty much limited to the gossip he hears on what you would call the "gay grapevine" which, as you can imagine, is lovely stuff indeed.
>
> Other than that, he knows that I don't like to tour, that I smoke too much pot, and that my albums still have a habit of going to number one.
>
> He will not be happy until I bang on his door in the middle of the night saying, "Please, please, help me, Elton. Take me to rehab."

A publicity photograph of George Michael dated 1990.
Author's collection

It's not going to happen.... Elton just needs to shut his mouth and get on with his own life.

The two buried the hatchet in 2011, when they reprised (yet again) their tried-and-true duet of "Don't Let the Sun Go Down on Me" at John's annual White Tie and Tiara Ball, but with Michael's death on Christmas Day, 2016, their friendship reached a sudden and tragic end.

Billy Joel

When Billy Joel and Elton John convened for their first Face to Face tour in 1994, consumer demand exceeded stadium capacities around the world. The 2001–2002 iteration of the tour raked in record revenues—at one point, Joel and John each reportedly earned one million dollars per show—to become the highest-grossing package tour in history. But it also became a juggernaut, with tensions festering between the two superstar musicians. Joel canceled several key performances, allegedly due to illness (though rampant speculation and police reports pointed to other, more inebriated causes), including an anticipated HBO concert special from London's Wembley Stadium, leaving John in the precarious position of either playing the gigs on his own or canceling them altogether. John fell ill on occasion as well, further compounding frustrations.

As Joel once jeered, in "Big Shot," "It's no big sin to stick your two cents in if you know when to leave it alone." Well, John didn't know when to leave it alone.

Speaking with *Rolling Stone* in 2011, for a cover story entitled "Elton Remembers" (recalling the magazine's historic 1970 long-form interview "Lennon Remembers," and, to a lesser extent, 1994's "Jagger Remembers"), John took Joel to task for slacking, among other dubious infractions. "At the end of the day, he's coasting," he said of the Piano Man, who hadn't released a new studio album of pop music since his 1993 LP, *River of*

Billy Joel, performing on January 17, 2014, at the Amalie Arena in Tampa, Florida.
Photo by Donald Gibson, Author's collection

```
IP0309  FL2      22    1    ADULT  EIP0309
EVENT CODE   SECTION/AISLE   ROW/BOX   SEAT        ADMISSION        EVENT CODE
$176.75  MAIN FLOOR            176.75 TAX11.45
$11.25           IN CONCERT                  PHONE
FL2    ELTON JOHN & BILLY JOEL       FL2
DS    4X        FACE TO FACE          DS711ZFS
22    1 ICE PALACE ARENA - TAMPA        22
ZFS2209          * * *               A 176.75
A24JAN2   SAT MAR 9 2002 7:30PM             1
```

A ticket stub from a Billy Joel/Elton John performance on March 2, 2002, in Tampa, Florida, during the pair's intermittent Face to Face tour.   *Author's collection*

Dreams. "And it upsets me. Billy's a conundrum. We've had so many canceled tours because of illnesses and various other things, alcoholism."

In a public response Joel struck a conciliatory, empathetic tone, saying, in part, "Elton is just being Elton." Behind the scenes, however, he was livid. Joel sent John a letter (as quoted in 2014's *Billy Joel: The Definitive Biography* by Fred Schruers) in which he wrote, "What gives you the omnipotent moral certainty and authority to justify the public humiliation of anyone—especially of someone to whom you should, at the very least, consider according a modicum of honor?" Joel ended the letter by stating, "We are done."

Both men having waged historic concert tours behind the Iron Curtain in the former Soviet Union, they know that even the most contentious relationships can be mended. The first such indication in their own Cold War was when John and Joel both attended the Songwriters Hall of Fame 44th Annual Induction and Awards Gala on June 14, 2013—John was bestowed the Johnny Mercer Award while Joel was on hand to induct Foreigner's Lou Gramm (who had produced his 1989 LP, *Storm Front*) and Mick Jones. They missed catching up in person, but each spoke with mutual benevolence toward the other during their respective moments onstage. The final détente, corroborated by a public hug and a photograph for posterity, occurred on October 15 of the same year, when Joel attended one of John's benefits for the Elton John AIDS Foundation.

"I want to thank him for coming tonight," John said from the podium. "It was an incredibly kind gesture. . . . I love you and I will be seeing a lot more of you, I think.

"11:30," he added. "My room."

Sheila Farebrother

The relationship between a mother and her son can be complicated, but the one between Elton John and his mother, Sheila Farebrother, had to withstand time, divorce, and, as it turns out, one of the nastiest feuds of all.

At the root of this nine-year mother/son feud was John's partner and, later, husband, David Furnish, who in 2008 cleaned house as far as getting rid of some of the key individuals, namely former personal assistant Bob Halley and former manager John Reid, both of whom had been a crucial part of John's professional inner circle for decades. John allegedly also insisted that Farebrother, in her eighties at the time, banish all such people from her life—an order she was not inclined to follow.

In a 2015 interview with the *Daily Mail*, Farebrother recounted the circumstances that led to her fallout with her only child, foremost that she would not be cutting off ties with Reid or Halley, the latter of whom lived close by and often checked on her wellbeing. "I had no intention of dropping John and Bob," Farebrother recalled, "and I told Elton so. He told me I thought more of Bob Halley than I did of my own son." As the disagreement intensified, so did the expletives, on both sides. "And to that I said to him, 'And you think more of that fucking thing you married than your own mother.' . . . Then, to my utter amazement, he told me he hated me. And he then banged the phone down. Imagine! To me, his mother!"

John never stopped subsidizing his mother's care and expenses, including hip-replacement surgery, but even with the birth of his and Furnish's two sons, Zachary and Elijah, he was hesitant to mend the bridges they had both burned. "I don't hate my mother," John told *Rolling Stone* in February 2016. "I look after her, but I don't want her in my life."

Upon the death of Farebrother's longtime husband, Fred (or Derf, as a young Reg Dwight had lovingly called him), John declined to attend the funeral.

Relations between the two began to thaw following Farebrother's ninetieth birthday, for which John reportedly sent his mother a gift, a bowl of white orchids—the accompanying card read, "Wow, 90! Congratulations. Love Elton, David, Zachary and Elijah." But he did not attend the lavish bash thrown in her honor, attended by Halley, former assistent and engineer, Stuart Epps, and many other individuals from his storied past. The most conspicuous attendee was Elton John impersonator Paul Bacon, leader of the Ultimate Elton Tribute Band, who had befriended Farebrother and was on hand to perform some of his doppelganger's greatest hits.

Mother and son reportedly reunited in person sometime in 2017, but it turned out to be a brief reconciliation. After a few years of declining health, the woman who had introduced her son to rock 'n' roll, before supporting his career with abiding enthusiasm, died on December 4, 2017. She was ninety-two.

"I only saw her last Monday," John wrote that morning, on his social media channels, "and I am in shock. Travel safe Mum. Thank you for everything. I will miss you so much."

The following night, John performed with his band at the Barclaycard Arena in Hamburg, Germany—one of the few major cities outside of England that Bluesology toured more than a half-century before. "This next song I wrote at her house," John said, prefacing a performance of "Your Song," "and I can remember every single minute of writing this song with Bernie. So, this is the song I want to dedicate to her. It's taken me from nowhere to somewhere, so thank you, Mum."

Nearly three months after Farebrother's death, the formal bequests of her will were made public, their details in part seeming like a slight against John. According to media reports, she left half of her fortune (£534,000, or nearly three quarters of a million dollars) to Bob Halley, whose continued friendship with Farebrother had allegedly caused John and his mother's nine-year rift in the first place. She split the other half of her fortune between John's half-brother, Frederick Farebrother, and her longtime friend, Deborah Woodward. Certainly, £534,000 is a negligible sum for John, whose net worth exceeds £300 million. Nonetheless, what he *did* inherit from his late mother—two family photographs and two ceramic urns (the contents of which were not disclosed)—left him with little more than memories.

27

It's Like Throwing a Switch on the Hands of Time

Rejuvenated in the Nineties

A t the dawn of the nineties, Elton John was a fortunate man. Having not only survived over fifteen years of serious substance abuse but also—after undergoing surgery on his throat in Australia in 1987—retained his very ability to sing, he'd saved his life simply by seeking help. Over six weeks in the summer of 1990, he had achieved his sobriety at Chicago's Parkside Lutheran Hospital—having overcome his addictions to both alcohol and cocaine while at the same time conquering his bulimia—and he entered his third full decade as Elton John with a renewed sense of purpose and vitality, and with his talent intact.

With the 1990 release of a career-spanning boxed set, *To Be Continued* . . . (which yielded the hit single "You Gotta Love Someone," a track that also appeared on the soundtrack to the motion picture, *Days of Thunder*), John was able to, in essence, begin again. As songwriting partner Bernie Taupin notes in the collection's liner notes, "I think the box set's good because it's sort of a milestone. That's that, a piece of history; take a nice long break and start all over again with something new."

Calling such a compilation *To Be Continued* . . . —particularly when it includes his most iconic, classic hits and timeless fan favorites—suggests either no shortage of chutzpah or blind optimism in predicting what lay ahead in the music John had yet to compose. No one could have foreseen the creative and critical windfall that would soon define his career in the decade to come. Having vowed never to score another film after his dissatisfying, contractually obligated experience working on *Friends* in 1971, his decision to collaborate with lyricist Tim Rice, with whom he'd

The 1990 UK CD single of "You Gotta Love Someone," which features on the soundtrack to *Days of Thunder* as well as on two compilations, the two-disc *The Very Best of Elton John* and the four-disc boxed set *To Be Continued . . .*   *Author's collection*

co-composed "Legal Boys" for his 1982 LP, *Jump Back!*, proved tremendously fortuitous.

Unlike any previous decade, in fact, John reached an unprecedented plateau as an artist in scoring the 1994 Disney feature film, *The Lion King*, a watershed at the box office and a catalyst in John's career. The circle of life, as it were, had returned Elton John to the apex of pop superstardom, reestablishing his presence among the relevant artists of the day, rather than with the legacy acts of a bygone era. While his appeal as a concert performer had sustained more or less unabated throughout his career, his newly revitalized profile necessitated more and more promotional appearances, including at annual music-award shows and on high-profile interview programs alongside the ultra-famous likes of Nirvana, Madonna, Oasis, Alanis Morissette, Garth Brooks, and Michael Jackson, among others. In short, *The Lion King* endowed John with an invaluable platform upon which his every creative move would generate substantial public attention and media coverage.

With his sobriety helping to enrich his albums with a renewed vitality, particularly in the first half of the decade, and the seismic success of *The Lion King* emboldening his work in the latter half, Elton John's studio albums in the nineties are unlike any he's released before or since. In this chapter, we examine those efforts.

The One (1992)

After a full year off from touring and recording, following his six-week stay in rehab, John emerged in 1992 with *The One*, the first album he'd

The One, released June 22, 1992, reached #8 in the US and peaked at #2 in the UK.

Author's collection

The UK CD single of "The One," the title track and Top 10 lead single from the album of the same name.   *Author's collection*

made sober in over seventeen years. Containing, in its title track, one of the most enduring love songs of his career, *The One* heralded a new era for Elton John, and, for his fans, a solid and eclectic return to form.

As an aside, John performed the title track on the 1992 MTV Video Music Awards, his performance coming directly after a performance by Nirvana, who ended theirs by trashing their equipment. In a subtle but sardonic nod to Cobain and company, John finished his performance by carefully chucking his piano bench off its raised platform. Cobain, who'd been bickering with Axl Rose, thought he would spew some spittle on Rose's piano keys before he sang Guns N' Roses' power ballad "November Rain" with Elton John. The only problem was, he spat on the wrong piano—he spat on John's piano, which John then unwittingly played.

Other album highlights include the pastoral ballad, "The North" and "The Last Song," the latter depicting a coming-to-terms moment between a distant father and his HIV-positive son.

Duets (1993)

The one album in his extensive canon that's most reflected a gratuitous bandwagon mentality—John has forsworn such album projects as those

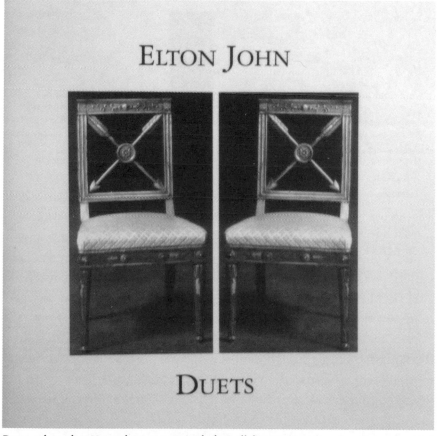

Duets, released on November 23, 1993, includes collaborations with such artists as Leonard Cohen, Little Richard, and Tammy Wynette.   *Author's collection*

A UK CD single of "Don't Go Breaking My Heart," as covered on 1993's *Duets* by John and RuPaul.   *Author's collection*

comprising the "American Songbook" or a Christmas collection—*Duets* found him collaborating with a string of different artists (save for the solo title track) on a mixed bag of both originals and covers, to invariably mixed results. Considering the covers, moments like the Kitty Lester lament "Love Letters" (with Bonnie Raitt) and the Cole Porter chestnut "True Love" (with Kiki Dee) have their charm. Still, the handful of Bernie Taupin originals represented in this collection offers more bang for one's buck, from "The Power," which finds John collaborating with his childhood idol Little Richard (who sings it straight soul, not in cartoonish wails and screeches), to "A Woman's Needs," delivered with country-music legend Tammy Wynette, whose soulful pathos and aching vulnerability recall the same quintessential qualities of her own classic sides.

On "Born to Lose," John duets with Leonard Cohen, who had just released one of the most searing, provocative albums of his own lengthy career, *The Future*. As John recalled in a 2014 Sirius Town Hall interview with veteran music journalist David Fricke, when Cohen, who handled the first line in the song, opened with, "Born to lose, I've lived my life in vain," John, preparing to come in on the second line, instead laughed. "It sounds like an ocean liner leaving Long Beach," John remembered telling the bemused crooner, adding, "It was the lowest note I'd ever heard."

Made in England (1995)

With *The Lion King* still roaring as a film and soundtrack phenomenon (and with Broadway in its sights), John already had his next studio album ready for release—and it was among the strongest, most enduring efforts he had composed since the seventies.

While *The Lion King* was virtually everywhere in 1994–1995, so was the spirit of the Beatles, whose *Anthology* television miniseries had aired in conjunction with the release of the titular multi-disc sets of previously unreleased or otherwise rare tracks. As the first studio album to follow *The Lion King*—in fact, the album's release was postponed to account for the overwhelming response of the soundtrack—hopes were high.

Its first single, "Believe," one of the boldest songs he'd ever composed, was actually the album's running title until shortly before its release on April 8, 1995. It reached #13 on the *Billboard* Hot 100, while ascending to #1 on the Adult Contemporary chart. As is noted on John's official website, the sustained crashing opening chord of the title track is a tribute to the Beatles' "A Hard Day's Night," while producer George Martin also provided strings to one of the other songs, "Latitude," in homage to "You've Got to Hide Your Love Away."

Following a lackluster showing for the album's second single (the title track), the third US single, "Blessed," fared better with critics and fans alike, reaching #2 on the *Billboard* Adult Contemporary chart. The album itself peaked at #3.

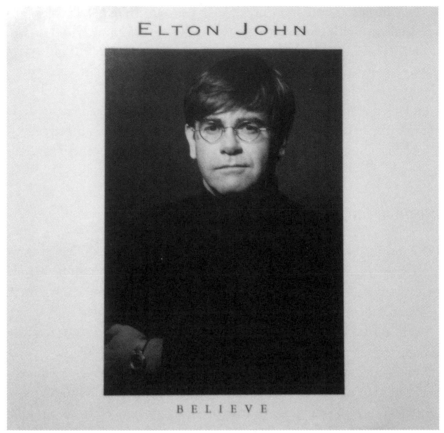

"Believe" reached #13 in the US and #15 in the UK in 1994 as the lead single from John's 1995 LP *Made in England*.   *Author's collection*

The Big Picture (1997)

Collected like a Whitman's Sampler of candied chocolates one gives a sweetheart on Valentine's Day, *The Big Picture* was at first touted as concentrating its theme on romantic love and relationships. In the years to follow, John would just about disown the album altogether, even though it yielded one surefire highlight, in "Something About the Way You Look Tonight," which he performed at his sixtieth birthday concert in 2007 at Madison Square Garden. Truth be told, the album's often piano-bereft production pales more than the quality of its best songs. "If the River Can Bend" suffuses a gospel shot of optimism, while "Live Like Horses" (originally written for *Made in England*) conjures an indefatigable sense of perseverance and triumph, which made it a prime selection for Luciano Pavarotti to send to the heavens in a shivering duet with John during one of the late Italian maestro's War Child benefit concerts.

28

And Some of Us Soar to the Stars

Scoring for Stage and Screen

Elton John has often described Bernie Taupin's lyrics as cinematic, and, in light of that storytelling context, his own scoring music for both stage and screen seems like a natural progression of his compositional talent.

While John has been an enthusiastic devotee of the theatrical arts since the earliest phases of his career, he seldom ventured into such territory as an artist—at least for a while. For instance, he was offered the leading male role in the 1971 film, *Harold and Maude* (which Bud Cort ultimately took) along with the chance to compose its soundtrack (which Cat Stevens ultimately wrote and recorded), but he turned down both requests, since his predominant obligation was to his music career at the time.

Other than writing a few songs that appear on the soundtrack to the 1971 film, *Friends*—Paul Buckmaster wrote the rest—John didn't embrace composing for motion pictures and Broadway productions until the nineties, when *The Lion King* roared into box-office immortality in both its stage and screen presentations.

This chapter offers an overview of Elton John's forays as a songwriter into the theatrical realms of motion pictures and musicals.

Friends (1971)

This film was directed by Lewis Gilbert, who at the time had already directed *Alfie* and the James Bond flick, *You Only Live Twice*—he would go on to direct two subsequent Bond films—while a torrent of other motion pictures lay in his future. Released on April 6, 1971, the official soundtrack features three songs written specifically for the film. Besides the title track, though, its most enduring highlights remain two songs composed for the then-unreleased studio LP, *Madman Across the Water*, "Can I Put You On" and "Honey Roll." With production by Gus Dudgeon and orchestral arrangements by Paul Buckmaster, the music bears the hallmarks that distinguished John's music during the most crucial period of his burgeoning career.

The opportunity came during John's first flush of success, and therefore wasn't engaged with the undivided attention songwriters most often pay w hen scoring a motion picture. Neither Taupin nor Buckmaster ever saw the film; Taupin hadn't even read the script. Indeed, the film's profile benefited more from its association with Elton John than he did from his association with it. Nevertheless, the soundtrack album failed to capitalize on his growing success, topping out at #36 in the States while not even troubling the UK albums charts in the slightest. It yielded a Top 40 single in the title track (which reached #34, to be exact). Nominated at the 1972 Grammy Awards in the category of "Best Original Score Written for a Motion Picture," the album lost to Isaac Hayes's soundtrack to *Shaft*.

After this, while several of his songs would subsequently appear in various films and on certain soundtracks, John would not write specifically for another motion picture again until 1994.

Tommy / "Pinball Wizard" (1975)

As featured in the 1975 Ken Russell film adaptation of the Who's 1969 rock opera, *Tommy*, John's scorching version of "Pinball Wizard" ranks alongside the original in terms of its quality and brazenness. While the single was not released in the States—it was eventually included on *Elton John's Greatest Hits II* in 1977—it reached #7 in the UK and has remained a popular selection, if not a regular staple, of John's live performances ever since.

The gigantic Doc Marten's platform boots that John wears in the film (as the "Local Lad" character) reside on permanent display at the Northampton Museum in England.

The Lion King (1994)

Considering his singular talent to compose melodies to nearly whatever set of words lands on top of his piano, isn't it peculiar that Elton John had not written for an animated feature film before *The Lion King*? Throughout the thirty-five years that preceded what remains his career's biggest windfall, he certainly wrote upbeat, even wacky songs that appealed (or could have

The official soundtrack to the 1994 Disney animated motion picture *The Lion King*, released on May 31, 1994. With over seven million copies sold to date, it is the all-time best-selling soundtrack to an animated film in US history.   *Author's collection*

appealed, had they been bigger hits) to the children-of-all-ages demo-graphic that swarmed box offices in 1994—songs like "Honky Cat" or "Honey Roll," or even a madcap rarity like "Take Me Down to the Ocean."

Lyricist Tim Rice—who, with composers from Andrew Lloyd Webber (*Jesus Christ Superstar, Phantom of the Opera*) to Alan Mencken (*Aladdin*), had inspired their own share of exuberant fans flocking box offices— must have sensed that John possessed this specific skill when, in the fall of 1990, he was asked by Disney executive Thomas Schumacher with whom he would like to work on a forthcoming animated feature. "Elton John" was the first name out of his mouth, but he had little faith that his request would be answered in the affirmative, let alone considered. Disney nevertheless approached John—*twice*—but both times to no avail. John's management reportedly never informed him about the offers,

A UK CD single of "Circle of Life," which hit #18 in the US and #11 in the UK, and features on the soundtrack to the 1994 Disney animated motion picture *The Lion King*. The song, with music by John and lyrics by Tim Rice, was nominated for "Best Original Song" at the 67th Annual Academy Awards, losing to "Can You Feel the Love Tonight?"—also composed by John and Rice for *The Lion King*.   *Author's collection*

however, such was Disney's reputation regarding copyright payment to songwriters (Disney also asked Paul McCartney, who was on his first world tour in thirteen years, and he declined as well). It took a third offer before a deal was finally struck (with the inclusion of score composer Hans Zimmer), presaging the historic windfall that followed.

The soundtrack album yielded three nominations for John and Rice at the 67th Annual Academy Awards on March 27, 1995, all in the category of "Best Original Song," with "Can You Feel the Love Tonight" taking the prize. "Circle of Life" and "Hakuna Matata" were also nominated.

"I get accosted in airports now by six-year-olds," John said, grinning mischievously, during a 1996 interview for *ABC in Concert*. "When you write something for *The Lion King*, something like that—I wrote it for children, the kids. That's what Disney wanted me to do. A lot of the Disney movies have very full Broadway scores, and they're beautiful, but they wanted to make it a pop score. And that's what I did. I wrote the songs with kids in mind. I mean, how could you not when you're writing about a warthog? But it's the kid in everybody, whether it's the six-year-old kid or the fifty-year-old kid."

By the time the stage musical premiered at Broadway's New Amsterdam Theater on October 15, 1997, the phenomenon (not to mention the anticipation) only intensified, with *The Lion King* going on to win the Tony Award for "Best Musical" in 1998.

The Muse (1999)

For this mostly forgettable film directed by Albert Brooks, the soundtrack (which, if it didn't have Elton John's name on it, probably wouldn't have garnered much publicity, either) features instrumentals only, save for the title track, which features lyrics by Bernie Taupin.

Elton John and Tim Rice's Aida (1999)

After their milestone success in composing the music for Disney's 1994 animated feature *The Lion King*, Elton John and Tim Rice reunited, hoping to capture lightning in a bottle once more, this time in composing the music for a Broadway adaptation of Verdi's opera *Aida*. The soundtrack album features songs performed by John and a host of additional artists, including Sting ("Another Pyramid"), Tina Turner ("Easy as Life"), Shania Twain ("Amneris' Letter"), Lenny Kravitz ("Like Father, Like Son,"), and LeAnn Rimes, with whom John sang the hit ballad, "Written in the Stars," the soundtrack's crowning achievement.

While the album did not necessarily educate the theater crowd on what to expect from the stage production, audiences nevertheless made

Elton John and Tim Rice's Aida, released on March 23, 1999, offered a preview of the Tony Award–winning musical production of *Aida*, which opened the following year on Broadway. With the notable exception of the hit Elton John/LeAnn Rimes duet "Written in the Stars," the album mostly features artists such as James Taylor, Tina Turner, and Lenny Kravitz performing John and Rice's compositions. *Author's collection*

Aida a smashing, enduring success. It won a total of four Tony Awards in 2000, with John and Rice in particular winning for "Best Original Score."

The Road to El Dorado (2000)

Heralding the first time John had collaborated with lyricist Tim Rice and composer Hans Zimmer since *The Lion King*, and now under the

The Road to El Dorado, released on March 14, 2000, in conjunction with the Dreamworks animated feature of the same name, features songs co-written by John and Tim Rice. The soundtrack includes guest performances by the likes of Randy Newman, the Backstreet Boys, and Don Henley and Timothy B. Schmit of the Eagles.   *Author's collection*

auspices of former Disney chairman Jeffrey Katzenberg's DreamWorks Animation, *The Road to El Dorado* found John composing an album boasting more than an ample amount of enjoyable moments. From love songs like "Someday Out of the Blue (Theme from El Dorado)" and "Without Question" to the zany-rhythmic rock of "16th Century Man," the soundtrack marks the debut of producer Patrick Leonard, who went on to produce *Songs from the West Coast* the following year.

But while the film has its charm (though not as much charm as the soundtrack), *The Road to El Dorado* was a box-office flop.

Billy Elliot the Musical (2005)

"Every child wants their father's approval," Elton John said to Katie Couric, in a 2008 interview with CBS News. "Every *son*, anyway." The emotional parallels of his life and that of the main character in the 2000 film, *Billy Elliot* inspired John and his partner, David Furnish, to develop a stage production. Composed with lyricist Lee Hall, *Billy Elliot the Musical* shares the story of a young boy who, having grown up in a harsh (and judgmental) miner's town, sought to escape his desperate conditions, along with his mining father's condemnation, by becoming a ballet dancer.

"Billy's dad eventually comes in and supports him in a way Elton's dad never really did," said Furnish, in a 2004 interview with the *Independent*. "There was a lot of tension and a lot of friction [in Elton's family], and there's so much of that in *Billy Elliot*."

The (based-on-a-true) story that struck a chord with Elton John succeeded in a major way with audiences and critics upon its official premiere in London's West End, at the Victoria Palace Theatre, on May 11, 2005. *Billy Elliot* officially opened on Broadway on November 13, 2008, at the Imperial Theatre, inspiring rave reviews there as well. All told, the musical won a slew of industry accolades, including four Laurence Olivier Awards and ten Tony Awards, among them "Best Musical."

Lestat (2006)

Inspired by author Anne Rice's *The Vampire Chronicles*, *Lestat* features songs written by John and longtime lyricist Bernie Taupin, making it the first musical the two legendary rock ' n' roll songwriters have collaborated on together.

Originally staged at the Curran Theatre in San Francisco from December 17, 2005, until January 29, 2006, the production underwent substantial edits after receiving negative reviews, in an attempt to make it more palatable to those who weren't necessarily familiar with Rice's writings. The critical drubbings continued after it opened at Manhattan's Palace Theater on March 25, 2006, however, and *Lestat* clo sed on May 28, after a mere thirty-nine performances. It was almost like potential fans were scared off or something.

Gnomeo and Juliet (2011)

In his first experience as the executive producer of a motion picture, Elton John reunited once more with former bandmate and arranger James Newton Howard, who laced this film's score with melodies and fragments from several of John's classic hits ("Crocodile Rock," "Bennie and the Jets," "Your Song"). The soundtrack also saw John collaborating with provocative protégé Lady Gaga on "Hello Hello," but their duet was not included on the official album release; it plays only in the film, with the soundtrack opting instead for John's solo version.

29

I Could Really Get Off Being in Your Shoes

Ten Notable Cover Songs

This Is Your Song

The songs of Elton John and Bernie Taupin have been recorded by hundreds of artists, most notably dating back to 1969, when Three Dog Night recorded "Lady Samantha," the band including the song on its sophomore album, *Suitable for Framing*. However, unlike, for instance, the Beatles, from whose music others have cultivated emphatic classics in their own right—like Stevie Wonder's funky rendition of "We Can Work It Out," or Joe Cocker's impassioned performance of "With a Little Help from My Friends"—very few (if any) have yielded a supplementary rendition of one of John's songs that bests his original.

Perhaps what makes his recordings so definitive is that listeners have regarded them as being quintessentially personal to John himself. For that reason, choosing and ranking the best cover versions of Elton John originals—as we will now do, in the first part of this chapter—becomes an all-the-more challenging and exciting task.

10. John Grant—"Sweet Painted Lady" (*Goodbye Yellow Brick Road: 40th Anniversary Deluxe Edition*, 2014)

Any number of far more prominent songs from John's most celebrated album probably should have yielded the best cover performance from the collection of covers included in this boxed set. But perhaps the relative obscurity of "Sweet Painted Lady" allows for just the right artist to embrace it in a unique and believable way. Alas, with his gruff, dispassionate vocal sounding eerily (and emotionally) removed, singer/songwriter John Grant emphasizes the implicit and clandestine seediness this underrated tribute to the titular lady of the night entails.

9. Bettye LaVette—"Don't Let the Sun Go Down on Me" (*Interpretations: The British Rock Songbook*, 2010)

While the original's shimmering production (courtesy of Gus Dudgeon) paid homage to the Phil Spector's Wall of Sound and the sumptuous soundscapes of the Beach Boys, the narrative John first delivered was consequently overshadowed. Soul firebrand Bettye LaVette reverses course with her own stunning version. Her voice suffused with grit and hard-fought wisdom, she distills the anthemic grandiloquence of John's classic *Caribou* performance to its emotional essence, while at the same time wrenching out all the weariness and desperation its lyrics portend.

8. Ellie Goulding—"Your Song" (*Lights*, 2010)

Taking on John's signature song would be a tall, daunting order for the most seasoned artist. Yet on her debut studio album, British singer/songwriter Ellie Goulding rendered "Your Song" with thoroughly enchanting, remarkable conviction. Her tender and resplendent vocal brims with the softest of trembles, resonating much like first-love butterflies, the intemerate perspective of the lyrics summoned elegantly to life.

7. Diana Krall—"Sorry Seems to Be the Hardest Word" (*Wallflower*, 2015)

Somber yet sultry, jazz chanteuse Diana Krall renders "Sorry" like a soliloquy, singing almost in a murmur, the results much like something someone would hear while eavesdropping on one end of a late-night telephone call from an adjacent room. And, indeed, she seems as compellingly regretful as the lyrics suggest, the blend of her rich vocal phrasing and subtle piano accompaniment lending credence to the song's most intimate expressions of despair.

6. Miranda Lambert—"We All Fall in Love Sometimes" (*My Sister's Keeper* soundtrack, 2009)

On an exquisite tribute album featuring no shortage of country music's finest—the roster includes Willie Nelson, Kacey Musgraves, Emmylou Harris, and Vince Gill—Miranda Lambert scorches them all. Reprising one of *Captain Fantastic's* most riveting moments, she takes to its Old West themes of sacrament and tradition like a method actor on a dramatic stage.

5. Sara Bareilles—"Goodbye Yellow Brick Road" (*Brave Enough: Live at the Variety Playhouse*, 2013)

On what is the most unique cover represented on this list, singer/songwriter Sara Bareilles delivers a harrowing rendition of one of John's most wistful compositions. Accompanying herself on keyboard during this 2013 performance in Atlanta, Georgia, she forgoes John's lush arrangement in favor of an altogether more stark and haunting motif, her voice ascending as if out of darkness into light.

"I've never heard anyone sing one of my songs like that, ever," John said, after witnessing Bareilles perform "Goodbye Yellow Brick Road" at the annual Hot Pink Party in 2014, a benefit for the Breast Cancer Research Foundation. "Because when someone sings your songs they usually copy you, and she made it her own."

4. Tina Turner—"The Bitch Is Back" (*Rough*, 1978)

In the lean years of her solo career following her violent split from her husband Ike, Tina Turner started over, performing on pitifully trivial stages and releasing music that failed to find the mass audience it deserved. Having performed this *Caribou* barnstormer during her solo Las Vegas revues during this time, she then recorded it on her 1978 LP, *Rough*, on which her signature sexuality and raw power is delivered with an onslaught of blazing electric guitars. Unfortunately, few people cared. In 1991, while at the height of her renewed success (having long since graduated from the middling-theater circuit to sell out football stadiums the world over), she re-recorded the track upon the occasion of the *Two Rooms* tribute album and documentary, but it lacked the visceral thrust of the version available on *Rough*.

3. Sting—"Come Down in Time" (*Two Rooms: Celebrating the Songs of Elton John and Bernie Taupin*, 1991)

An upright bass, sparse piano (played by John, here credited as Nancy Treadlight), and one of the most evocative vocals of his career were all the Police's erstwhile front man required to render the most soulful cover performance on the entire *Two Rooms* tribute album. "I was an English

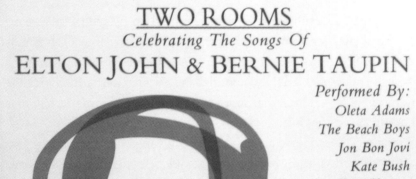

Two Rooms: Celebrating the Songs of Elton John and Bernie Taupin, which features Elton John guesting on piano credited as "Nancy Treadlight" on Sting's cover of "Come Down in Time."
Author's collection

student when *Tumbleweed Connection* came out, and 'Come Down in Time' was my favorite track," Sting notes in the LP's liner notes. "I love Bernie's lyrics and it's just one of those songs you wished you'd written yourself."

2. George Michael—"Idol" (*Symphonica*, 2014)

Listening now to Elton John on the 1976 *Blue Moves* original, "Idol" is a melancholy homage, its lyrics at once celebrating Elvis Presley in his fifties-era prime while lamenting his fading vitality and relevance in the late seventies. In contrast, listening now to George Michael singing it on what would become the final album of his lifetime, the song resounds like a requiem for a gifted superstar who never lost his musical genius in life but rather in premature death. And, much like Michael's legacy, this stunningly gorgeous live performance will continue to resonate with listeners as nothing short of timeless.

1. Aretha Franklin—"Border Song" (*Young, Gifted, and Black*, 1972)

By any reckoning, the Queen of Soul's gospel-tinged rendition of "Border Song," which appeared on her 1972 LP, *Young, Gifted, and Black*, reigns as the superior Elton John cover. Drawing out the song's gospel inflections to their umpteenth degree, Franklin translates "Border Song" into a plea for peace and brotherhood of man. In 1993, John and Franklin performed the song together—their grand pianos bookending each other onstage— on the latter's television special *Duets*, during which they also powered through a scorching performance of Lady Soul's epic "Spirit in the Dark."

You Were Made for Me

By contrast, considering that he has enjoyed the good fortune of having Bernie Taupin write the lyrics to most of the songs he has recorded throughout his fifty-year career—not to mention the other lyricists he has collaborated with, like Gary Osborne ("Blues Eyes," "Little Jeannie") and Tim Rice ("Circle of Life," "Can You Feel the Love Tonight")—for Elton John to record another artist's song most often suggests a specific, special occasion. In other words, the man doesn't lack for outside material.

What becomes evident in examining the relatively few such songs John has interpreted on official releases, though, is his profound respect for the original artists behind them, and, in particular, their songwriters.

10. "I'm Your Man" (Written by Leonard Cohen)

Only two years after collaborating with Leonard Cohen on a deliciously morose rendition of "Born to Lose," John tackled one of the late Canadian singer/songwriter's naughtiest, most evocative confections. Embracing its lyrical conceit full-tilt, he enlivens the slow percussive tease of the original in favor of a fearsome vocal drenched in a gung-ho, glam-rock glitz.

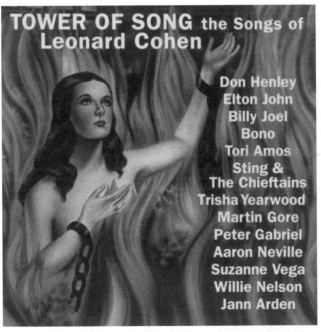

Tower of Song: The Songs of Leonard Cohen, released on September 26, 1995, collected some of the Canadian bard's biggest fans including Billy Joel, Tori Amos, and Willie Nelson to sing his praises through his songs.   *Author's collection*

9. "A Song for You" (Written by Leon Russell)

During his historic 1986 Tour de Force of Australia with the Melbourne Symphony Orchestra, John unfurled a medley of love songs (including "Blue Eyes" and "I Guess That's Why They Call It the Blues") that included this Leon Russell standard. Definitive renditions by Donny Hathaway and the Carpenters exist in a rarified space all their own, but Russell had been a singular influence for John since the earliest days of the latter's career, the enigmatic Master of Space and Time having attended the second night of John's fabled August 1970 residency at the Troubadour in Los Angeles and encouraged his subsequent efforts. Until John recorded *The Union* with his idol in 2010, this brief live performance remained the sole "tribute" available for fans. Not officially released in audio form until 1988, as a bonus cut on the British CD single for "A Word in Spanish," this impassioned rendition of this oft-interpreted love song is well worth seeking out.

8. "Stand by Your Man" (Written by Tammy Wynette and Billy Sherrill)

On the posthumous tribute album, *Tammy Wynette . . . Remembered*, John plays it straight (more or less) with a faithful rendition of what is perhaps the late country legend's signature song. Only five years prior to this 1998 recording, John and Wynette had provided the standout moment on the former's *Duets* album with "A Woman's Needs," which was also included on Wynette's 1994 LP, *Without Walls*. Their unlikely collaboration was cheekily described at the time by John as a meeting of "the queen of country and the queen of England."

7. "Whole Lotta Shakin' Goin' On" (Written by Dave "Curlee" Williams)

Though the Rocket Man didn't cross paths in person with the Killer until 2015, when they both were on the bill at the New Orleans Jazz Festival, John had revered Jerry Lee Lewis since he first heard "Great Balls of Fire" as an impressionable young child. His lifelong adoration for Lewis's music and awe at his prodigious skills as a pianist shine through in this rollicking and indisputably exuberant performance, available on the rambunctious 2001 collection, *Good Rockin' Tonight—The Legacy of Sun Records*.

6. "Chapel of Love" (Written by Jeff Barry, Ellie Greenwich, and Phil Spector)

John delivers this Dixie Cups classic in a boisterous revamp packed with more punch than a Wall of Sound, summoning the standout moment from the otherwise lackluster 1994 soundtrack to *Four Weddings and a Funeral*.

5. "Blueberry Hill" (Written by Vincent Rose, Larry Stock, and Al Lewis)

With the devastation wrought by Hurricane Katrina still wrenchingly fresh in the hearts and minds of New Orleans natives, one of the Big Easy's favorite sons—and one of rock 'n' roll's founding fathers—was saluted with the 2007 star-packed, two-disc set, *Goin' Home: A Tribute to Fats Domino*. Among such venerable artists as Neil Young, Randy Newman, Lucinda Williams, and Paul McCartney, the Rocket Man handled the Fat Man's signature tune as though embracing an old friend, instilling the performance with the kind of love and respect he reserves for only his most beloved musical heroes.

4. "True Love" (Written by Cole Porter)

First featured in the 1956 musical, *High Society*, starring Bing Crosby and Grace Kelly, this Cole Porter classic is likely one John encountered as a young child on the radio programs that played in his family's house in Pinner. Two decades later, he most assuredly heard George Harrison's version on his 1976 LP, *Thirty Three & 1/3*. Nearly two decades later still, John and Kiki Dee evoked splendid chemistry together, going full circle to rekindle the original's rhapsodic magic on their hit 1993 duet, which peaked at #2 on the UK's Adult Contemporary chart.

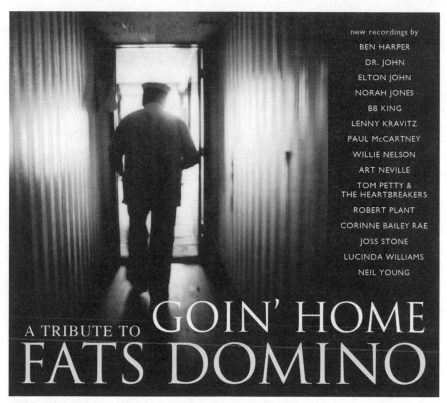

new recordings by
BEN HARPER
DR. JOHN
ELTON JOHN
NORAH JONES
BB KING
LENNY KRAVITZ
PAUL McCARTNEY
WILLIE NELSON
ART NEVILLE
TOM PETTY &
THE HEARTBREAKERS
ROBERT PLANT
CORINNE BAILEY RAE
JOSS STONE
LUCINDA WILLIAMS
NEIL YOUNG

A TRIBUTE TO GOIN' HOME
FATS DOMINO

Besides Elton John, *Goin' Home: A Tribute to Fats Domino*, released on September 25, 2007, boasts such venerable artists as B.B. King, Lucinda Williams, Robert Plant, and Tom Petty and the Heartbreakers, all playing classics made famous by the Fat Man.   *Author's collection*

3. "I Love You All the Time" (Written by Jesse Hughes and Joshua Homme)

In the wake of the terrorist attack during an Eagles of Death Metal concert at the Bataclan in Paris on November 13, 2015 , a wide roster of artists was recruited to cover the band's song, "I Love You All the Time" on behalf of the Play It Forward campaign, with all proceeds benefiting the Sweet Stuff Foundation, which provides for musicians and their families in need of victim relief. Of the various takes recorded and released to date—an ever-growing list includes versions by Kings of Leon, Chelsea Wolfe, and My Morning Jacket—John's 2016 rendition is by far the most

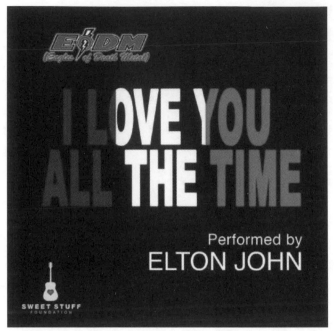

John joined a host of artists in covering the Eagles of Death Metal's "I Love You All the Time" following the terrorist attack during the band's performance at the Bataclan in Paris, France, on November 13, 2015.   *Author's collection*

striking, the vivacious pace of EODM's original dialed down to become a somber, unnervingly sober anthem.

2. "Pinball Wizard" (Written by Pete Townshend)

The Who's Pete Townshend's frenetic, finger-picking overture is transformed into a torrid piano assault on John's 1974 dynamic version, enlivening this most iconic rock anthem with the sort of invincible vigor that even the most die-hard fans of the Who should emphatically respect.

Among them is Chris Charlesworth, former editor and journalist at *Melody Maker*. "To tell you the truth," he says, "it was probably the best track on that *Tommy* soundtrack album. And you know why, because Elton insisted on having his own band play, whereas the rest was done with just session musicians or it was done with musicians who weren't used to playing together. Whereas Elton said, 'No, I'm bringing in my own band to do this.' He wasn't going to take any risks."

At first, Rod Stewart was supposed to record the song and play the title character in the Who's film version of their rock opera, *Tommy*, but John talked him out of it. Townshend later beseeched John to take on the role, which he jumped at (angering Stewart in the process), culminating in one of rock's all-time great covers. The song remains a staple of John's live concerts to this day. John incorporated bits of the Who's "I Can't Explain" into the film performance; the Who returned the favor, so to speak, with a comparatively anemic cover of "Saturday Night's Alright for Fighting / Take Me to the Pilot" on the 1992 LP, *Two Rooms: Celebrating the Songs of Elton John and Bernie Taupin*.

1. "Lucy in the Sky with Diamonds" (Written by John Lennon and Paul McCartney)

Having arranged their historic three-song performance on Thanksgiving 1974 at Madison Square Garden, and having sung backing vocals on John Lennon's 1974 LP, *Walls and Bridges*, most notably on the #1 single "Whatever Gets You Thru the Night," John wished to record one of Lennon's songs. He asked the former Beatle which one he would prefer, and Lennon suggested "Lucy," as at that point no one had recorded it yet. The song now chosen, John invited Lennon to Caribou Ranch in Colorado to take part in the 1975 session, for which he is credited on the album sleeve as alter ego Dr. Winston O'Boogie. Pretty much replicating the flow and feel of the original, John also recorded Lennon's *Mind Games* cut "One Day at a Time" as the B-side.

30

Read 'Em, as They Say, and Weep

Awards, Records, and Distinctions

Popular success does not always coincide with critical acclaim, but Elton John has proven over the past fifty years that both such achievements are indeed possible. In the nearly fifty years since "Your Song" introduced him to listeners of all persuasions, John has received countless honors, awards, prizes, distinctions, records, and proclamations, including five Grammy Awards, five Brit Awards, twelve Ivor Novello awards, and a BRITs Icon Award. In addition, he was named a Commander of the Order of British Empire in 1996, a MusiCares Person of the Year honoree in 2000, and a Kennedy Center honoree in 2004. He has also achieved the following:

Thirty Consecutive Years with at Least One Top 40 Hit

From "Your Song" in 1970 through "Written in the Stars" in 1999, John notched up at least one single in the US Top 40, breaking Elvis Presley's previous record of twenty-two straight years. (The title track from John's 1992 LP, *The One*, released in 1992, broke the record.) Besides the virtues of his longevity as a relevant rock 'n' roll artist, John has proven that while fads change and technology evolves, melodies are perennial. There is no substitute for fundamental talent, whether it materializes on a computerized studio, an electric keyboard, or an acoustic grand piano. The musical styles John encountered through these thirty consecutive years call to mind a plethora of pop music variations.

Seven Consecutive #1 Albums in the US

If his thirty-year streak of achieving at least one Top 40 hit per year best reflects John's musical consistency over the long haul, his run of seven consecutive US #1 albums—*Honky Château, Don't Shoot Me I'm Only the Piano Player, Goodbye Yellow Brick Road, Caribou, Greatest Hits, Captain Fantastic and the Brown Dirt Cowboy*, and *Rock of the Westies*—best reflects the concentrated dominance he exerted in his prime. The quality of the last album, coupled with anticipation for the next one, resulted in unprecedented sales figures for John as the hot streak perpetuated through the mid-seventies.

First Album to Debut at #1 in the US: *Captain Fantastic and the Brown Dirt Cowboy* (1975)

The sales figure that mattered the most in the music industry in the seventies was millions of dollars, not today's yardstick of millions of copies sold. Nevertheless, for Elton John's 1975 autobiographical LP, *Captain Fantastic and the Brown Dirt Cowboy*, to debut at #1 on the *Billboard* 200 album chart was an unprecedented milestone at the time. None of Elvis Presley's albums had achieved the same feat. Neither had any albums by the Beatles, the Rolling Stones, or Led Zeppelin. Stevie Wonder achieved as much with his 1976 double album, *Songs in the Key of Life*, but only after Elton John did so first—and second, as the follow-up to *Captain Fantastic and the Brown Dirt Cowboy*, 1975's *Rock of the Westies*, also debuted at #1.

Songwriters Hall of Fame (1992)

It's fitting that Elton John and Bernie Taupin were inducted into the Songwriters Hall of Fame two years before they were inducted into the Rock and Roll Hall of Fame. At the core of their partnership—and at the root of their fifty-year relationship—is songwriting. John has often said that without Taupin's lyrics, he'd have nothing to sing. Well, without a song set to music, neither one of them would have a career.

Rock and Roll Hall of Fame (1994)

"The Rock and Roll Hall of Fame honors the musicians who make the music that not only becomes the soundtrack to our lives but it actually helps us get through each day *of* our life," a strikingly earnest Axl Rose said in 1994, at the same Waldorf Astoria ceremony that saw Paul McCartney poignantly induct John Lennon as a solo artist. "And for myself as well as many others, no one has been there more for inspiration than Elton John."

Unless they are performers who write their own songs (like, say, Bruce Springsteen or Joni Mitchell), songwriters do not get inducted to the Rock and Roll Hall of Fame. And so, when Elton John was inducted in 1994, it was technically without Bernie Taupin, his primary lyricist. John has always credited Taupin as being more important in the scheme of things than even he is, as in the pair's lyrics-first arrangement, a song wouldn't exist without Taupin first writing down the words. So John not only brought Taupin to the stage to be recognized during his acceptance speech but also gave him his trophy.

"I kind of feel [I'm] cheating, standing up here accepting this," John said in his brief acceptance speech, "because without Bernie, there wouldn't have been any Elton John at all."

Academy Award for "Best Original Song": "Can You Feel the Love Tonight" (1995)

"Can You Feel the Love Tonight" had already won the Golden Globe for "Best Original Song," as well as the Grammy for "Best Male Pop Vocal Performance," by the time of the 67th Annual Academy Awards commenced on March 27, 1995. However, if anyone still needed a reminder of how big a phenomenon Disney's *The Lion King* had been in 1994 (besides the fact that it was the highest-grossing film worldwide in 1994), consider that in the Oscars category of "Best Original Song," three of the five nominations comprised songs that Elton John and Tim Rice had composed. They were so favored to walk out of that ceremony with a trophy that John and Rice should've been snapping their fingers and humming "Hakuna

Matata"—"It's our problem-free philosophy"—without a care in the world on their way in.

Polar Music Prize (1995)

Recognized among the most prestigious music-related honors in the world, this award (founded by former Abba lyricist Stig Anderson) is, according to the Polar Music Prize website, "awarded to individuals, groups and institutions in recognition of exceptional achievements." After a watershed year as co-composer of the soundtrack to Disney's *The Lion King*, John was named the Laureate of the Polar Music Prize 1995. "I can't do anything unless I'm good at it," he said on June 26, 1995, upon accepting the prize in Stockholm, Sweden. "I'm not one of those persons who get pleasure out of doing something and being mediocre . . . if I'm going to be mediocre at something, I don't want to do it. That's part of my personality."

Knighthood (1998)

Distinguished in the list of recipients published on New Year's Eve, 1997, John was knighted by Queen Elizabeth II on February 24, 1998, as the citation proclaimed, "for services to music and charitable services." Inside Buckingham Palace, dressed as conventionally formally as the royal family could have hoped, John approached the Queen in order to accept his honor. Unfortunately, the Lord Chamberlain announced him as "John Elton," unwittingly recalling Groucho Marx's ribbing a quarter of a century earlier (see chapter 7). Regardless, before John's mother and stepfather, and his partner, David Furnish, Her Majesty the Queen dubbed the investiture sword on each of John's shoulders as he knelt before her, recasting the man born Reginald Kenneth Dwight in a government-subsidized council house as Sir Elton Hercules John, CBE. "They don't come much bigger than this," he said afterward, standing outside the palace before the assembled press. "I love my country, and to be recognized in such a way—I can't think of anything better."

Second-Highest-Selling Single of All Time: "Candle in the Wind 1997" (1997)

The original version of "Candle in the Wind," from John's 1973 double LP, *Goodbye Yellow Brick Road*, took on a life of its own in the wake of Princess Diana's tragic death in Paris on August 31, 1997, with innumerable public and private remembrances popping up all over England during which the song was played. Upon receiving an invitation to perform at Diana's memorial service on September 6, 1997, at Westminster Abbey, John appealed to Bernie Taupin to rewrite the lyrics to "Candle in the Wind," withdrawing all inferences to Marilyn Monroe, while instead reflecting imagery and emotions more closely associated with the loss of the late Princess of Wales.

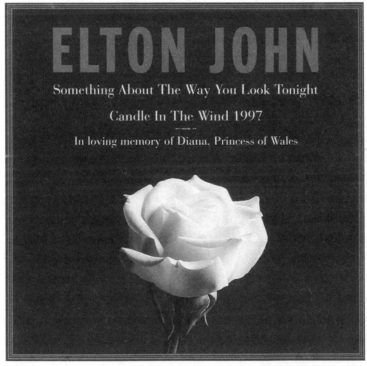

Released on September 13, 1997, as a double A-side single along with "Something About the Way You Look Tonight," "Candle in the Wind 1997" has sold over thirty-three million copies to date.   *Author's collection*

After performing the song live at the memorial service, John recorded the song at Townhouse Studios in West London, with George Martin producing and a string quartet and oboe complementing John's piano and vocal.

Released on September 13, 1997 as a double A-side single, along with "Something About the Way You Look Tonight" (which featured on John's forthcoming LP, *The Big Picture*), the song has sold over thirty-three million copies to date, with proceeds benefitting various charities the princess supported via the Diana, Princess of Wales Memorial Fund. At the time of writing, it is the second-highest-selling single of all time, behind Bing Crosby's version of "White Christmas," which has sold fifty million copies, according to the *Guinness Book of World Records*.

"Grammy Legend Award" (2000)

Retrospective honors such as this are often bestowed as consolation prizes for legendary artists who aren't properly recognized for the work that has most contributed to their legends. Led Zeppelin, for instance, won their first Grammy—the "Lifetime Achievement Award"—in 2005; the band didn't win in a competitive category until 2014, when the two-disc live set, *Celebration Day*, won "Best Rock Album."

Elton John had won four Grammy awards by the time the 42nd Annual Grammy Awards aired live on CBS television on February 23, 2000—he has won five trophies to date—but he had yet to attend or perform at any previous ceremony. On the occasion of his receiving the "Grammy Legend Award," a noncompetitive prize for which recipients are announced well in advance, John not only showed up but performed as well.

"In an age of Stratocasters and wah-wah pedals, Elton John made it cool to be a piano player," said Billy Joel, who presented the award before John and his band performed "Philadelphia Freedom," with the Backstreet Boys (then at the peak of their popularity) singing backup. "Now he is a knight, and in the United Kingdom he should be addressed as Sir Elton, but here in the good ol' USA, his friends can still call him Sharon."

Songwriter's Hall of Fame "Johnny Mercer Award" (2013)

More than two decades after they were inducted into the Songwriters Hall of Fame, Elton John and Bernie Taupin were recognized at the forty-fourth annual induction ceremony with the even more prestigious "Johnny Mercer Award," bestowed to those songwriters whose compositions have achieved the greatest possible distinction within popular culture.

In his acceptance speech, Taupin said of John, "I got somebody who put wings to my songs, took them all over the world, and made them belong to people, made them special to people, wrote things that made people believe those songs were their own, made people believe that we wrote the soundtrack of their life."

Harvard Foundation "Humanitarian of the Year" (2017)

On November 6, 2017, in homage to his founding of and contributions to the Elton John AIDS Foundation, John was bestowed with the "Humanitarian of the Year" award from the Harvard Foundation.

In his acceptance speech, noting how the fifties were ultra-conservative, John remarked on how the seismic "big bang" of such rock 'n' roll rebels as Elvis Presley, Little Richard, Fats Domino, and Jerry Lee Lewis during that era altered his adolescent existence and charted his course as a musician. "I would never have been a great concert pianist. Neither did I want to be a great concert pianist. I wanted to beat the *shit* out of the piano."

31

This Life of Mine Seemed Surreal at Times

Befriending the Beatles

A kind word goes a long way. As an emerging artist, Elton John enjoyed the praise of fans and critics alike, yet the encouragement of or a kind word from an established artist could go a long way in boosting his self-confidence. To receive such praise from one (or two) of the Beatles meant more than all the critical acclaim in the world.

Though not friends straightaway, John and Taupin did run in some of the same circles as the Beatles, particularly when they were signed by Dick James, who created Northern Songs as an exclusive publishing house for Lennon and McCartney. What the Beatles provided, though, was a template for how things should be done by songwriters who produce their own material.

John Lennon

In John Lennon's infamous 1970 interview with *Rolling Stone* editor-in-chief and co-founder Jann Wenner (an extensive conversation later immortalized as *Lennon Remembers*), the former Beatle discussed some of his favorite Beatles songs, singling out "Help!" and "Strawberry Fields Forever" for their emotional authenticity. In referencing the latter, he said, "It's like that Elton John one where he talks to himself, sort of singing"—presumably alluding to "Your Song's" "Anyway, the thing is, what I really mean" section—"which I thought was nice. It reminded me of that." Nearly four years before the two were introduced by mutual acquaintance Tony

King, to even be mentioned by Lennon at this still unproven point in his career—let alone complimented by him—could not have been higher praise for the emerging singer/songwriter.

In a 1975 *Rolling Stone* interview, Lennon went even further in his praise. "I remember hearing Elton John's 'Your Song,' heard it in America—it was one of Elton's first big hits—and remember thinking, *Great, that's the first new thing that's happened since we happened.* It was a step forward. There was something about his vocals that was an improvement on all of the English vocals until then."

Paul McCartney

Though their bond is not as strong as John's friendships with the other member of the Fab Four, the two have become arguably among the most beloved British artists of the past half-century (and inarguably the UK's most successful songwriters of all time), and their shared longevity has yielded more than a few shared moments in the studio and onstage, including the Concert for New York City after the 9/11 attacks.

In *Tin Pan Alley: The Rise of Elton John,* author Ken Haywood describes a 1968 session at Abbey Road Studios by Barron Knights, whose song "An Olympic Record" featured John on piano. With only twenty minutes left in their session, Paul McCartney—who by 1968 didn't have to worry about such matters as how long sessions should last, even if they cost him insane amounts of money—invited John and Barron Knights founding member Peter Langford (and, according to other reminiscences, Bernie Taupin as well) to listen to a new song he'd just written called "Hey Jude," which would soon be released at the Beatles' twentieth single, with the John Lennon–penned "Revolution" on the B-side.

George Harrison

In the wake of the *Elton John* album's success, John received a telegram from George Harrison, complimenting and encouraging his effort. The gesture provided the young artist with an invaluable validation of his talent, and in the years to come it would serve as the foundation of a mutual respect and friendship.

John was part of an all-star band including both Ringo Starr and Phil Collins on drums at the Prince's Trust gala on July 6, 1987, at the Royal Albert Hall in London, where he performed, among many other classics with many other classic acts, with Harrison on "While My Guitar Gently Weeps" and "Here Comes the Sun."

In 1987, John played on Harrison's comeback album, *Cloud Nine*, appearing on three songs. And in the wake of Harrison's death from lung cancer on November 29, 2001, John performed "Something" in his honor.

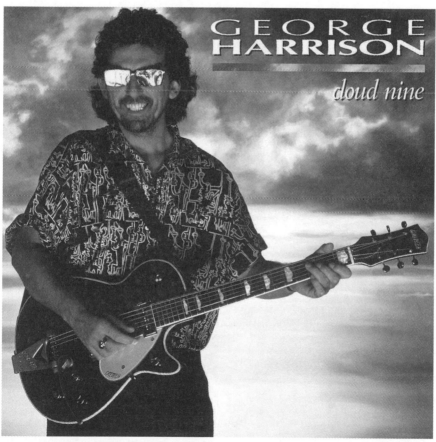

George Harrison's 1987 LP *Cloud Nine*, which features Elton John playing keyboards on three tracks.   *Author's collection*

Ringo Starr

The once and former Richard Starkey, and the once and former Reginald Dwight, have come a long way. In 1974, John and Taupin composed "Snookeroo," which appeared on the Beatles drummer's album, *Goodnight Vienna*, expressly for Starr—one of the few times since their days as staff songwriters at Dick James Music that the pair has written for another artist.

John appeared with mutual friend Marc Bolan in the film, *Born to Boogie*, which Starr directed, performing three songs (including "Children of the Revolution" and "Tutti Frutti").

32

I Was Playing Rock 'n' Roll and You Were Just a Fan

The Official Live Releases

While the recording studio is where Elton John first made his name, the concert stage is where he has earned and increasingly sustained his legend. One of the world's most invigorating and in-demand live performers for nearly a half-century, John has underscored his sartorial flash and flamboyance with earnest, serious musicianship. Having paid his dues during the mid-to-late sixties in London's pubs and rhythm-and-blues nightclubs as a keyboardist and erstwhile vocalist in Bluesology, by the time he'd earned some recognition in the early seventies he was already a stage veteran. Through his every subsequent phase and musical evolution—as he pushed the boundaries of performance art, as his wardrobes got louder and more grandiose—he has continued to serve and even test his most fundamental talents.

With over four thousand live performances to his name, John perhaps surprisingly hasn't released a copious amount of official live recordings—certainly not when compared to the outputs of, say, the Rolling Stones or Bruce Springsteen. Nevertheless, whether in audio or video format, each of his live recordings illustrates John as an artist at specific points or periods in his career, interpreting moments from his catalogue with both sentience and soul.

11–17–70 (1971 LP/CD)

Issued in April 1971, amid a concentrated run of Elton John albums—
Tumbleweed Connection was released barely six months before, with the
Friends film soundtrack having come out just two months prior—John's
first official live album showcases the artist as a dynamic concert performer, a perspective that wasn't particularly apparent on his studio
albums. (It was also devised, incidentally, to thwart the lucrative efforts
of bootleggers who had already profited from distributing the performance to John's more resourceful fans.) For those accustomed only to

The live LP *11-17-70*, released on April 9, 1971, highlights an eighty-minute performance
delivered by John, bassist Dee Murray, and drummer Nigel Olsson at A&R Recording
Studios in Manhattan on that date. Originally released by Dick James Music to stem sales of
unauthorized bootlegged copies, *11-17-70* or *17-11-70*, as it is titled in the UK is now considered one of the greatest live albums of all time.   *Author's collection*

humming along to radio-friendly ballads like "Your Song," the distinction proved a stark and perhaps startling one.

Recorded on the titular date at New York City's WABC studio before an assembled audience that included Mary Travers of Peter, Paul, and Mary fame, the out-of-sequence track listing offers a grab-bag assortment from a proper full-length performance, revealing John in boisterous, often bombastic form thanks in no small part to the thunderous complement of drummer Nigel Olsson and bassist Dee Murray. However, due either to oversaturation or the album's fractured length or its relative dearth of hits, *11–17–70* barely registered on the Top 40 in Britain, and though it fared somewhat better in the States by reaching #11, it soon enough descended to the bargain bins on both sides of the Atlantic. Still, a barnstorming "Take Me to the Pilot" and a torrid, eighteen-minute version of "Burn Down the Mission"—the latter including bits of Arthur "Big Boy" Crudup's "My Baby Left Me" and the Beatles' "Get Back"—resonate all these years later as compelling live moments. A new official version, fleshed out but still not complete or in sequence, was released exclusively on vinyl for Record Store Day in 2017.

Here and There (1976 2LP/2CD)

Delivered on April 30, 1976, *Here and There* fulfilled the final installment of John's contract with Dick James Music, pairing two distinct yet fairly representative performances from 1974—one from the Festival Hall in London, the other from Madison Square Garden in New York City. Though originally omitted from inclusion in the set, three songs performed in New York on Thanksgiving with John Lennon, in what would be the former Beatle's final concert appearance—"Whatever Gets You Thru the Night," "Lucy in the Sky with Diamonds," and "I Saw Her Standing There"—were added to the remastered 1995 version. Beginning with John's next studio LP, *Blue Moves*, all of his subsequent albums would be released on his own label, Rocket Records.

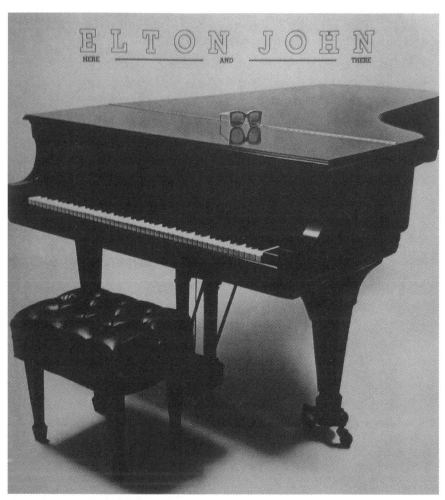

Here and There, released on April 30, 1976, as the final contractual obligation between John and Dick James Music, compiles a 1974 performance at Royal Festival Hall and a 1976 performance at Madison Square Garden.   *Author's collection*

To Russia with Elton: A Single Man in Concert with Ray Cooper (1979 VHS/Digital Video)

In mid-1979, Elton John became the first major western rock 'n' roll star to perform behind the Iron Curtain—Boney M. and Cliff Richard had played there prior, but neither boasted John's stature or cache of hit songs—with four concerts at the Great October Hall in Leningrad (May 21–24) and four more at the Rossya Hotel in Moscow (May 25–28).

On the road for the first time since announcing his retirement in August 1976 following six sold-out performances at New York City's Madison Square Garden, John remained wary on the idea of touring, at least with a full band—he had performed one benefit gig in 1977, at London's Wembley Arena, with guitarist Davey Johnstone's band, China, backing him, but he nixed the idea of a full-fledged tour from the stage that very night—but he nevertheless recruited percussionist Ray Cooper for select accompaniment. Smack dab in the middle of a trek ostensibly in support of his latest album, *A Single Man* (which found John writing for the first time without Bernie Taupin in favor of *War of the Worlds* lyricist Gary Osborne), John and Cooper played five warm-up performances in Israel (first in Jerusalem, then in Tel Aviv) before traveling—with families, management, and a modest film crew in tow—to the Soviet Union.

The concert film chronicles John's historic visit in general, and above all his live performances (divided into two sets, the first one solo and the second with Cooper), tickets for which had mostly been gobbled up by Russian government officials—not exactly the most enthusiastic rock 'n' roll–loving audience. In fact, during the first performance, John stares out to the faces in the prime seats, baffled at their stoic reactions, having not been previously informed of the "official" arrangement. Once the bulk of the apathetic lawmen had left their posts for home, though, the genuine fans perched at the back of the venue dashed to the front, succumbing to the unbridled energy and enthusiasm emanating from the artist onstage. Cooper is shown in the film beseeching the audience at every turn to clap and stomp and shout, punctuating the herky-jerky rhythm of "Bennie and the Jets" like a man possessed, and injecting songs like "Funeral for a Friend" and "Part Time Love" with fire-and-brimstone intensity.

Of course, these performances transpired at the dawn of the Cold War's last decade, a time when Soviet tolerance of rock music remained (as it had for decades before) at a dispassionate low. However, that an openly bisexual pop star known for wearing outrageous stage costumes festooned with vivid feather boas and glittery hats and glasses was allowed to enter the country, and indeed entertain the Russian masses, had as much to do with marketing—Moscow was set to host the 1980 Summer Olympics, and the Soviet Union needed all the favorable publicity it could muster—as it did with evolving perceptions of western culture.

Live in Australia with the Melbourne Symphony Orchestra (1987 CD/VHS)

His voice was shot. Amid moments like "The King Must Die" and "Madman Across the Water," in fact, John sounds like he's damn near gagging, his desperation mitigated only by his dogged determination to persevere through the nearly three-hour, nationally televised performance.

Throat problems had plagued John for several months, but soon after embarking upon a twenty-seven-date tour of Australia with his thirteen-piece band and the Melbourne Symphony Orchestra (conducted by his former keyboardist James Newton Howard), the matter turned dire. His voice deteriorated from painfully hoarse to nonfunctional, causing one date on the itinerary to be canceled altogether—the first such cancelation of John's career to date. Having consulted a physician prior to the tour's highly publicized final shows in December at the Sydney Entertainment Centre, where a live album and concert film were set to be recorded and broadcast on national television, John was forewarned that nodules in his throat

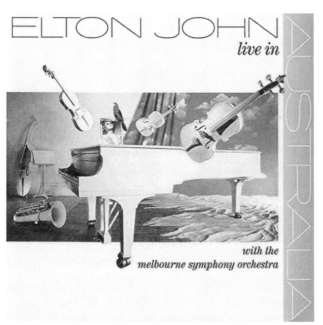

Live in Australia with the Melbourne Symphony Orchestra, released on July 6, 1987, includes a hit live version of "Candle in the Wind," which reached #6 in the US and #5 in the UK.   *Author's collection*

could very well be malignant, and could thus put an end to his singing career once and for all. The nodules, removed in surgery the following January, proved to be benign—but for all he knew until then, particularly onstage in Sydney, his fate hung in the balance.

Live in Australia captures Elton John in the throes not only of a crisis but indeed of his own mortality. As a result, it's arguably the strongest and most captivating live album in his catalogue.

Elton John—Live in Barcelona (1992 DVD)

A recording of the complete performance on July 21, 1992, at Ministadio CF in Barcelona, on his world tour in support of *The One*—John's first album after emerging from rehab, his sobriety intact, his talent undiminished—this was his first live release since the Tour de Force performance in Sydney, Australia, with the Melbourne Symphony Orchestra. Still in his keyboard phase, John sat center stage atop a Versace-designed platform, its gold accentuations giving a royal distinction.

One Night Only: The Greatest Hits Live at Madison Square Garden (2000 CD/DVD)

At times, *One Night Only* feels like one of the most representative and accessible, and at others, one of the most atypical, documents of a regular Elton John concert. Produced by Phil Ramone (whose superstar credentials include albums by Billy Joel, Ray Charles, Tony Bennett, and Karen Carpenter) and culled from two performances (October 20 and 21, 2000), the CD includes a generous selection of the as-advertised greatest hits—the DVD boasts a complete performance—but some of the most definitive ones are rendered as duets with select veteran friends and then-rising stars.

You can't fault John for wanting to shake things up, thirty years into his career, but who wants to hear "Your Song" sung by anyone but him, especially when he's sitting right there on the stage? Some collaborations work better than others, like "Goodbye Yellow Brick Road" with Billy Joel, whose obvious ease with the 1973 pastoral classic owes much to the fact that he'd performed it on his own during his and John's Face to Face tours in the mid-to-late '90s, when John didn't even play it himself. Another such highlight, unsurprisingly, is "Don't Go Breaking My Heart," which finds John and original duet partner, Kiki Dee, rekindling their old spark with the sort of chemistry that can only surface between old friends. Speaking of old friends, these concerts marked the return of the original Elton John Band drummer, Nigel Olsson, whose singular playing and harmonies had helped define John's signature '70s material in the first place.

An officially sanctioned bobble-head commemorating John's performances at New York City's Madison Square Garden on October 20–21, 2000, which were recorded and released on both CD and DVD, as *One Night Only: The Greatest Hits* and *One Night Only: The Greatest Hits Live at Madison Square Garden*, respectively.   *Author's collection*

New York City has long held a special significance for John, dating back to his earliest gigs there in 1970, as the opening act for Derek and the Dominos. Madison Square Garden, in particular, holds no shortage of resonance either, not least of all due to his Thanksgiving 1974 performance there, which featured John Lennon. Whenever John has played the venue in more recent years, he has usually dusted off the seldom-performed "Empty Garden," which he and Bernie Taupin composed in the late Beatle's honor in the aftermath of his 1980 assassination. Here, though, John maintains more of an upbeat vibe, delivering a faithful rendition of the *Abbey Road* classic "Come Together"—just one of the many benefits of the DVD that the CD lacks. Indeed, *One Night Only* succeeds far more as a complete visual live document than it does as an abbreviated audio one.

Elton 60: Live at Madison Square Garden (2007 DVD)

It's a shame this wasn't released in-full as a live album—a cursory, way-too-condensed digital version is available on iTunes—because it is just about the best official, latter-day Elton John concert film available. Beginning with the all-too-appropriate "Sixty Years On" and including nearly every hit fans could hope to hear, along with several well-selected deep cuts ("Holiday Inn," "Hercules," "Where to Now, St. Peter?"), John delivers a superb three-hour set, has his birthday cake, and eats it, too.

Elton John—The Million Dollar Piano (2014 DVD)

Following the tremendous success of *The Red Piano*, which closed in 2009 after a highly celebrated and lucrative five-year run, Elton John returned to the Colosseum stage at Caesars Palace in 2011 to premiere an all-new revue. *Elton John—The Million Dollar Piano*, which captures a show from

A banner formerly hanging from the rafters inside Madison Square Garden, commemorating John's sixtieth performance at the venue on his birthday, March 25, 2007—a record that stood until Billy Joel's ongoing residency enabled the Piano Man to seize the distinction.   *Author's collection*

2012, reveals the Las Vegas production to be a magnificent confluence of music and multimedia, complete with a technologically tricked-out, custom-made Yamaha grand piano (at a cost of four million dollars, to be exact) and a stage set festooned with the sort of majestic, Baroque-inspired grandiosity that probably reminds the Rocket Man of one of his living rooms.

"It has to be a little over the top," John says in a supplemental, behind-the-scenes featurette. "It's Vegas."

Such multimedia extravagance no doubt enriched the overall experience for those actually in attendance, but its impact is understandably a bit muted for those viewing at home. Still, the show is sensational, as John and his band sail through a diverse survey of one of pop music's preeminent catalogs. If his voice lacks some of the finesse of old—the distinctive high notes on "Tiny Dancer" and "Goodbye Yellow Brick Road," for instance, are handled by backup singers these days—his passion is as strong as ever. Indeed, the hits are invested with the conviction and vitality they deserve, yet the concert's most thrilling moments come from back-to-back album tracks, "Better Off Dead" and "Indian Sunset," the latter featuring legendary percussionist Ray Cooper in a tour de force performance. Longtime fans will also recognize bassist Bob Birch, who committed suicide later the same year. If this turns out to be the last commercially released concert with him on the stage, it will stand as a most rewarding farewell.

33

I'm Not Dying and I'm Far from Gone

A Twenty-First-Century Music Man

It wasn't nostalgia that compelled Elton John to make his most definitive and unassailable albums of his career in the early to mid-seventies. It was, simply, the desire (not to mention the talent) to create the best, most indelible music he could compose. While he has certainly turned out several commendable albums and songs in the decades since, there have been also a number of moments where that original desire seemed to be forsaken in favor of specific marketing strategies or blatant commerciality.

For a number of reasons—the breakout, award-winning triumphs of his efforts on the silver screen, particularly with Disney's *The Lion King*, along with his Broadway success like *Aida*, not to mention the ongoing stability of his relationship with partner David Furnish—John has in recent years felt more secure than he has since the halcyon days when "Rocket Man" and "Daniel" ascended the charts.

So much of Elton John's personal life has been underscored by insecurity, but what underscores much of the music that has come forth in his latter days has been a self-confidence—that after a half-century of fighting demons, both emotional and physical, he has finally reached a place wherein he feels comfortable in his own skin. That sense of security translates throughout the music he has made in recent years. He makes the kinds of albums he most desires, rather than out of contractual obligation, which has manifested in working with idol Leon Russell on *The Union*, or creating a reprisal of his most autobiographical work on *The*

Captain and the Kid, or in an exaltation of his most fundamental joys on *Wonderful Crazy Night*.

Whether each and every new project yielded the kind of critical praise and popular approval he had become accustomed to in the past wasn't the point. The point was that he was making the kinds of music he most enjoyed, with the musicians and producers with whom he most wanted to work.

Whatever John's ambition to recapture the glory days of his career, the death of Gus Dudgeon in 2002 obliterated such open-ended ambitions once and for all. As his recording career moved into the twenty-first century, John approached each subsequent album with marked discretion, almost like he was deliberating on a film or stage production. Intervals between studio albums have stretched longer as well. The days of two albums per year are, if not long since impossible, nevertheless long since gone.

After Everything I've Ever Learned

Even when some of his songs held up, John's albums of the past decade have allowed for too much gloss, too much fluff to pop through. Getting back to basics, or at least as back to basics as possible, became a battle cry. With the release of *Songs from the West Coast*, John redeemed himself, summoning songs that sound like what Elton John should have sounded like in his fifties if he hadn't strayed too far from his roots. The album's dedication to alt.country singer/songwriter Ryan Adams, who had recently split from his band Whiskeytown to go solo with his 2000 LP, *Heartbreaker*, is the key to the whole endeavor. Produced by Pat Leonard, the album was on the way to being the comeback effort of the decade, with its first single, "I Want Love," climbing the charts.

After the terrorist attacks of September 11, 2001, however, the context of "I Want Love" shifted. It became a solemn anthem in the face of evil. When John appeared at Madison Square Garden for the Concert for New York City in October of the same year, singing this song, it was embraced through eyes of grief and extreme adversity like a sobering, sacred hymn.

A UK CD single of "I Want Love," the lead single from John's 2001 LP *Songs from the West Coast*. While the song peaked at #7 in the UK, it reached only #110 in the US. Nevertheless, its poignancy increased in the aftermath of the 9/11 terror attacks, especially after John performed it six weeks later at Madison Square Garden, during the benefit Concert for New York.   *Author's collection*

The one-take video, starring actor Robert Downey Jr., walking solitary through a vacant yet opulent mansion, personalized the desperation evoked by the lyrics—"I want love, but it's impossible"—his dark eyes burning into the camera, searching for some inkling of solace from the other side.

John had decided to stop appearing in his own videos—a quick look at the *Tantrums and Tiaras* scene where he is apoplectic over his loathing of making them gives one a suitable reference for this decision—and this, ironically, yielded one of the most indelible videos of his career.

But I See Hope in Every Cloud

The American South looms large on 2004's *Peachtree Road*, which in its most organic moments recalls the styles, if not the sonic textures, of *Tumbleweed Connection* or *Honky Château*. Indicative of its street-block title, John recorded this one in his home away from home, Atlanta, Georgia, and, for the first time in his career, he produced it himself.

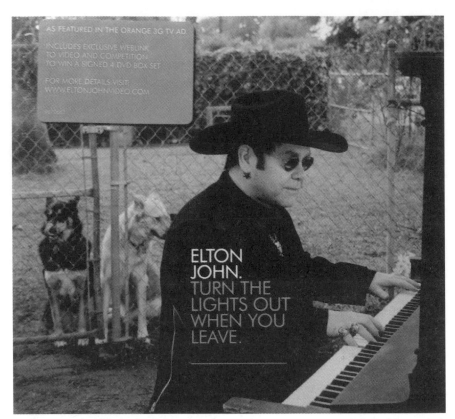

A UK CD single of "Turn the Lights Out When You Leave," a country-style ballad from John's 2004 LP *Peachtree Road*.   *Author's collection*

"On the last album [*Songs from the West Coast*], [producer] Pat Leonard got me back to doing stuff that was much more simple, playing piano, doing what I do best," John said in 2004, in an interview with *Billboard* magazine. "Trying to be Elton, not trying to be anybody else. That really paid off, and then this album I decided to produce myself, which I'd never done before. I knew I wanted to make an organic record like *Tumbleweed* [*Connection*] or *Madman* [*Across the Water*], with a band playing, which we did on *Songs from the West Coast*, so [I decided] to continue it, but using my band."

The approach worked, as John summons moments of bittersweet country flourishes ("Porch Swing in Tupelo," "Turn the Lights Out When You Leave") to complement moments of back-porch gospel grace ("Answer in the Sky" "All That I'm Allowed"), mixed with bits of friskiness ("They

Call Her the Cat") and hard-won self-reflection ("My Elusive Drug"). Unfortunately, his revived and realized inspiration didn't translate to record sales, with the album reaching a disappointing #17 on the *Billboard* Hot 100 album chart in the US, while bowing even lower, at #21, in the UK.

Strong Enough to Hold the Weight of Time

Composed as the thematic sequel—a bookend, really—to 1975's auto-biographical *Captain Fantastic and the Brown Dirt Cowboy*, 2006's *The Captain and the Kid* recalls the lean and green years of Elton John and Bernie Taupin back when they were struggling songwriters in the fading days of England's fabled Tin Pan Alley. Revisiting their shared history allows for even more nostalgia this time around, with songs like "Postcards from Richard Nixon" and "Old 67" summoning memories like cherished scrapbook clippings. "The Bridge" is the emotional crux of the album, its simple marriage of lyric and melody yielding one of John's most affecting recorded moments of the decade.

Don't Abandon the Light

Long after his most weird and wonderful days chasing his fortunes on the yellow brick road, Elton John found himself on safari in Africa, listening to Leon Russell's *Greatest Hits* collection on his iPod, sobbing. "I started to cry, it moved me so much," John told the *New York Times* in 2010, reflecting not only on Russell's music but also his increasing obscurity in recent years. "His music takes me back to the most wonderful time in my life, and it makes me so angry that he's been forgotten."

That wonderful time in John's life was the early seventies, when he first traveled to America, making his national debut at Doug Weston's storied Troubadour club in West Hollywood. On the second night of his six-date residency, as he barnstormed through "Burn Down the Mission," John recognized Russell in the audience, listening, watching, turning his nerves to jelly. As mentor and protégé, the two toured together, but, in subsequent years, lost touch. John continued burning out his fuse out here alone as Russell's spotlight dimmed, his fame diminishing into a haze of one-nighters lined like polka dots across the country, his old bus feeling the endless interstate miles.

On 2010's *The Union*, mentor and protégé came together once more. Produced by T Bone Burnett and featuring songs written both by Russell and with Bernie Taupin, the album thrives on a musical gumbo spiced with rhythm and blues, gospel, and rock 'n' roll, two boogie-woogie pianos pounding out plenty of sanctified grooves in a gothic resurrection.

"He is a better piano player than I am," John said in a joint interview with Russell in 2010, on NPR's *Morning Edition*. "As far as gospel and stuff like that, that's why I wanted to make this album. He is my idol."

I'm Counting on a Memory

Produced by T Bone Burnett, *The Diving Board* was conceived as a three-piece arrangement (John on piano, along with bassist Raphael Saadiq and drummer Jay Bellerose) with slight embellishments—a "parlor record," as Burnett has often described it. As John explained in 2013, to the *Independent*, "A lot of the takes were first takes, and the first track on the album is a solo piano track, which I've never done before."

As Taupin reflected in the same interview, "We'll sit down, and I might say, 'I kind of see this as a Gram Parsons kind of song.' Or 'there's a very Ray Charles feel to this.' He likes bullet points. But then he'll go off on a tangent and take it totally somewhere else. But I never argue with his melodic stylings, because the guy is a genius as far as I'm concerned."

One of the standout moments on the album is "Oceans Away," the words to which Taupin wrote in homage to veterans of World War II, and specifically to Captain Robert Taupin, his father, who died on June 23, 1994, aged eighty-three.

"They're miserable songs," John told the *Guardian* in 2013, "and I love to sing miserable songs. If misery is done well, it's fantastic."

Elton John, performing on November 11, 2007, at the Germain Arena in Estero, Florida, on his world tour in support of *Rocket Man: The Definitive Hits*.
Photo by Donald Gibson, Author's collection

I Looked Up and Felt My Feet Lift Off the Ground

Unlike on *The Union* and *The Diving Board*, which feature select session players—musicians within producer T Bone Burnett's custom stable— John's touring band played on 2016's *Wonderful Crazy Night*, which contributes to the album's loose, joyous vibe. In fact, John beseeched lyricist

Bernie Taupin to dial down the sorrow (a long-since familiar and favorite wellspring of inspiration for both men) in the songs he wrote.

"I said, 'no sad songs,'" John told the *Los Angeles Times*, in a brief interview published on January 12, 2016. "We could both write sad songs every five minutes, but I wanted something to reflect where I am right now. I have a great career, a great partner, two wonderful children, and life couldn't be better. I wanted to make a record that reflects that."

Appendix 1
Get a Little Action In: Side Jobs and Sessions

In the earliest days of his songwriting partnership with Bernie Taupin—when the likes of Lulu and Tom Jones covered their songs but failed to turn them into hits—Elton John supplemented his weekly stipend from Dick James Music by playing on songs by other artists, at times uncredited or attributed to an alias. As his success flourished in the seventies, such sessions were neither logistically feasible nor financially necessary; nevertheless, John made time for select artists. His loyalty to friends as well as his enthusiasm for emerging artists has inspired him, on occasion, to contribute to a wide spectrum of recordings.

Though by no means definitive, this chapter surveys some of John's most essential side jobs and sessions from throughout his career.

Alice in Chains

"Black Gives Way to Blue" (*Black Gives Way to Blue*, 2009): piano

Argosy

"Mr. Boyd" (single, 1970): piano
"Imagine" (single, 1970): piano

Rick Astley

"Wonderful You" (*Free*, 1991): piano
"Behind the Smile" (*Free*, 1991): piano

Kevin Ayers

"Toujours La Voyage" (*Sweet Deceiver*, 1976): piano
"Circular Letter" (*Sweet Deceiver*, 1976): piano
"Guru Banana" (*Sweet Deceiver*, 1976): piano

Marc Bolan and T. Rex

"Children of the Revolution" (*Born to Boogie* soundtrack, 1972): piano

Long John Baldry

"Let's Burn Down the Cornfield" (*It Ain't Easy*, 1971): piano
"Mr. Rubin" (*It Ain't Easy*, 1971): piano
"Rock Me When He's Gone" (*It Ain't Easy*, 1971): piano
"Flying" (*It Ain't Easy*, 1971): piano
"Come Back Again" (*Everything Stops for Tea*, 1972): backing vocals
"Wild Mountain Tyme" (*Everything Stops for Tea*, 1972): backing vocals
"Iko Iko" (*Everything Stops for Tea*, 1972): backing vocals
"Jubilee Crowd" (*Everything Stops for Tea*, 1972): backing vocals

The Barron Knights

"An Olympic Record" (single, 1968): piano

Blue

"Victim" (*Fools Party*, 1979): piano
"Love Stings" (*Fools Party*, 1979): piano

Jon Bon Jovi

"Billy Get Your Guns" (*Blaze of Glory* soundtrack, 1990)
"Dyin' Ain't Much of a Living" (*Blaze of Glory* soundtrack, 1990)

Bread and Beer Band

"Breakdown Blues" (single, 1969): piano
"Dick Barton Theme (The Devil's Gallop)" (single, 1969): piano

Jackson Browne

"Redneck Friend" (1973): piano (credited as Rockaday Johnnie)

Cindy Bullens

"Dream #29 (One True Love)" (*Dream #29*, 2005): piano

Brandi Carlisle

"Caroline" (*Give Up the Ghost*, 2009): piano and vocals

Bright Light Bright Light

"I Wish We Were Leaving" (single, 2014): backing vocals
"All in the Name" (*Choreography*, 2016): backing vocals
"Symmetry of Two Hearts" (*Choreography*, 2016): backing vocals
"Running Back to You" (*Choreography*, 2016): backing vocals

Tina Charles

"Good to Be Alive" (single, 1969): backing vocals
"Same Old Story" (single, 1969): backing vocals

China

"Shameful Disgrace" (*China*, 1977): piano

Kiki Dee

"The Last Good Man in My Life" (single, 1973): piano

Lonnie Donegan

"Diggin' My Potatoes" (*Puttin' on the Style*, 1978): piano
"Puttin' on the Style" (*Puttin' on the Style*, 1978): piano

Lesley Duncan

"Help Me Jesus" (*Sing Children Sing*, 1971): piano
"Mr. Rubin" (*Sing Children Sing*, 1971): piano

Simon Dupree and the Big Sound

"Give it All Back" (single, 1969): piano

Judith Durham

"Skyline Pigeon" (*Climb Ev'ry Mountain*, 1970): piano

Bob Dylan

"2 X 2" (*Under the Red Sky*, 1990): piano

Fall Out Boy

"Save Rock and Roll" (*Save Rock and Roll*, 2013): piano and vocal

Fairfield Parlour

"Just Another Day" (single, 1970): piano and backing vocals

Family Dogg

"A Way of Life" (single, 1969): piano

George Harrison

"Cloud 9" (*Cloud 9*, 1987): electric piano
"Devil's Radio" (*Cloud 9*, 1987): piano
"Wreck of the Hesperus" (*Cloud 9*, 1987): (piano)

The Hollies

"Perfect Lady Housewife" (*Moving Finger*, 1969): organ and backing vocals
"He Ain't Heavy (He's My Brother)" (single, 1969): piano and backing vocals

"I Can't Tell the Bottom from the Top" (single, 1969): piano and backing vocals

Hurts

"Help" (*Exile*, 2013): piano

Davey Johnstone

"Keep Right On" (*Smiling Face*, 1973): piano

Tom Jones

"Delilah" (single, 1968): piano and backing vocals
"Daughter of Darkness" (*Daughter of Darkness,* 1970): backing vocals

John Lennon

"Whatever Gets You Thru the Night" (*Walls and Bridges*, 1974): piano and backing vocals
"Surprise Surprise" (*Walls and Bridges*, 1974): piano and backing vocals

Eddie Murphy

"Yeah" (*Love's Alright*, 1993): backing vocals

Olivia Newton-John

"The Rumour" (*The Rumour*, 1988): piano and vocal

Nigel Olsson

"Only One Woman" (*Nigel Olsson*, 1975): piano
"In Good Time" (single, 1975): backing vocals
"Showdown" (*Changing Tides*, 1986): piano
"Saturday Night" (*Changing Tides*, 1986): piano

Mal Pope

"If I Wasn't There" (*Old Enough to Know Better*, 2010): backing vocals
"How It Hurts" (*Old Enough to Know Better*, 2010): backing vocals

Queens of the Stone Age

"Fairweather Friends" (Album: . . . *Like Clockwork*, 2013): piano and vocals

Radio Heart Featuring Gary Numan

"Strange Thing" (*Radio Heart*, 1987): piano
"The Victim" (*Radio Heart*, 1987): piano

Bruce Roberts

"Emerald" (*Intimacy*, 1995): piano and backing vocals
"The Man Who Loves You" (*Intimacy*, 1995): backing vocals

Brian and Brenda Russell

"Tell Me When the Whistle Blows" (*Word Called Love*, 1976): piano

Saxon

"Northern Lady" (*Rock the Nations*, 1986): piano
"Party 'Til You Puke" (*Rock the Nations*, 1986): piano

The Scaffold

"Lily the Pink" (single, 1968): backing vocals

Neil Sedaka

"Steppin' Out" (*Steppin' Out*, 1976): piano and backing vocals

Scissor Sisters

"I Don't Feel Like Dancing" (*Ta Dah*, 2006): piano

"Intermission" (*Ta Dah*, 2006): piano

Ringo Starr

"Snookeroo" (*Goodnight Vienna*, 1974): piano

Rod Stewart

"Let Me Be Your Car" (*Smiler*, 1974): piano and backing vocals

Sting

"Come Down in Time" (*Two Rooms: Celebrating the Songs of Elton John and Bernie Taupin*, 1991): piano (credited as Nancy Treadlight)

Bernie Taupin

"Love (The Barren Desert)" (*He Who Rides the Tiger*, 1980): backing vocals
"Citizen Jane" (*Tribe*, 1987): backing vocals
"Billy Fury" (*Tribe*, 1987): backing vocals

Timbaland

"2 Man Show" (*Timbaland Presents Shock Value*, 2007): piano

Wham!

"Edge of Heaven" (*Music from the Edge of Heaven*, 1986): piano

Kanye West

"All of the Lights" (*My Beautiful Dark Twisted Fantasy*, 2010): piano and backing vocals

Appendix 2
Discography

Empty Sky (June 3, 1969)

"Empty Sky" / "Val-Hala" / "Western Ford Gateway" / "Hymn 2000" / "Lady What's Tomorrow" / "Sails" / "The Scaffold" / "Skyline Pigeon" / "Gulliver / Hay Chewed"

Elton John (April 10, 1970)

"Your Song" / "I Need You to Turn To" / "Take Me to the Pilot" / "No Shoe Strings on Louise" / "First Episode at Hienton" / "Sixty Years On" / "Border Song" / "The Greatest Discovery" / "The Cage" / "The King Must Die"

Tumbleweed Connection (October 30, 1970)

"Ballad of a Well-Known Gun" / "Come Down in Time" / "Country Comfort" / "Son of Your Father" / "My Father's Gun" / "Where to Now, St. Peter?" / "Love Song" / "Amoreena" / "Talking Old Soldiers" / "Burn Down the Mission"

Friends (Original Motion Picture Soundtrack) (April 6, 1971)

"Friends" / "Honey Roll" / "Variations on Friends" / "Theme (The First Kiss)" / "Seasons" / "Variations on Michelle's Song (A Day in the Country)" / "Can I Put You On" / "Michelle's Song" / "I Meant to Do My Work Today (A Day in the Country)" / "Four Moods" / "Seasons Reprise"

11–17–70 (May 10, 1971)

"Bad Side of the Moon" / "Amoreena" / "Take Me to the Pilot" / "Sixty Years On" / "Honky Tonk Women" / "Can I Put You On" / "Burn Down the Mission / My Baby Left Me / Get Back"

Madman Across the Water (November 5, 1971)

"Tiny Dancer" / "Levon" / "Razor Face" / "Madman Across the Water" / "Indian Sunset" / "Holiday Inn" / "Rotten Peaches" / "All the Nasties" / "Goodbye"

Honky Château (May 19, 1972)

"Honky Cat" / "Mellow" / "I Think I'm Going to Kill Myself" / "Susie (Dramas)" / "Rocket Man (I Think It's Going to Be a Long, Long Time)" / "Salvation" / "Slave" / "Amy" / "Mona Lisas and Mad Hatters" / "Hercules"

Don't Shoot Me I'm Only the Piano Player (January 26, 1973)

"Daniel" / "Teacher I Need You" / "Elderberry Wine" / "Blues for Baby and Me" / "Midnight Creeper" / "Have Mercy on the Criminal" / "I'm Gonna Be a Teenage Idol" / "Texan Love Song" / "Crocodile Rock" / "High Flying Bird"

Goodbye Yellow Brick Road (October 5, 1973)

Disc 1: "Funeral for a Friend / Love Lies Bleeding" / "Candle in the Wind" / "Bennie and the Jets" / "Goodbye Yellow Brick Road" / "This Song Has No Title" / "Grey Seal" / "Jamaica Jerk-Off" / "I've Seen That Movie Too"

Disc 2: "Sweet Painted Lady" / "The Ballad of Danny Bailey (1903-34)" / "Dirty Little Girl" / "All the Girls Love Alice" / "Your Sister Can't Twist (But She Can Rock 'N' Roll)" / "Saturday Night's Alright for Fighting" / "Roy Rogers" / "Social Disease" / "Harmony"

Caribou (June 28, 1974)

"The Bitch Is Back" / "Pinky" / "Grimsby" / "Dixie Lily" / "Solar Prestige a Gammon" / "You're So Static" / "I've Seen the Saucers" / "Stinker" / "Don't Let the Sun Go Down on Me" / "Ticking"

Greatest Hits (November 8, 1974)

"Your Song" / "Daniel" / "Honky Cat" / "Goodbye Yellow Brick Road" / "Saturday Night's Alright for Fighting" / "Rocket Man (I Think It's Going to Be a Long, Long Time)" / "Bennie and the Jets" / "Don't Let the Sun Go Down on Me" / "Border Song" / "Crocodile Rock"

Captain Fantastic and the Brown Dirt Cowboy (May 23, 1975)

"Captain Fantastic and the Brown Dirt Cowboy" / "Tower of Babel" / "Bitter Fingers" / "Tell Me When the Whistle Blows" / "Someone Saved My Life Tonight" / "Gotta Get a Meal Ticket" / "Better Off Dead" / "Writing" / "We All Fall in Love Sometimes" / "Curtains"

Rock of the Westies (October 4, 1975)

"Yell Help / Wednesday Night / Ugly" / "Dan Dare (Pilot of the Future)" / "Island Girl" / "Grow Some Funk of Your Own" / "I Feel Like a Bullet (In the Gun of Robert Ford)" / "Street Kids" / "Hard Luck Story" / "Feed Me" / "Billy Bones and the White Bird"

Here and There (April 30, 1976)

Disc 1: "Skyline Pigeon" / "Border Song" / "Take Me to the Pilot" / "Country Comfort" / "Love Song" / "Bad Side of the Moon" / "Burn Down the Mission" / "Honky Cat" / "Crocodile Rock" / "Candle in the Wind" / "Your Song" / "Saturday Night's Alright for Fighting"

Disc 2: "Funeral for a Friend / Love Lies Bleeding" / "Rocket Man (I Think It's Going to Be a Long, Long Time)" / "Take Me to the Pilot" / "Bennie and the Jets" / "Grey Seal" / "Daniel" / "You're So Static" / "Whatever Gets You Thru the Night" / "Lucy in the Sky with Diamonds" / "I Saw Her Standing There" / "Don't Let the Sun Go Down on Me" / "Your Song" / "The Bitch Is Back"

Blue Moves (October 22, 1976)

Disc 1: "Your Starter For . . ." / "Tonight" / "One Horse Town" / "Chameleon" / "Boogie Pilgrim" / "Cage the Songbird" / "Crazy Water" / "Shoulder Holster"

Disc 2: "Sorry Seems to Be the Hardest Word" / "Out of the Blue" / "Between Seventeen and Twenty" / "The Wide-Eyed and Laughing" / "Someone's Final Song" / "Where's the Shoorah?" / "If There's a God in Heaven (What's He Waiting For?)" / "Idol" / "Theme from a Non-Existent TV Series" / "Bite Your Lip (Get Up and Dance)"

Greatest Hits Volume II (September 13, 1977)

"The Bitch Is Back" / "Lucy in the Sky with Diamonds" / "Tiny Dancer" / "I Feel Like a Bullet (In the Gun of Robert Ford)" / "Someone Saved My Life Tonight" / "Philadelphia Freedom" / "Island Girl" / "Grow Some Funk of Your Own" / "Levon" / "Pinball Wizard"

A Single Man (October 16, 1978)

"Shine on Through" / "Return to Paradise" / "I Don't Care" / "Big Dipper" / "It Ain't Gonna Be Easy" / "Part-Time Love" / "Georgia" / "Shooting Star" / "Madness" / "Reverie" / "Song for Guy"

Victim of Love (October 13, 1979)

"Johnny B. Goode" / "Warm Love in a Cold World" / "Born Bad" / "Thunder in the Night" / "Spotlight" / "Street Boogie" / "Victim of Love"

21 at 33 (May 13, 1980)

"Chasing the Crown" / "Little Jeannie" / "Sartorial Eloquence" / "Two Rooms at the End of the World" / "White Lady White Powder" / "Dear God" / "Never Gonna Fall in Love Again" / "Take Me Back" / "Give Me the Love"

The Fox (May 20, 1981)

"Breaking Down Barriers" / "Heart in the Right Place" / "Just Like Belgium" / "Nobody Wins" / "Fascist Faces" / "Carla / Etude / Fanfare / Chloe" / "Heels of the Wind" / "Elton's Song" / "The Fox"

Jump Up! (April 9, 1982)

"Dear John" / "Spiteful Child" / "Ball and Chain" / "Legal Boys" / "I Am Your Robot" / "Blue Eyes" / "Empty Garden (Hey, Hey Johnny)" / "Princess" / "Where Have All the Good Times Gone" / "All Quiet on the Western Front"

Too Low for Zero (May 1, 1983)

"Cold as Christmas (In the Middle of the Year)" / "I'm Still Standing" / "Too Low for Zero" / "Religion" / "I Guess That's Why They Call It the Blues" / "Crystal" / "Kiss the Bride" / "Whipping Boy" / "Saint" / "One More Arrow"

Breaking Hearts (July 9, 1984)

"Restless" / "Slow Down Georgie (She's Poison)" / "Who Wears These Shoes?" / "Breaking Hearts (Ain't What It Used to Be)" / "Li'l 'Frigerator" / "Passengers" / "In Neon" / "Burning Buildings" / "Did He Shoot Her?" / "Sad Songs (Say So Much)"

Ice on Fire (November 4, 1985)

"This Town" / "Cry to Heaven" / "Soul Glove" / "Nikita" / "Too Young" / "Wrap Her Up" / "Satellite" / "Tell Me What the Papers Say" / "Candy by the Pound" / "Shoot Down the Moon"

Leather Jackets (October 15, 1986)

"Leather Jackets" / "Hoop of Fire" / "Don't Trust That Woman" / "Go It Alone" / "Gypsy Heart" / "Slow Rivers" / "Heartache All Over the World" / "Angeline" / "Memory of Love" / "Paris" / "I Fall Apart"

Live in Australia with the Melbourne Symphony Orchestra (June 13, 1987)

"Sixty Years On" / "I Need You to Turn To" / "The Greatest Discovery" / "Tonight" / "Sorry Seems to Be the Hardest Word" / "The King Must Die" / "Take Me to the Pilot" / "Tiny Dancer" / "Have Mercy on the Criminal" / "Madman Across the Water" / "Candle in the Wind" / "Burn Down the Mission" / "Your Song" / "Don't Let the Sun Go Down on Me"

Elton John's Greatest Hits Volume III (*1979–1987*) (November 12, 1987)

"I Guess That's Why They Call It the Blues" / "Mama Can't Buy You Love" / "Little Jeannie" / "Sad Songs (Say So Much)" / "I'm Still Standing" / "Empty Garden (Hey, Hey Johnny)" / "Heartache All Over the World" / "Too Low for Zero" / "Kiss the Bride" / "Blue Eyes" / "Nikita" / "Wrap Her Up"

Reg Strikes Back (June 24, 1988)

"Town of Plenty" / "A Word in Spanish" / "Mona Lisas and Mad Hatters (Part Two)" / "I Don't Wanna Go on with You Like That" / "Japanese Hands" / "Goodbye Marlon Brando" / "The Camera Never Lies" / "Heavy Traffic" / "Poor Cow" / "Since God Invented Girls"

The Complete Thom Bell Sessions (February 1, 1989)

"Nice and Slow" / "Country Love Song" / "Shine on Through" / "Mama Can't Buy You Love" / "Are You Ready for Love" / "Three Way Love Affair"

Sleeping with the Past (August 29, 1989)

"Durban Deep" / "Healing Hands" / "Whispers" / "Club at the End of the Street" / "Sleeping with the Past" / "Stone's Throw from Hurtin'" / "Sacrifice" / "I Never Knew Her Name" / "Amazes Me" / "Blue Avenue"

To Be Continued . . . (November 8, 1990)

Disc 1: "Come Back Baby" / "Lady Samantha" / "It's Me That You Need" / "Your Song" (Piano Demo) / "Rock and Roll Madonna" / "Bad Side of the Moon" / "Your Song" / "Take Me to the Pilot" / "Border Song" / "Sixty Years On" / "Country Comfort" / "Grey Seal" (Original Version) / "Friends" / "Levon" / "Tiny Dancer" / "Madman Across the Water" / "Honky Cat" / "Mona Lisas and Mad Hatters"

Disc 2: "Rocket Man (I Think it's Going to Be a Long, Long Time)" / "Daniel" / "Crocodile Rock" / "Bennie and the Jets" / "Goodbye Yellow Brick Road" / "Funeral for a Friend" / "Love Lies Bleeding" / "Whenever You're Ready (We'll Go Steady Again)" / "Saturday Night's Alright for Fighting" / "Jack Rabbit" / "Harmony" / "Screw You" / "Step into Christmas" / "The Bitch Is Back" / "Pinball Wizard" / "Someone Saved My Life Tonight"

Disc 3: "Philadelphia Freedom" / "One Day at a Time" / "Lucy in the Sky with Diamonds" / "I Saw Her Standing There" (Live 1974) / "Island Girl" / "Sorry Seems to Be the Hardest Word" / "Don't Go Breaking My Heart" / "I Feel Like a Bullet (In the Gun of Robert Ford)" (Live 1977) / "Ego" / "Song for Guy" / "Mama Can't Buy You Love" / "Cartier" / "Little Jeannie" / "Donner Pour Donner" / "Fanfare" / "Chloe" / "The Retreat" / "Blue Eyes

Disc 4: "Empty Garden (Hey, Hey Johnny)" / "I Guess That's Why They Call It the Blues" / "I'm Still Standing" / "Sad Songs (Say So Much)" / "Act of War" / "Nikita" / "Candle in the Wind" (Live 1986) / "Carla / Etude" (Live 1986) / "Don't Let the Sun Go Down on Me" (Live 1986) / "I Don't Wanna Go on with You Like That" (Shep Pettibone Mix) / "Give Peace a Chance" / "Sacrifice" / "Made for Me" / "You Gotta Love Someone" / "I Swear I Heard the Night Talkin'" / "Easier to Walk Away"

The Very Best of Elton John (October 1, 1990)

Disc 1: Your Song" / "Rocket Man (I Think it's Going to Be a Long, Long Time)" / "Honky Cat" / "Crocodile Rock" / "Daniel" / "Goodbye Yellow Brick Road" / "Saturday Night's Alright for Fighting" / "Candle in the Wind" / "Don't Let the Sun Go Down on Me" / "Lucy in the Sky with Diamonds" / "Philadelphia Freedom" / "Someone Saved My Life Tonight" / "Pinball Wizard" / "The Bitch Is Back"

Disc 2: "Don't Go Breaking My Heart" / "Bennie and the Jets" / "Sorry Seems to Be the Hardest Word" / "Song for Guy" / "Part-Time Love" / "Blue Eyes" / "I Guess That's Why They Call It the Blues" / "I'm Still Standing" / "Kiss the Bride" / "Sad Songs (Say So Much)" / "Passengers" / "Nikita" / "I Don't Wanna Go on with You Like That" / "Sacrifice" / "Easier to Walk Away" / "You Gotta Love Someone"

The One (June 22, 1992)

"Simple Life" / "The One" / "Sweat It Out" / "Runaway Train" / "Whitewash County" / "The North" / "When a Woman Doesn't Want You" / "Emily" / "On Dark Street" / "Understanding Women" / "The Last Song"

Rare Masters (October 20, 1992)

Disc 1: "I've Been Loving You" / "Here's to the Next Time" / "Lady Samantha" / "All Across the Havens" / "It's Me That You Need" / "Just Like Strange Rain" / "Bad Side of the Moon" / "Rock and Roll Madonna" / "Grey Seal" (Original Version) / "Friends" / "Michelle's Song" / "Seasons" / "Variation on Michelle's Song (A Day in the Country)" / "Can I Put You On" / "Honey Roll" / "Variation on Friends" / "I Meant to Do My Work Today (A Day in the Country)" / "Four Moods" / "Seasons Reprise"

Disc 2: "Madman Across the Water" (Original Version) / "Into the Old Man's Shoes" / "Rock Me When He's Gone" / "Slave" (Alternate Fast Version) / "Skyline Pigeon" (Piano Version) / "Jack Rabbit" / "Whenever You're Ready (We'll Go Steady Again)" / "Let Me Be Your Car" / "Screw You (Young Man's Blues)" / "Step into Christmas" / "Ho! Ho! Ho! (Who'd Be a Turkey at Christmas)" / "Sick City" / "Cold Highway" / "One Day at a Time" / "I Saw Her Standing There" (Live with John Lennon) / "House of Cards" / "Planes" / "Sugar on the Floor"

Duets (November 30, 1993)

"When I Think About Love (I Think About You)" / "The Power" / "Shakey Ground" / "True Love" / "If You Were Me" / "A Woman's Needs" / "Old Friend" / "Go on and On" / "Don't Go Breaking My Heart" / "Ain't Nothing Like the

Real Thing" / "I'm Your Puppet" / "Love Letters" / "Born to Lose" / "Don't Let the Sun Go Down on Me" / "Duets for One"

The Lion King (*Original Motion Picture Soundtrack*) (May 31, 1994)

"Circle of Life" (with Carmen Twillie) / "I Just Can't Wait to Be King" (Jason Weaver) / "Be Prepared" (Jeremy Irons) / "Hakuna Matata" (Nathan Lane and Ernie Sabella) / "Can You Feel the Love Tonight" (Joseph Williams and Sally Dworsky) / "This Land" (Instrumental) / "To Die For" (Instrumental) / "Under the Stars" (Instrumental) / "King of Pride Rock" (Instrumental) / "Circle of Life" / "I Just Can't Wait to Be King" / "Can You Feel the Love Tonight"

Made in England (March 21, 1995)

"Believe" / "Made in England" / "House" / "Cold" / "Pain" / "Belfast" / "Latitude" / "Please" / "Man" / "Lies" / "Blessed"

Love Songs (November 6, 1995)

"Can You Feel the Love Tonight" / "The One" / "Sacrifice" / "Daniel" / "Someone Saved My Life Tonight" / "Your Song" / "Don't Let the Sun Go Down on Me" (Live with George Michael) / "Believe" / "Blue Eyes" / "Sorry Seems to Be the Hardest Word" / "Blessed" / "Candle in the Wind" (Live 1986) / "You Can Make History (Young Again)" / "No Valentines" / "Circle of Life"

The Big Picture (September 22, 1997)

"Long Way from Happiness" / "Live Like Horses" / "The End Will Come" / "If the River Can Bend" / "Love's Got a Lot to Answer For" / "Something About the Way You Look Tonight" / "The Big Picture" / "Recover Your Soul" / "January" / "I Can't Steer My Heart Clear of You" / "Wicked Dreams"

The Lion King (*Original Broadway Cast Recording*) (November 14, 1997)

"Circle of Life" / "Grasslands" / "The Morning Report" / "The Lioness Hunt" / "I Just Can't Wait to Be King" / "Chow Down" / "They Live in You" / "Be

Prepared" / "The Stampede" / "Rafiki Mourns" / "Hakuna Matata" / "One by One" / "The Madness of King Scar" / "Shadowland" / "The Lion Sleeps Tonight" / "Endless Night" / "Can You Feel the Love Tonight?" / "He Lives in You (Reprise)" / "Simba Confronts Scar" / "King of Pride Rock (Circle of Life Reprise)"

Elton John and Tim Rice's Aida (March 23, 1999)

"Another Pyramid" (Sting) / "Written in the Stars" (Elton John and LeAnn Rimes) / "Easy as Life" (Tina Turner and Angelique Kidjo) / "My Strongest Suit" (Spice Girls) / "I Know the Truth" (Elton John and Janet Jackson) / "Not Me" (Boyz II Men) / "Amneris' Letter" (Shania Twain) / "A Step Too Far" (Elton John, Heather Headley, and Sherie Rene Scott) / "Like Father Like Son" (Lenny Kravitz) / "Elaborate Lives" (Heather Headley) / "How I Know You" (James Taylor) / "The Messenger" (Elton John and Lulu) / "The Gods Love Nubia" (Kelly Price) / "Enchantment Passing Through" (Dru Hill) / "Orchestral Finale"

The Muse (Original Motion Picture Soundtrack) (August 24, 1999)

"Driving Home" / "Driving to Universal" / "Driving to Jack's" / "Walk of Shame" / "Better Have a Gift" / "The Wrong Gift" / "The Aquarium" / "Are We Laughing" / "Take a Walk with Me" / "What Should I Do?" / "Back to the Aquarium" / "Steven Redecorates" / "To the Guesthouse" / "The Cookie Factory" / "Multiple Personality" / "Sarah Escapes" / "Back to Paramount" / "Meet Christine" / "The Muse" / "The Muse" (Remix by Jermaine Dupri)

The Road to El Dorado (Original Motion Picture Soundtrack) (March 14, 2000)

"El Dorado" / "Someday Out of the Blue (Theme From El Dorado)" / "Without Question" / "Friends Never Say Goodbye" / "The Trail We Blaze" / "16th Century Man" / "The Panic in Me" / "It's Tough to Be a God" / "Trust Me" / "My Heart Dances" / "Queen of Cities" / "Cheldorado" (Instrumental) / "The Brig" (Instrumental) / "Wonders of the New World" (Instrumental)

Elton John and Tim Rice's Aida (*Original Broadway Cast Recording*) (June 6, 2000)

"Every Story Is a Love Story" / "Fortune Favors the Brave" / "The Past Is Another Land" / "Another Pyramid" / "How I Know You" / "My Strongest Suit" / "Enchantment Passing Through" / "My Strongest Suit" (Reprise) / "Dance of the Robe" / "Not Me" / "Elaborate Lives" / "The Gods Love Nubia" / "A Step Too Far" / "Easy as Life" / "Like Father Like Son" / "Radames' Letter" / "How I Know You" (Reprise) / "Written in the Stars" / "I Know the Truth" / "Elaborate Lives" (Reprise) / "Enchantment Passing Through" (Reprise) / "Every Story Is a Love Story" (Reprise)

Elton John—One Night Only: The Greatest Hits (November 20, 2000)

"Goodbye Yellow Brick Road" / "Philadelphia Freedom" / "Don't Go Breaking My Heart" / "Rocket Man (I Think It's Going to Be a Long, Long Time)" / "Daniel" / "Crocodile Rock" / "Sacrifice" / "Can You Feel the Love Tonight" / "Bennie and the Jets" / "Your Song" / "Sad Songs (Say So Much)" / "Candle in the Wind" / "The Bitch Is Back" / "Saturday Night's Alright for Fighting" / "I'm Still Standing" / "Don't Let the Sun Go Down on Me" / "I Guess That's Why They Call It the Blues"

Songs from the West Coast (October 1, 2001)

"The Emperor's New Clothes" / "Dark Diamond" / "Look Ma, No Hands" / "American Triangle" / "Original Sin" / "Birds" / "I Want Love" / "The Wasteland" / "Ballad of the Boy in the Red Shoes" / "Love Her Like Me" / "Mansfield" / "This Train Don't Stop There Anymore"

Greatest Hits 1970–2002 (November 11, 2002)

Disc 1: "Your Song" / "Tiny Dancer" / "Honky Cat" / "Rocket Man (I Think It's Going to Be a Long, Long Time)" / "Crocodile Rock" / "Daniel" / "Saturday Night's Alright for Fighting" / "Goodbye Yellow Brick Road" / "Candle in the Wind" / "Bennie and the Jets" / "Don't Let the Sun Go Down on Me" / "The Bitch Is Back" / "Philadelphia Freedom" / "Someone Saved My Life Tonight"

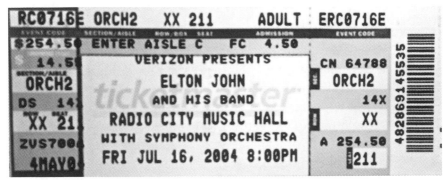

A ticket stub from Elton John's performance on July 16, 2004, at Radio City Music Hall, featuring his touring band as well as a full symphony orchestra and choir.   *Author's collection*

/ "Island Girl" / "Don't Go Breaking My Heart" / "Sorry Seems to Be the Hardest Word"

Disc 2: "Blue Eyes" / "I'm Still Standing" / "I Guess That's Why They Call It the Blues" / "Sad Songs (Say So Much)" (Single Edit) / "Nikita" / "Sacrifice" / "The One" / "Kiss the Bride" / "Can You Feel the Love Tonight" / "Circle of Life" / "Believe" (Radio Edit) / "Made in England" (Radio Edit) / "Something About the Way You Look Tonight" (Edit Version) / "Written in the Stars" / "I Want Love" / "This Train Don't Stop There Anymore" / "Song for Guy" (Single Version)

Peachtree Road (November 9, 2004)

"Weight of the World" / "Porch Swing in Tupelo" / "Answer in the Sky" / "Turn the Lights Out When You Leave" / "They Call Her the Cat" / "Freaks in Love" / "All That I'm Allowed (I'm Thankful)" / "I Stop and I Breathe" / "Too Many Tears" / "It's Getting Dark in Here" / "I Can't Keep This from You"

Billy Elliot the Musical (*The Original Cast Recording*) (February 07, 2006)

"The Stars Look Down" / "Shine" / "Grandma's Song" / "Solidarity" / "Expressing Yourself" / "The Letter" / "Born to Boogie" / "Angry Dance" / "Merry Christmas Maggie Thatcher" / "Deep into the Ground" / "He Could Be a Star" / "Electricity" / "Once We Were Kings" / "The Letter" / "Finale"

The Captain and the Kid (September 18, 2006)

"Postcards from Richard Nixon" / "Just Like Noah's Ark" / "Wouldn't Have You Any Other Way (NYC)" / "Tinderbox" / "And the House Fell Down" / "Blues Never Fade Away" / "The Bridge" / "I Must Have Lost It on the Wind" / "Old '67" / "The Captain and the Kid"

Rocket Man: The Definitive Hits (March 27, 2007)

Disc 1: "Bennie and the Jets" / "Philadelphia Freedom" / "Daniel" / "Rocket Man (I Think It's Going to Be a Long, Long Time)" / "I Guess That's Why They Call It the Blues" / "Tiny Dancer" / "Don't Let the Sun Go Down on Me" (Live with George Michael) / "I Want Love

Disc 2: Candle in the Wind" (Album Version) / "Crocodile Rock" / "I'm Still Standing" / "Saturday Night's Alright for Fighting" / "Your Song" / "Sorry Seems to Be the Hardest Word" / "Sacrifice" / "Goodbye Yellow Brick Road" / "Tinderbox" / "Are You Ready for Love" ('79 Version Radio Edit)

The Union (October 19, 2010)

"If It Wasn't for Bad" / "Eight Hundred Dollar Shoes" / "Hey Ahab" / "Gone to Shiloh" / "Jimmie Rodgers' Dream" / "There's No Tomorrow" / "Monkey Suit" / "The Best Part of the Day" / "A Dream Come True" / "When Love Is Dying" / "I Should Have Sent Roses" / "Hearts Have Turned to Stone" / "Never Too Old (To Hold Somebody)" / "In the Hands of Angels"

Gnomeo and Juliet (Original Motion Picture Soundtrack) (February 8, 2011)

"Hello Hello" (Album Version) / "Crocodile Rock" (with Nelly Furtado) / "Saturday Night's Alright for Fighting" / "Don't Go Breaking My Heart" / "Love Builds a Garden" / "Your Song" / "Rocket Man (I Think It's Going to Be a Long, Long Time)" / "Tiny Dancer" / "Bennie and the Jets" / "Gnomeo and Juliet" (Instrumental) / "Dandelions" (Instrumental) / "Bennie and the Bunnies" (Instrumental) / "Terrafirminator" (Instrumental) / "The Tiki, Tiki, Tiki Room" (Instrumental)

The Diving Board (September 16, 2013)

"Oceans Away" / "Oscar Wilde Gets Out" / "A Town Called Jubilee" / "The Ballad of Blind Tom" / "Dream #1" (Instrumental) / "My Quicksand" / "Can't Stay Alone Tonight" / "Voyeur" / "Home Again" / "Take This Dirty Water" / "Dream #2" (Instrumental) / "The New Fever Waltz" / "Mexican Vacation (Kids in the Candlelight)" / "Dream #3" (Instrumental) / "The Diving Board"

Wonderful Crazy Night (February 5, 2016)

"Wonderful Crazy Night" / "In the Name of You" / "Claw Hammer" / "Blue Wonderful" / "I've Got 2 Wings" / "A Good Heart" / "Looking Up" / "Guilty Pleasure" / "Tambourine" / "The Open Chord"

Diamonds (November 10, 2017)

Disc 1: "Your Song" / "Tiny Dancer" / "Rocket Man (I Think It's Going to be a Long, Long Time)" / "Honky Cat" / "Crocodile Rock" / "Daniel" / "Saturday Night's Alright for Fighting" / "Goodbye Yellow Brick Road" / "Candle in the Wind" / "Bennie and the Jets" / "The Bitch Is Back" / "Philadelphia Freedom" / "Island Girl" / "Someone Saved My Life Tonight" / "Don't Go Breaking My Heart" / "Sorry Seems to Be the Hardest Word" / "Little Jeannie"

Disc 2: "Song for Guy" / "Blue Eyes" / "I'm Still Standing" / "I Guess That's Why They Call It the Blues" / "Sad Songs (Say So Much)" / "Nikita" / "I Don't Wanna Go on with You Like That" / "Sacrifice" / "Don't Let the Sun Go Down on Me" (with George Michael) / "Something About the Way You Look Tonight" / "I Want Love" / "Can You Feel the Love Tonight" / "Are You Ready for Love?" / "Electricity" / "Home Again" / "Looking Up" / "Circle of Life"

Disc 3: "Skyline Pigeon" / "Lucy in the Sky with Diamonds" / "Pinball Wizard" / "Mama Can't Buy You Love" / "Part-Time Love" / "Victim of Love" / "Empty Garden (Hey, Hey Johnny)" / "Kiss the Bride" / "That's What Friends Are For" (with Dionne Warwick, Stevie Wonder, and Gladys Knight) / "The One" / "True Love" (with Kiki Dee) / "Believe" / "Live Like Horses" (with Pavarotti) / "Written in the Stars" (with LeAnn Rimes) / "This Train Don't Stop There Anymore" / "Good Morning to the Night" (Elton vs. Pnau) / "Step into Christmas"

Selected Bibliography

Bernardin, Claude, and Tom Stanton. *Rocket Man: The Encyclopedia of Elton John*. Westport, Connecticut: Greenwood Press, 1995.

Bockris, Victor, and Liz Derringer. "New Again: Bernie Taupin." *Interview*, July 8, 2015. Accessed December 16, 2017. www.interviewmagazine.com/music/new-again-bernie-taupin.

Brown, Mick. "Bernie Taupin: 'Lyricist? I Think of Myself as a Storyteller.'" *Telegraph*, September 16, 2013. Accessed December 15, 2017. www.telegraph.co.uk/culture/music/rockandpopfeatures/10306999/Bernie-Taupin-Lyricist-I-think-of-myself-as-a-storyteller.html.

Cassata, Mary Anne. "Bernie Taupin: A Gifted Lyricist." *American Songwriter*, November 1, 1996. Accessed December 17, 2017. americansongwriter.com/1996/11/berne-taupin-a-gifted-lyricist.

Clark, Rick. "Gus Dudgeon, 1942–2002." *Mix Online*, October 1, 2002. Accessed December 26, 2017. www.mixonline.com/recording/gus-dudgeon-1942-2002-364951.

Cole, George. "Elton John, the Beach Boys and the Fine Art of Pop Alchemy." *Guardian*, September 30, 2010. Accessed December 27, 2017. www.theguardian.com/music/2010/sep/30/arranging-brian-wilson-paul-buckmaster.

Dawson, Julian. *And on Piano . . . NICKY HOPKINS: The Extraordinary Life of Rock's Greatest Session Man*. San Francisco: Backstage Press, 2011.

Doran, John. "A Demon in the Drift: Kate Bush Interviewed." *Quietus*, March 21, 2014. Accessed December 31, 2017. www.thequietus.com/articles/07364-kate-bush-interview-2.

Doyle, Tom. *Captain Fantastic: Elton John's Stellar Trip Through the '70s*. New York: Ballantine Books, 2017. Kindle Edition.

Fussman, Cal. "Bernie Taupin: What I've Learned." *Esquire*, January 1, 2012. Accessed December 15, 2017. www.esquire.com/entertainment/interviews/a11922/bernie-taupin-quotes-0112.

Greene, Andy. "Elton John and Bernie Taupin Look Back At 'Goodbye Yellow Brick Road.'" *Rolling Stone*, March 14, 2014. Accessed December

17, 2017. www.rollingstone.com/music/news/elton-john-and-bernie
-taupin-look-back-at-goodbye-yellow-brick-road-20140314.

Greenfield, Robert. "Elton John: 'He's Our Neil Young'—A Classic Interview
from the Vaults." *Guardian*, July 12, 2012. Accessed January 2, 2018. www
.theguardian.com/music/2012/jul/17/elton-john-interview

Hagen, Joe. *Sticky Fingers: The Life and Times of Jann Wenner and Rolling
Stone Magazine*. New York: Alfred A. Knopf, 2017.

Hayward, Keith. *Elton John: From Tin Pan Alley to the Yellow Brick Road*.
Bedford, England: Wymer Publishing, 2015. Kindle Edition.

Hayward, Keith. *Tin Pan Alley: The Rise of Elton John*. London: Soundcheck
Books LLP, 2013. Kindle Edition.

Hill, Jim. "'The Lion King: Twenty Years on Broadway and Around the World'
Reveals How Close This Hit Show Came to Not Happening." *Huffington
Post*, December 20, 2017. Accessed January 3, 2018. www.huffington-
post.com/entry/the-lion-king-twenty-years-on-broadway-and-around_
us_5a3afa62e4b06cd2bd03d7d0.

Hoskyns, Barney (ed.). *Glam! Bowie, Bolan, and the Glitter Rock Revolution*.
London: Backpages Ltd, 2011. Kindle Edition.

John, Elton. *Love Is the Cure: On Life, Loss, and the End of AIDS*. New York:
Little, Brown & Company, 2012.

Jury, Louise. "Elton John Writes 'Billy Elliot' the Musical Because 'He's
Like Me.'" *Independent*, June 22, 2004. Accessed January 4, 2018. www
.independent.co.uk/arts-entertainment/theatre-dance/news/elton-john
-writes-billy-elliot-the-musical-because-hes-like-me-733199.html.

Kania, Carrie (ed.). *Two Days That Rocked the World: Elton John Live at Dodger
Stadium: Photographs by Terry O'Neill*. Suffolk, United Kingdom: ACC Art
Books Ltd., 2015.

Lassell, Michael. *Elton John and Tim Rice's Aida: The Making of a Broadway
Musical*. New York: Disney Editions, 2000.

Light, Alan. "A Superstar Puts One of His Early Influences Back in the
Spotlight." *New York Times*, October 18, 2010. Accessed January 3, 2018.
www.nytimes.com/2010/10/19/arts/music/19leon.html.

Massey, Howard. *Behind the Glass II: Top Record Producers Tell How They
Craft the Hits*. Milwaukee: Backbeat Books, 2009.

McKinley, James C. Jr. "Still Making Music Together, Far Apart: Elton John and
Bernie Taupin Are Back with 'Diving Board.'" *New York Times*, September
27, 2013. Accessed December 24, 2017. www.nytimes.com/2013/09/

29/arts/music/elton-john-and-bernie-taupin-are-back-with-diving-board.html.

Mower, Sarah. "Domenico Dolce Apologizes for His Controversial Remarks." *Vogue*, August 14, 2015. Accessed December 17, 2017. www.vogue.com/article/dolce-and-gabbana-synthetic-babies-apology.

Norman, Philip. *Elton John: The Biography*. New York: Harmony Books, 1991.

Parker, Ian. "He's a Little Bit Funny." *New Yorker*, August 26, 1996. Accessed January 4, 2018. www.newyorker.com/magazine/1996/08/26/hes-a-little-bit-funny.

Peachey, Paul. "Elton John Producer Died Drink-Driving." *Independent*, November 8, 2002. Accessed December 26, 2017. www.independent.co.uk/news/uk/home-news/elton-john-producer-died-drink-driving-126767.html.

Petridis, Alexis. "Elton John: 'When I Was on Drugs There Was A Monstrous Side to Me.'" *Guardian*, September 15, 2013. Accessed December 7, 2017. www.theguardian.com/music/2013/sep/15/elton-john-drugs-monstrous-side.

Questlove. *Soul Train: The Music, the Dance, and Style of a Generation*. New York: HarperCollins, 2013. Kindle Edition.

Ramone, Phil, with Charles Granata. *Making Music—The Scenes Behind the Music*. New York: Hyperion, 2007.

Reynolds, Simon. *Shock and Awe: Glam Rock and Its Legacy from the Seventies to the Twenty-First Century*. New York: Dey Street Books, 2017. Kindle Edition.

Rosen, Craig. "Bernie Taupin: The Billboard Interview." *Billboard*, October 4, 1997.

Rosenthal, Elizabeth J. *His Song: The Musical Journey of Elton John*. New York: Watson-Guptill Publications, 2001.

Scaggs, Austin. "Elton John: The Rolling Stone Interview." *Rolling Stone*, February 17, 2011.

Schruers, Fred. *Billy Joel: The Definitive Biography*. New York: Three Rivers Press, 2014. Kindle Edition.

Sexton, Paul. "I'm the Ultimate Fan, Searching for Stuff I Can't Hear on the Radio." *Billboard*, November 20, 2004.

Soundbreaking: Stories from the Cutting Edge of Recorded Music, 2016.

Tantrums and Tiaras, 1995.

Time Magazine. "Elton John: Rock's Captain Fantastic." New York: Time, Inc., 2016. Kindle Edition.

White, Timothy. "Elton John: The Billboard Interview." *Billboard*, October 4, 1997.

Wigg, David. "Why My Son Elton Hasn't Spoken to Me for Seven Years: In This Blistering Interview, Elton John's Mother Tells of the Day the Star Said He Hated Her—and How She Blames His Husband for Their Bitter Rift." *Daily Mail*, March 27, 2015. Accessed December 7, 2017. www .dailymail.co.uk/news/article-3015303/Elton-John-hasn-t-spoken-seven -years.html.

Wolfson, Sam. "Vegas Knights: A Conversation with Sir Elton John." *Noisey*, December 4, 2015. Accessed December 18, 2018. noisey.vice.com/en_au/ article/rzegpj/rocket-hour-conversation-with-elton-john-in-las-vegas.

Zollo, Paul. *More Songwriters on Songwriting*. Boston: Da Capo Press, 2016. Kindle Edition.

Index

THE FAQ SERIES

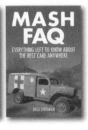

Prices, contents, and availability
subject to change without notice.

Johnny Cash FAQ
by C. Eric Banister
Backbeat Books
9781480385405................. $24.99

KISS FAQ
by Dale Sherman
Backbeat Books
9781617130915....................... $24.99

Led Zeppelin FAQ
by George Case
Backbeat Books
9781617130250 ....$22.99

Lucille Ball FAQ
by James Sheridan
and Barry Monush
Applause Books
9781617740824.......................$19.99

M.A.S.H. FAQ
by Dale Sherman
Applause Books
9781480355897.......................$19.99

Michael Jackson FAQ
by Kit O'Toole
Backbeat Books
9781480371064 ....$19.99

Modern Sci-Fi Films FAQ
by Tom DeMichael
Applause Books
9781480350618 .... $24.99

Monty Python FAQ
by Chris Barsanti, Brian Cogan,
and Jeff Massey
Applause Books
9781495049439 ....$19.99

Morrissey FAQ
by D. McKinney
Backbeat Books
9781480394483.................. $24.99

Neil Young FAQ
by Glen Boyd
Backbeat Books
9781617130373.......................$19.99

Nirvana FAQ
by John D. Luerssen
Backbeat Books
9781617134500....................... $24.99

Pearl Jam FAQ
by Bernard M. Corbett and
Thomas Edward Harkins
Backbeat Books
9781617136122 ....$19.99

Pink Floyd FAQ
by Stuart Shea
Backbeat Books
9780879309503...................$19.99

Pro Wrestling FAQ
by Brian Solomon
Backbeat Books
9781617135996....................... $29.99

Prog Rock FAQ
by Will Romano
Backbeat Books
9781617135873 .... $24.99

Quentin Tarantino FAQ
by Dale Sherman
Applause Books
9781480355880 .... $24.99

Robin Hood FAQ
by Dave Thompson
Applause Books
9781495048227 ....$19.99

**The Rocky Horror
Picture Show FAQ**
by Dave Thompson
Applause Books
9781495007477 ....$19.99

Rush FAQ
by Max Mobley
Backbeat Books
9781617134517 ....$19.99

Saturday Night Live FAQ
by Stephen Tropiano
Applause Books
9781557839510..................... $24.99

Seinfeld FAQ
by Nicholas Nigro
Applause Books
9781557838575..................... $24.99

Sherlock Holmes FAQ
by Dave Thompson
Applause Books
9781480331495..................... $24.99

The Smiths FAQ
by John D. Luerssen
Backbeat Books
9781480394490.................. $24.99

Soccer FAQ
by Dave Thompson
Backbeat Books
9781617135989....................... $24.99

The Sound of Music FAQ
by Barry Monush
Applause Books
9781480360433................... $27.99

South Park FAQ
by Dave Thompson
Applause Books
9781480350649................... $24.99

Star Trek FAQ
(Unofficial and Unauthorized)
by Mark Clark
Applause Books
9781557837929.......................$19.99

Star Trek FAQ 2.0
(Unofficial and Unauthorized)
by Mark Clark
Applause Books
9781557837936.....................$22.99

Star Wars FAQ
by Mark Clark
Applause Books
9781480360181..................... $24.99

Steely Dan FAQ
by Anthony Robustelli
Backbeat Books
9781495025129 ....$19.99

Stephen King Films FAQ
by Scott Von Doviak
Applause Books
9781480355514..................... $24.99

Three Stooges FAQ
by David J. Hogan
Applause Books
9781557837882.....................$22.99

TV Finales FAQ
by Stephen Tropiano and
Holly Van Buren
Applause Books
9781480391444 ....$19.99

The Twilight Zone FAQ
by Dave Thompson
Applause Books
9781480396180 ....$19.99

Twin Peaks FAQ
by David Bushman and
Arthur Smith
Applause Books
9781495015861.......................$19.99

UFO FAQ
by David J. Hogan
Backbeat Books
9781480393851 ....$19.99

Video Games FAQ
by Mark J.P. Wolf
Backbeat Books
9781617136306 ....$19.99

The Who FAQ
by Mike Segretto
Backbeat Books
9781480361034 .... $24.99

The Wizard of Oz FAQ
by David J. Hogan
Applause Books
9781480350625 .... $24.99

The X-Files FAQ
by John Kenneth Muir
Applause Books
9781480369740.................... $24.99